THE
EQUILIBRISTS

Curated by Gary Carrion-Murayari
and Helga Christoffersen with Massimiliano Gioni

ΔΕΣΤΕ

THE EQUILIBRISTS

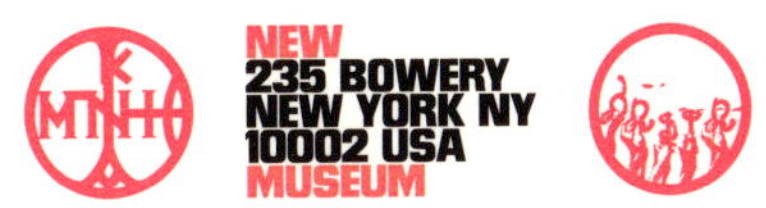

Participating Artists

LOUKIA ALAVANOU
b. 1979, Athens, Greece; lives
and works in Belgium

DIMITRIS AMELADIOTIS
b. 1979, Thessaloniki, Greece; lives
and works in Thessaloniki, Greece

MARIA ANASTASSIOU
b. 1982, Nicosia, Cyprus; lives and
works in London, United Kingdom

ELENI BAGAKI
b. 1979, Crete, Greece; lives
and works in Athens, Greece

MARGARITA BOFILIOU
b. 1979, Athens, Greece; lives
and works in Athens, Greece

MARIANNA CHRISTOFIDES
b. 1980, Nicosia, Cyprus; lives
and works in Cologne, Germany

MANOLIS DASKALAKIS-LEMOS
b. 1989, Athens, Greece; lives
and works in Athens, Greece

PETROS EFSTATHIADIS
b. 1980, Liparo, Greece; lives
and works in Liparo, Greece

EIRENE EFSTATHIOU
b. 1980, Athens, Greece; lives
and works in Athens, Greece

ZOI GAITANIDOU
b. 1981, Athens, Greece; lives
and works in Athens, Greece

GIORGOS GERONTIDES
b. 1987, Athens, Greece; lives
and works in Thessaloniki, Greece

STELIOS KALLINIKOU
b. 1985, Limassol, Cyprus; lives
and works in Nicosia, Cyprus

YANNIS KARPOUZIS
b. 1984, Athens, Greece; lives
and works in Athens, Greece

LITO KATTOU
b. 1990, Nicosia, Cyprus; lives and
works in London, United Kingdom
and Athens, Greece

KERNEL
f. 2009, Athens, Greece; based
in Athens, Greece

IOANNIS KOLIOPOULOS
b. 1986, Athens, Greece; lives and
works in Komi, Tinos Island, Greece

CHRYSANTHI KOUMIANAKI
b. 1985, Heraklion Crete, Greece;
lives and works in Athens, Greece

ORESTIS MAVROUDIS
b. 1988, Athens, Greece; lives
and works in Berlin, Germany

IRINI MIGA
b. 1981, Larissa, Greece; lives
and works in New York, United
States of America

OLGA MIGLIARESSI-PHOCA
b. 1981, Athens, Greece; lives
and works in Athens, Greece

PETROS MORIS
b. 1986, Lamia, Greece; lives
and works in Athens, Greece

PERSEFONI MYRTSOU
b. 1986, Thessaloniki, Greece;
lives and works in Berlin, Germany
and Istanbul, Turkey
& EVA GIANNAKOPOULOU
b. 1977, Athens, Greece; lives
and works in Berlin, Germany
and Athens, Greece

MALVINA PANAGIOTIDI
b. 1985, Athens, Greece; lives
and works in Berlin, Germany
and Athens, Greece

ALIKI PANAGIOTOPOULOU
b. 1980, Athens, Greece; lives
and works in Athens, Greece

EVA PAPAMARGARITI
b. 1987, Larissa, Greece; lives
and works in London, United Kingdom

ZOË PAUL
b. 1987, London, United Kingdom;
lives and works in Athens, Greece

SOFIA STEVI
b. 1982, Athens, Greece; lives
and works in Athens, Greece
and London, United Kingdom

ANASTASIS STRATAKIS
b. 1985, Thessaloniki, Greece;
lives and works in Athens
and Thessaloniki, Greece

VALINIA SVORONOU
b. 1991, Athens, Greece; lives
and works in London, United
Kingdom and Athens, Greece

PAKY VLASSOPOULOU
b. 1985, Athens, Greece; lives
and works in Athens, Greece

MYRTO XANTHOPOULOU
b. 1981, Helsinki, Finland; lives
and works in Athens, Greece

NATALIE YIAXI
b. 1980, Nicosia, Cyprus; lives
and works in Nicosia, Cyprus

Lisa Phillips
Toby Devan Lewis Director, New Museum, New York

Director's Foreword: New Museum

"The Equilibrists" is a unique joint project between the New Museum, the DESTE Foundation, and the Benaki Museum, which offers a timely look at a new generation of Greek and Cypriot artists. The exhibition brings together 33 artists and collaborations whose works reflect the diverse activities of artists working both within Greece and further abroad. Amid challenging political and social circumstances, these artists have continued to innovate in ways that enrich their local artistic scenes and resonate with the contemporary art world more broadly. The artists selected for this exhibition represent only a small sampling of the many promising young artists currently working in or emerging from Greece, and they hint at the intrepid artis-run initiatives that are active throughout Greece and Cyprus.

This exhibition is an example of the New Museum's robust global initiatives and partnerships. The New Museum's mission has long been to identify and showcase exciting new artists and ideas from around the world, and in recent years this mission has expanded to include a range or projects that take place outside the museum and in collaboration with institutions, foundations, and artists internationally. "The Equilibrists" serves an extension of the New Museum's signature Triennial exhibitions, which are similarly dedicated to identifying international emerging artists whose work is changing the discourse and impact of art-making today.

The New Museum has enjoyed a long partnership with DESTE Foundation for Contemporary Art and I would like to thank Dakis Joannou for inviting the New Museum to collaborate on this important project and making it possible for our curators to undertake such a rich and productive research process. I am grateful to the Benaki Museum for hosting this special exhibition and allowing the work of these promising young artists to be seen by both a local and international audience.

I would also like to thank the curators of the exhibition, Gary Carrion-Murayari, Helga Christoffersen, and Massimiliano Gioni, as well as curatorial intern, Lauren Young, for their efforts on all aspects of this exhibition. The team at the DESTE Foundation—Regina Alivisatos, Natasha Polymeropoulos, Kleio Silvestrou, and Eugenia Stamatopoulou—have overseen the planning and logistics of the installation with hard work and precision. This catalogue was designed by K2 Design in Athens and I would to thank Yiannis Kouroudis, Menelaos Kouroudis, and Yiannis Kondilis for their thoughtful design.

The New Museum is also grateful to the curators, artists, and writers who served as advisors on this project for their insight and generosity in suggesting artists and paths of inquiry for the show, and the artists' galleries for all their support. Finally, I would like to thank all of the participating artists in the exhibition for their participation in this project and the extraordinary work that they have produced.

Olivier Descotes

Director, Benaki Museum, Athens

Director's Foreword: Benaki Museum

"The Equilibrists" is a promising project that has resulted from the fruitful collaboration of the Benaki Museum, the New Museum, and the DESTE Foundation. This exhibition aims to reveal the creative potential of young Greek and Cypriot artists who, despite the challenges they have faced in their approaches to art-making, continue to navigate a changing social landscape in order to foster dialogues and exchanges that further enrich the contemporary art scene.

"The Equilibrists" evokes the nimbleness and inventiveness of this generation, and features a diverse group of 33 artists and artistic collaborations working in Greece and Cyprus, as well as in London, Berlin, and New York. While their artistic achievements are alone worthy of appreciation, there are many common threads that tie their works together thematically. Some of these artists—Eirene Efstathiou, Malvina Panagiotidi, and Olga Migliaressi-Phoca, for example—share an interest in public space as a stage for social expression, political action, and the evocation of historical memory. Others, including Petros Moris, Myrto Xanthopoulou, and Aliki Panagiotopoulou, make works that consider the urban environment through an archeological lens and connect ancient history with contemporary life by excavating and accumulating materials and language. Sofia Stevi, Giorgos Gerontides, and Dimitris Ameladiotis adopt a performative and improvisational approach to painting and sculpture, generating rich compositions and narratives from modest materials. Zoë Paul and Zoi Gaitanidou use craft-based techniques to create utopian visions for the future, whereas Eva Papamargariti and Valinia Svoronou combine video with other mediums to explore how our experience of landscapes and bodies are changing through the increasing ubiquity of digital technology.

Hosting this exhibition is immensely important for the Benaki Museum in that it furthers our primary and fundamental objectives—to support young artists and to foster artistic exchanges. I wish to express my warm thanks to the New Museum and DESTE for this collaboration and to all who have contributed to the success of this project.

President, DESTE Foundation for Contemporary Art

Preface

One of the principal aims of DESTE has always been to promote and support Greek contemporary culture. At our current moment, many young artists are responding to the economic crisis in Greece with an energy with which they are generating new ideas and pushing the limits of what is possible in very difficult circumstances. The exhibition "The Equilibrists" serves as a platform for these young artists, exposing many of them to an international audience for the first time.

This exhibition follows in the tradition of the biannual DESTE Prize, which since 1999 has given Greek and Cypriot artists the opportunity to enter into dialogue with artists and viewers internationally. The members of the DESTE Prize jury are museum directors, artists, writers, and curators who come together from all over the world to learn about these Greek and Cypriot artists' projects. As a result, new networks and friendships are formed and webs of reciprocal exchange and influence occur naturally.

"The Equilibrists" features the work of 33 young artists. Held at the Benaki Museum, and curated by Gary Carrion-Murayari and Helga Christoffersen with Massimiliano Gioni of the New Museum, New York, the exhibition celebrates 33 years of DESTE's collaborations. This project is exemplary of the kinds of collaborations that I value above all else, and it has been more rewarding than I could have ever imagined.

Over the last three decades, DESTE's many alliances and collaborations have taken risks to create new paths of communication and to expand participation in the dialogues around art. DESTE's projects are always enriched by ideas that are shared in an informal and personal manner. We don't box things in. We let the chips fall where they may. Time takes care of the rest.

Gary Carrion-Murayari

Kraus Family Curator, New Museum, New York

The Equilibrists

As with the origins many forms of skilled athleticism, the roots of funambulism (or tightrope walking) can be traced back to classical Greece. And although the term equilibrist—meaning one adept at feats of balancing—appeared only in the eighteenth century, images of acrobats can be found in Greek art dating back to at least 300 BCE. Early on, tightrope walking was isolated from the athletic endeavors featured in the early Olympic Games, like running, jumping, and wrestling. While on purely athletic terms, tightrope walking is just as physically rigorous as other events, the intellectual concentration it requires in concert with bodily control—in addition to the tightrope walker's ability to seize control away from gravity and to maintain precarious positions—produces a unique spectacle. This exhibition of young Greek and Cypriot artists borrows this term, not to denote an overall thematic of acrobatics, but rather to express a shared sensibility of poise and skillfulness and a common ability to wrest a sense of balance and stability from a tumultuous, entropic world.

This exhibition features over 30 artists working in Athens, Thessaloniki, Cyprus, Berlin, London, and New York. In many ways, these artists are most unified by their heterogeneity—with works in painting, sculpture, drawing, film, and video, many often move across mediums and even into other disciplines like writing, architecture, design, and dance. The artists in the exhibition also vary in age from their mid-twenties to mid-thirties. In many cases, the stylistic diversity visible in artists only a decade apart seems to stretch the definition of a distinct generation, but this group of artists is unavoidably linked through their shared experience of the ongoing financial crisis in Greece.

To say that the political and social upheaval that resulted from this crisis has shaped young Greeks today is an understatement. In 2013, researcher and policy analyst Athanassios Gouglas outlined the parameters that unite a majority of this generation. As he describes: "Today, when we talk about the young generation in Greece, we are talking about an actual generation whose members, born between 1979 and 2000, are exposed to concrete historical problems, this time around primarily social and economic: a) a prolonged period of economic dependency, which may last till the mid-thirties; b) precarity c) generational tension beyond conventional notions of generational gap; and d) the momentous formative event of the 2010 debt crisis." The tenuous prospects for this so-called "young precariat" would come as no surprise to local or international observers, but young Greek and Cypriot artists' responses to this era of uncertainty have been remarkably nuanced. The degree to which individual artists address this condition in their works, or engage with larger notions of Greek history, identity, and contemporaneity, varies greatly. One of the main goals of this exhibition is to acknowledge the set of conditions that are continuing to shape this generation, while demonstrating the ways in which this shared precarity has not resulted in stylistic uniformity.

This exhibition is inevitably a small cross-section of the works being made by the rich artistic community in Athens and by Greek and Cypriot artists domestically and abroad. The range of these artists' activities and contributions extends far beyond the concrete objects in this show to encompass artist-run spaces, residency programs, publications, and numerous collectives and joint projects both formal and informal. In Athens in particular, these activities exist within a network of dialogues and collaborations among local artists, curators, and writers of who have built and maintained an active and layered artistic scene with limited market support and in the midst of historic economic and political instability. These continuing initiatives provide critical and sustained responses to the ongoing crisis. Among these significant efforts are the most recent Athens Biennial (2015–17), which is unfolding over two years and through exhibitions, workshops, performances, and screenings, and the magazine *South as a State of Mind*, which over the past four years has carefully articulated the challenges of the crisis and Greece's shifting identity in relationship to the rest of Europe. In their collaborative and durational nature, these projects are complex and responsive platforms that befit the social realities they are addressing.

Nearly all of the artists in "The Equilibrists" participate in one or another of these initiatives and simultaneously maintain independent studio practices through which they continue to make concrete objects despite the fact that commercial sales opportunities are limited and exhibitions are often self-organized. This commitment to object-making reflects the way in which all of these young artists attempt to arrest the flow of images, the transformation of materials, and the flux of history. Some address political and social change as it affects the landscape of public space; others channel uncertainty through humble materials or formal and linguistic improvisation; and others balance historical and vernacular traditions with speculative visions of the future.

Each of these artists strikes a balance between different registers of time and methods of dealing with changes in the material world. Against precarity and material uncertainty, they each maintain a faith in physical object-making.

The artists whose works visualize the effects of the crisis often do so by acknowledging the layers of history that exist in urban space and the ways in which the crisis has warped the experience of time. Yannis Karpouzis's photographs of Athens capture the sense of stasis that has gripped Athens over the past decade, using photography to "suspend time that has already stalled." Eirene Efstathiou's subtle paintings juxtapose two volatile Decembers in Greek history: the beginning of the Greek Civil War in 1944 and the violent riots of December 2008. Malvina Panagiotidi's wax facades of purportedly haunted houses in Athens evoke the architectural specters that afflict the city's changing landscape, while Marianna Christofides's moving portrait of an Adriatic fisherman brings to mind the innumerable individuals whose livelihoods have been made anachronistic in the new economy.

Other artists look further afield to contested notions of identity and community that are often played out in public space. Stelios Kallinikou's series *Local Studies* documents the artist's journey across the divided city of Nicosia in Cyprus in search of a common urban landscape that transcends the politics separating the Greek south from the Turkish north. Persefoni Myrtsou and Eva Giannakopoulou's ongoing series of videos, The Brides of Maltepe, uses their own experiences of cross-cultural marriage to explore the tensions and sympathies between Greek and Turkish culture and across geographic and social settings. In her large-scale prints, Olga Migliaressi-Phoca compresses the conflicts among various individual identities and communities by collaging together images of graffiti she encounters in cities like Mykonos and Istanbul. Through a study of urban architecture and infrastructures, the Athens-based collective KERNEL examines the contested ownership of public space and the effects of the global economy on individuals and resources. Manolis Daskalakis-Lemos also addresses infrastructure and social discontent through his multi-media works. In sculpture, photography, and painting, he references the utopian fantasies of the avant-garde and the contemporary fantasy that a serendipitous discovery of oil could solve Greece's economic crisis.

To a certain degree, intersections of the past and present have long been a concern for Greek artists, prompting them to reexamine elements of historical Greek culture with a critical eye. Margarita Bofiliou's lyrical paintings and drawings have a transhistorical sensibility that recalls the sagas of classical Greek tragedy but also evokes political caricatures that resonate with the social challenges of contemporary Greece. In her work, the historical past is seen as a potential burden but also as raw material that can be reconfigured by individuals who are generating new personal narratives.

The relationship between historical narrative and speculative fiction also comes to the forefront in the works of Zoë Paul and Zoi Gaitanidou. For Paul, this relationship entails using traditional or archaic methods, like weaving and bead-making, to create works that appear as remnants of an imagined vision of the past. Gaitanidou produces intricate and incredibly labor-intensive embroidered tapestries that feature imagery that merges exotic natural landscapes and science-fiction fantasies of the future. In both cases, the artists' inventive and deliberate approaches to materials and process reconsider the nature of artifacts and their uses in constructing new narratives. The efforts of the protagonist of Orestis Mavroudis's film, who tinkers with outdated materials to construct a flying machine, offers a parallel to this theme. The chance of flight seems unlikely, but the man remains hopeful.

The tension between past and present extends to more formal strategies of making in the works of artists like Petros Moris, Myrto Xanthopoulou, Aliki Panagiotopoulou, and Ionnis Koliopoulos, in which classical Greek tradition and an awareness of Greek history coincide with ideas about artifacts and the lives of objects. Moris adopts the excavation methodologies of archeology and illustrates serial forms of an almost biological accumulation in his steel, plaster, and concrete installations, while Xanthopoulou and Panagiotopoulou accumulate fragments of objects, languages, and images in works that straddle categories like painting and sculpture, or research and poetry. Koliopoulos seeks a kind of balance between past and present in his new series *Primal Objectives*, which consists of photographs of temporary sculptures combined with delicate drawings, woodblock prints, and subtly altered postcards and snapshots. These artists' critical engagement with different kinds of material history hints at a broader impulse towards preservation and conservation in the face of inevitable deterioration and destruction.

The precariousness of the material world prompts other artists to adopt a performative approach to producing paintings, sculptures, drawings, and photographs. Giorgos Gerontides collects an array of discarded objects in order to produce enigmatic typologies and elegantly improvised kinetic sculptures. Petros Efstathiadis's theatrical constructions, built in his home village in the north of Greece, are assembled for the camera but suggest the presence of an unseen, eccentric builder fabricating his own idiosyncratic universe. Dimitris Ameladiotis draws from an even more chaotic morass of detritus, which he coaxes into tightly compressed sculptural assemblages. Sofia Stevi's painted fabrics and household objects are comprised of lively and exquisite biomorphic forms that suggest hidden energy flows and cosmic bodies transported into surreal domestic scenes. Irini Miga echoes this transformation of quotidian settings in works that animate fragments of architecture and delicately reconstruct everyday items with a forensic attention to detail. This embrace of humble materials and incidental constructions is linked to the volatility of present, but also seems to posit a belief in the vibrancy of the material world.

Natalie Yiaxi and Eleni Bagaki offer a playful approach to the relationship between language and objects. Yiaxi's recent floor sculpture consists of everyday objects and tactile ceramic constructions arranged in a sculptural analog of concrete poetry. Accompanied by fragments of songs that Yiaxi recorded, the work is lyrical and evocative of memories both personal and universal. Bagaki also begins with a practice based in writing. Her texts are confessional, visceral, and exuberant—qualities that she translates into videos and installations in which language is a tool of social mediation as well as a bridge to the world of images. Maria Anastassiou also starts with a textual source in her mixed-media video *Gravity* (2015), visually interpreting a poem into a kaleidoscopic demonstration of the materiality of film.

Chrysanthi Koumianaki, Paky Vlassopoulou, and Anastasis Stratakis also connect performance, labor, and materials to varying effect. Koumianaki's works in sculpture, photography, and drawing involve layers of historical research and trace the artist's attempts to translate the physical languages of dance, manufacturing, and political protest into abstract forms. Vlassopoulou's sculptural constructions also evoke the esoteric pursuit of knowledge. Her sculptural installation *33,478* (2014) comprises fragments of torn books and shards of marble in a patchworked wooden vitrine, suggesting an attempt at learning beyond language and history. The quietness of this work also recalls Stratakis's minimal drawings—laborious renderings of almost imperceptibly detailed surfaces of walls, which radically transform the architectural sites they depict.

Finally, many artists working in moving images explore issues around visuality and materiality in both analog and digital forms. Loukia Alavanou's film *The Green Room* (2015–16) centers on a young Belgian painter with a vision disorder that causes her eyesight to flicker—a condition that serves as a metaphor for the temporal and psychological dislocations produced by cinema. Moving into the digital realm, Valinia Svoronou's videos and sculptures create networks of bodies and surfaces that transcend the boundaries between the virtual and the real, while Eva Papamargariti's animations and printed fabrics create their own visual universe, visualizing how digital landscapes have infected and suffused life beyond these virtual realms. And although her works are static, Lito Kattou's sculptures suggest an interface of bodies, surfaces, and cosmologies, appearing as if tools brought back from an uncertain technological future.

It would be easy to characterize the works of this new generation of artists as symptomatic of their uncertain political and social positions and their tenuous prospects for the future, but it is more valuable to consider their richly diverse works as a set of propositions for how to think with materials. These artists' works display a confidence in their ability to understand and affect the world around them by creating objects and images that are more than just commodities. These artists are remarkably committed to experimentation and alchemical transformation, and the works they produce, regardless of medium, manage to hold the competing forces of the material world in tension—even if only for a brief moment. These strategies of experimentation and transformation feel necessarily forceful and optimistic for confronting the challenges faced by these artists, both within Greece and beyond, and even if the degree to which these young artists directly address the crisis in Greece varies, a concern for changing social and the political conditions is visible in nearly all the works they produce. The works assembled for this exhibition, in combination with the temporal and ephemeral activities in which these artists are engaged, stand as propositions for how to walk a tightrope amid the vibrations of a constantly shifting world.

1. – 8. *The Green Room*, 2015–16 (stills)
Stereoscopic 3D video, color, and sound, 4:07 min

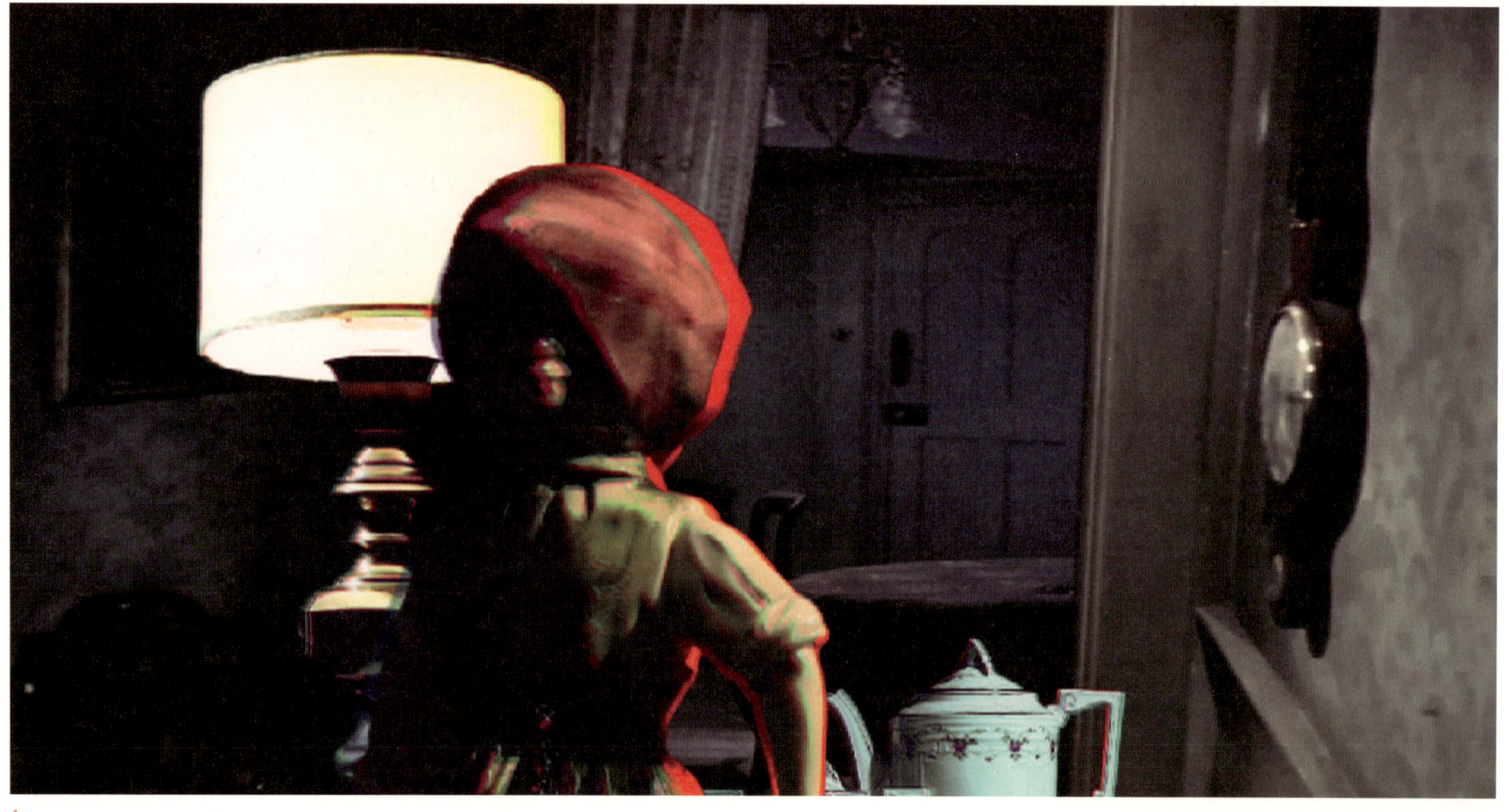

1

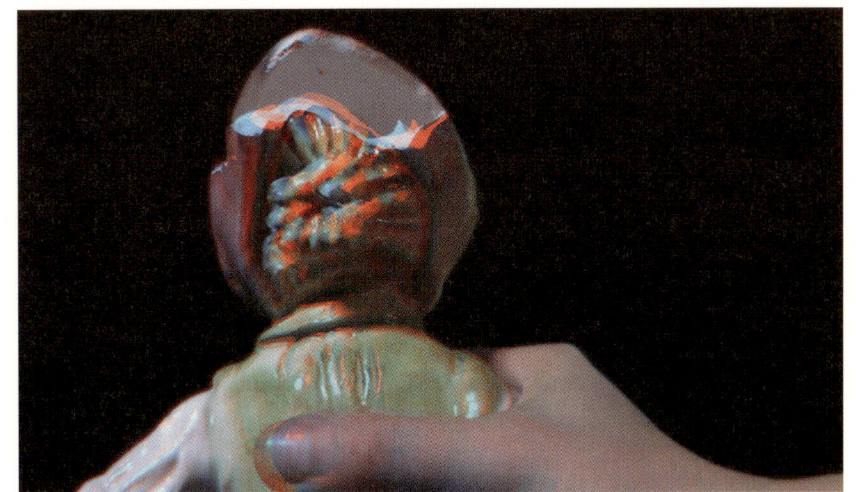

2

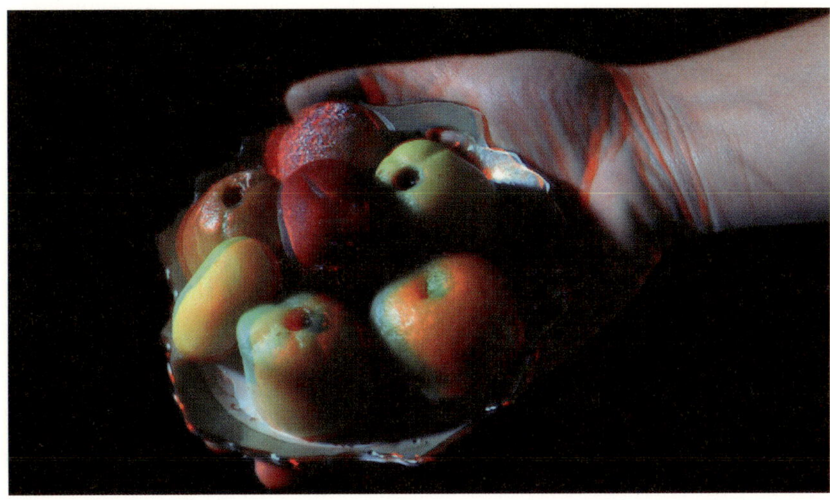

3

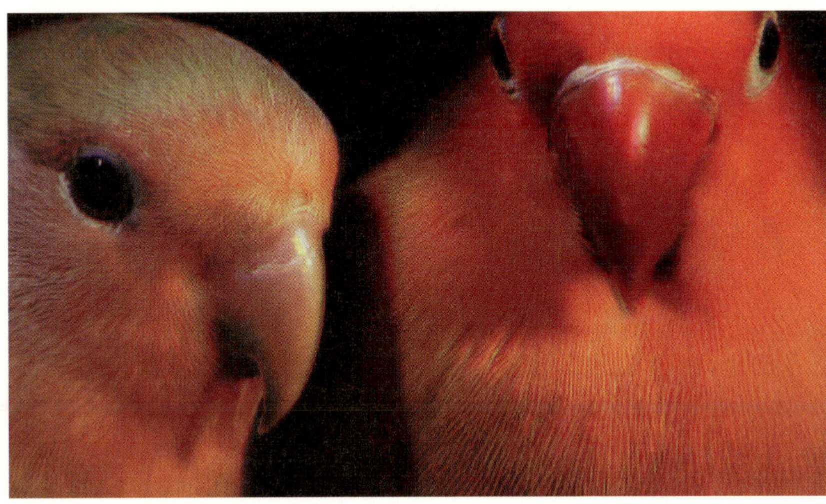

4

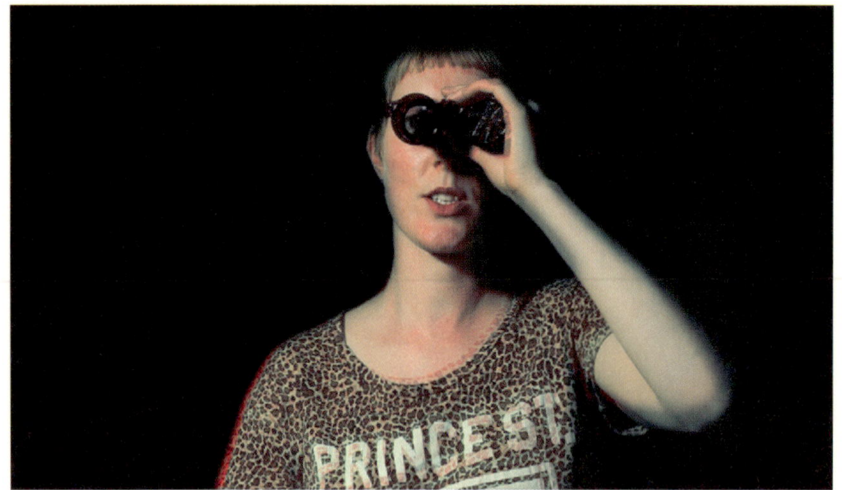

5

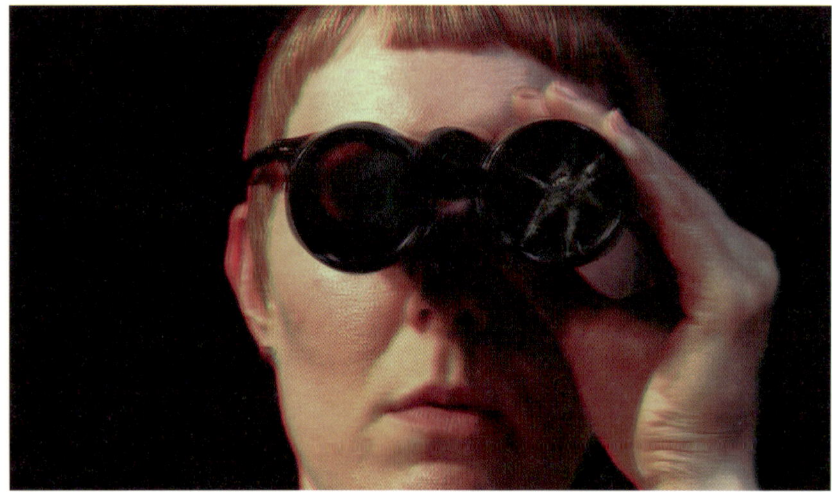

6

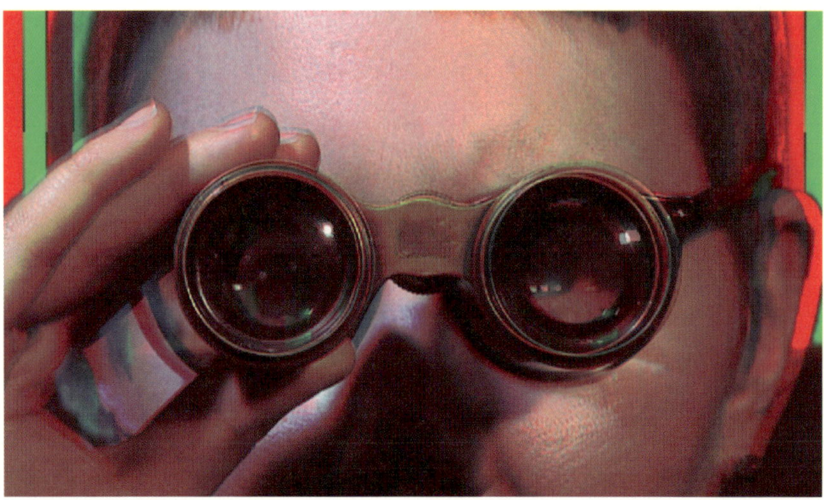

7

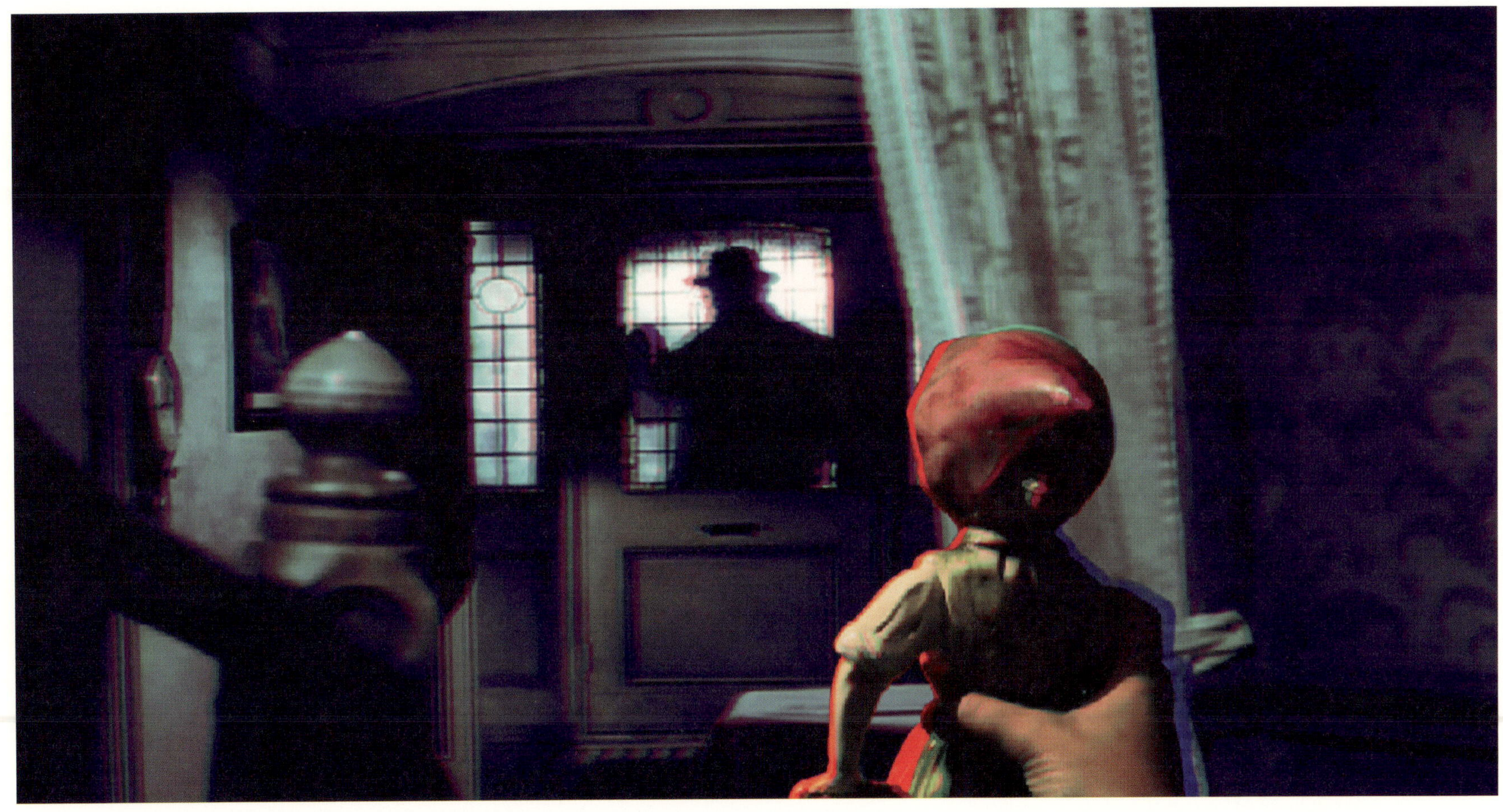

1. *Untitled*, 2012
Mixed media, 52 x 48 x 18 cm

2. *Untitled*, 2015
Mixed media, 70 x 12 x 12 cm

3. *Untitled*, 2014
Mixed media, 38 x 49 x 36 cm

4. *Untitled*, 2012
Mixed media, 40 x 36 x 19 cm

5. *I Would Like This Artwork to Exist Without Any Name!*, 2013
Mixed media, 25 x 18 x 15 cm

6. *Untitled*, 2015
Mixed media, 70 x 86 x 37 cm

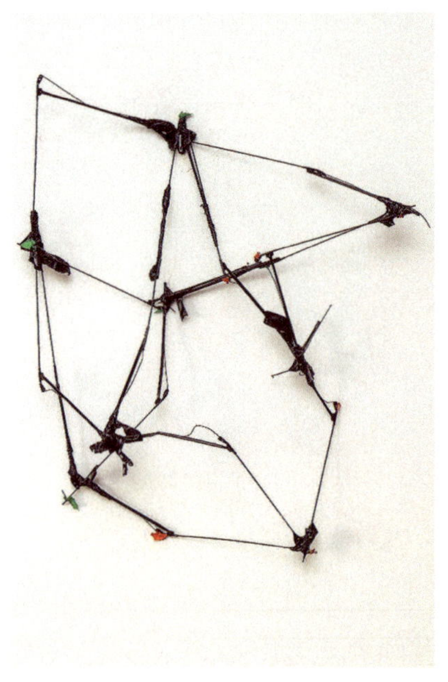

1

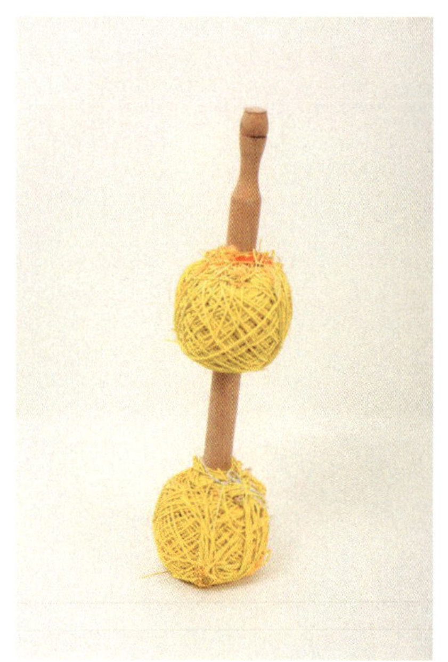

2

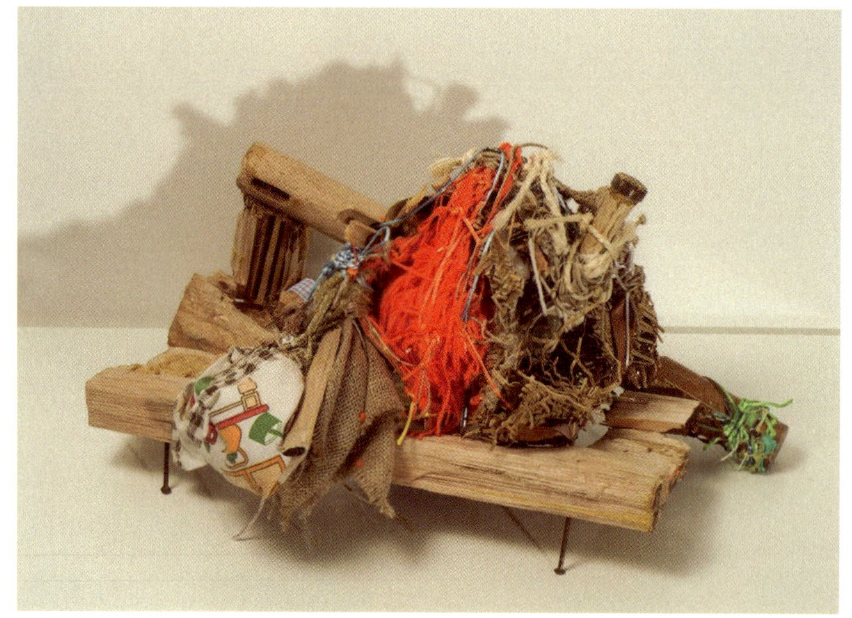

3

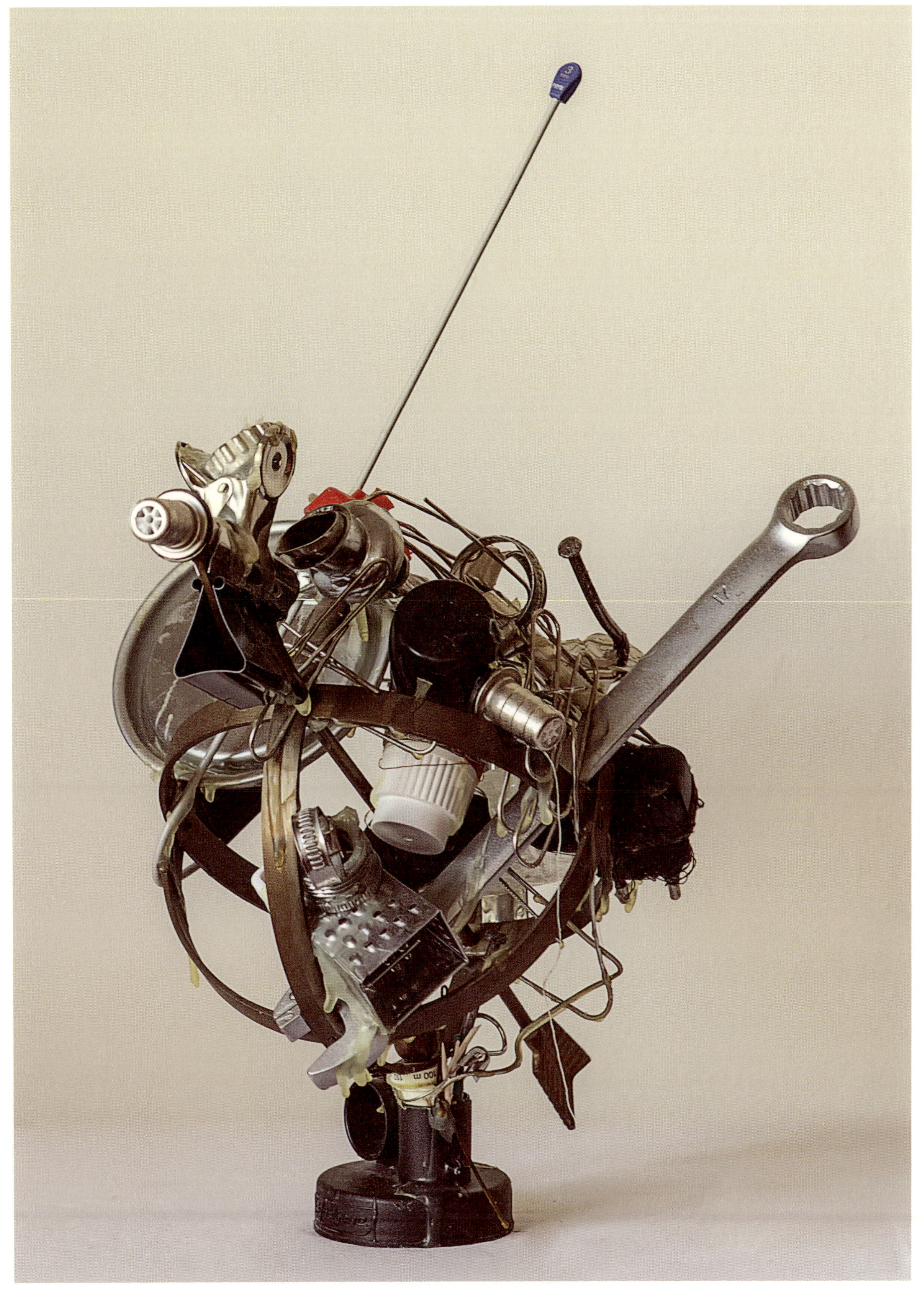

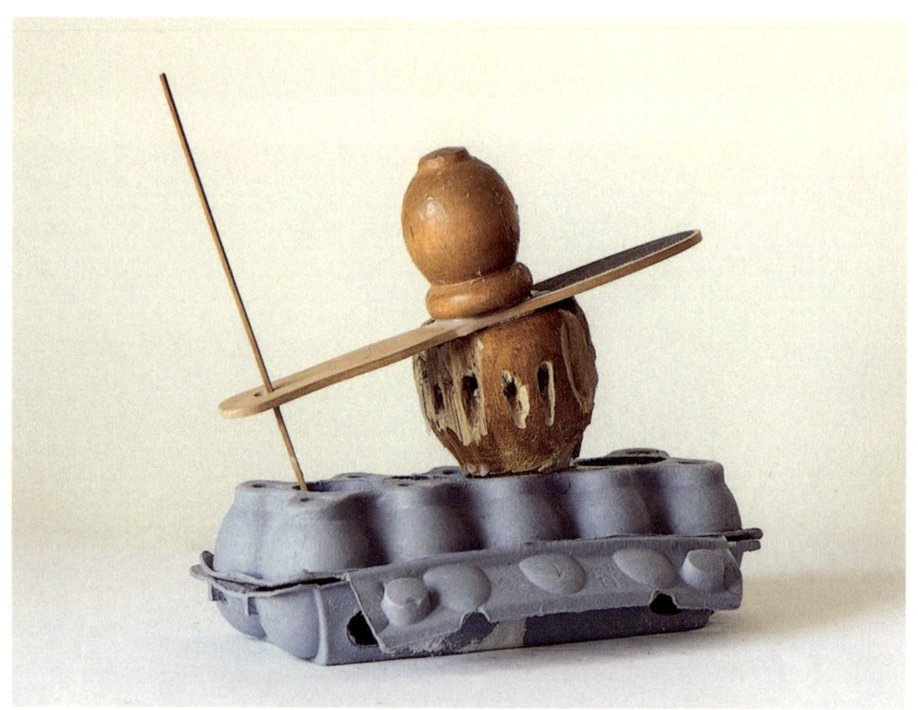

5

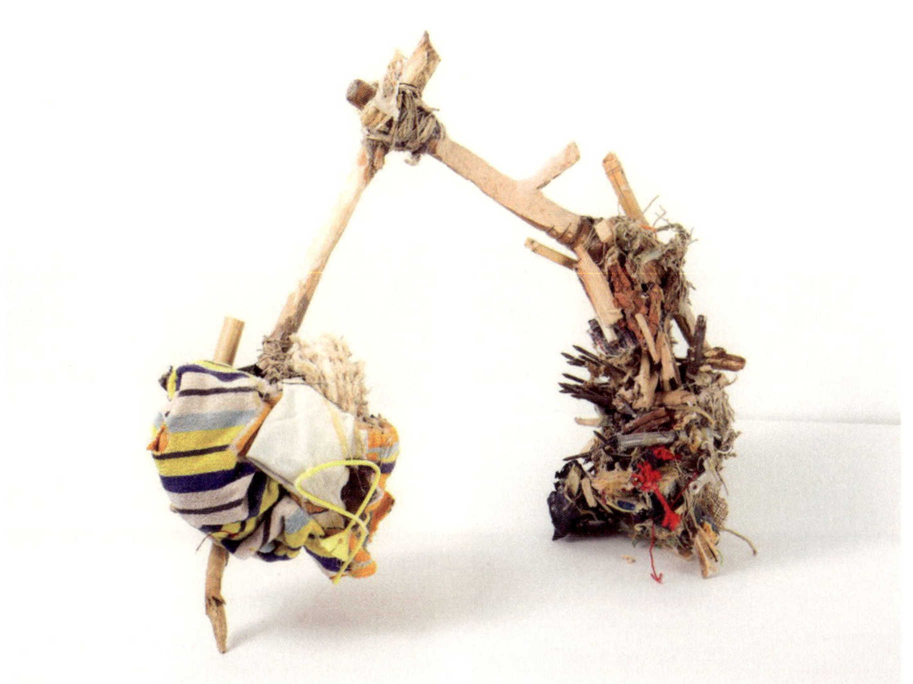

6

1. – 5. *Gravity*, 2015 (stills)
HD video, found video, digitized 16mm film, color, and found sound, 1:38 min

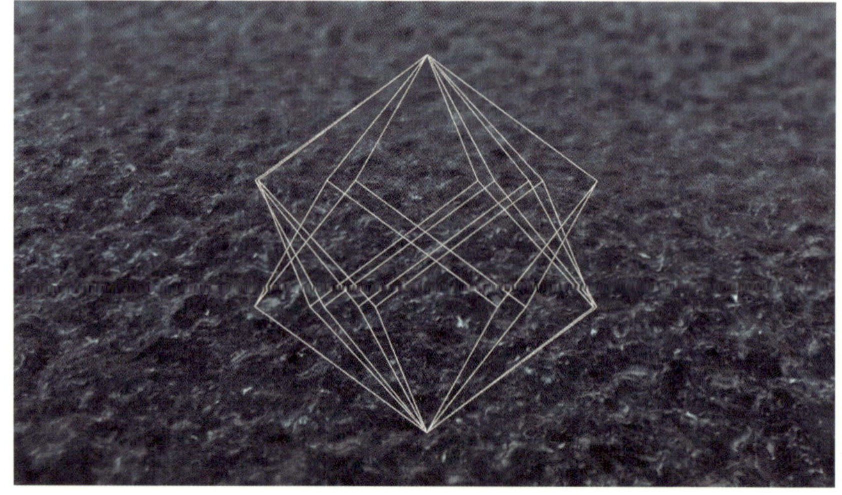

1

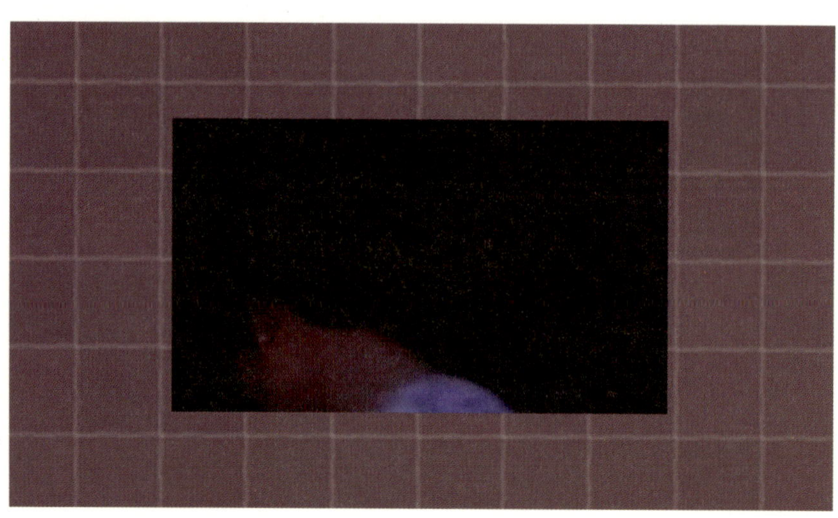

2

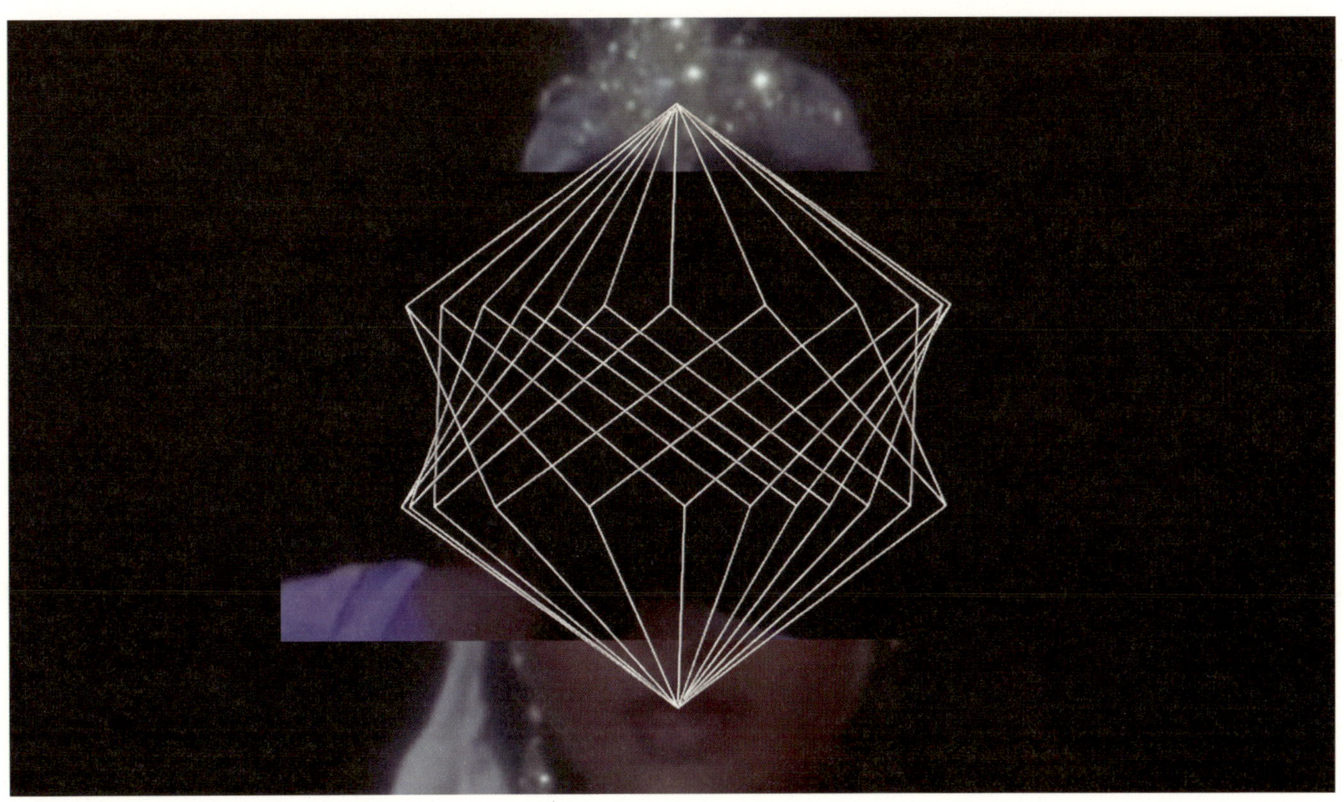

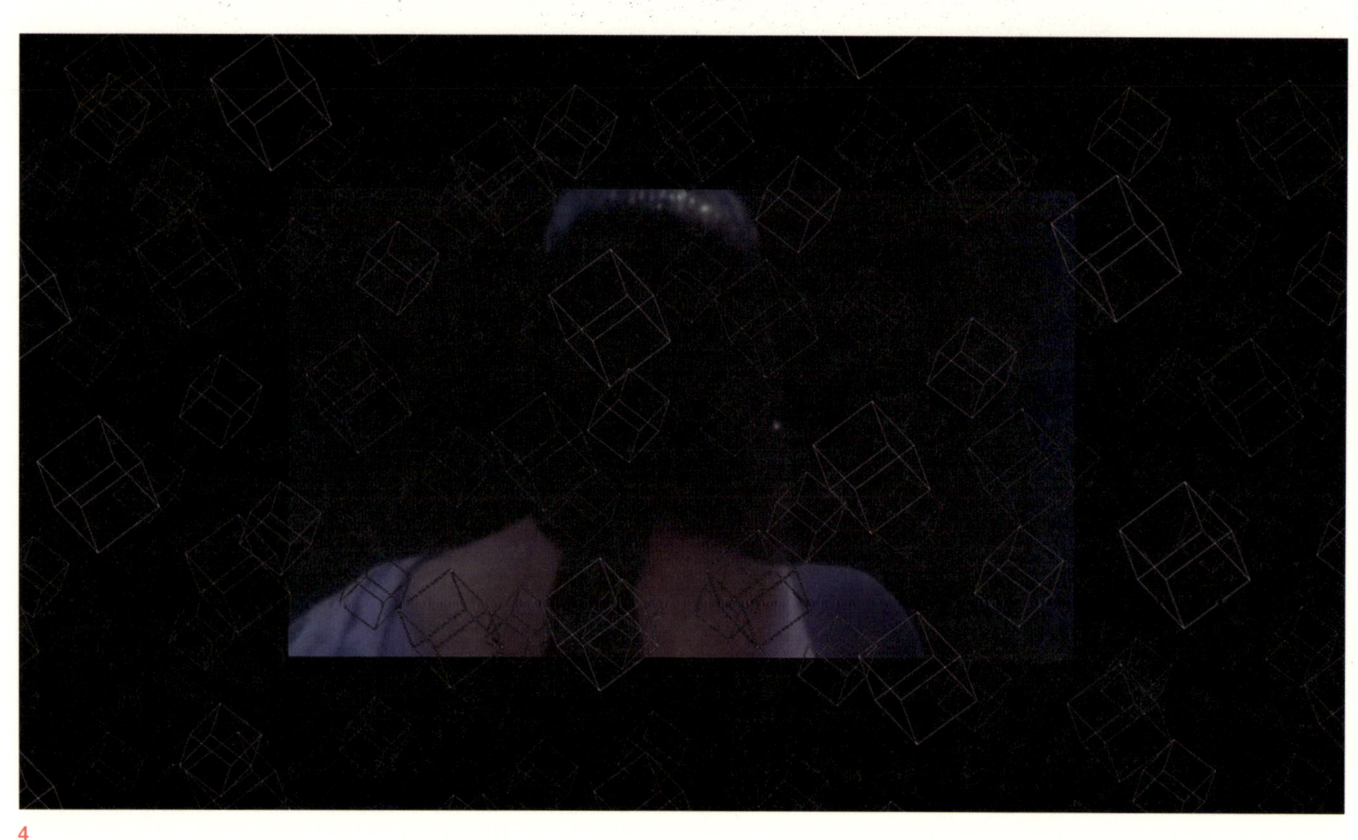

4

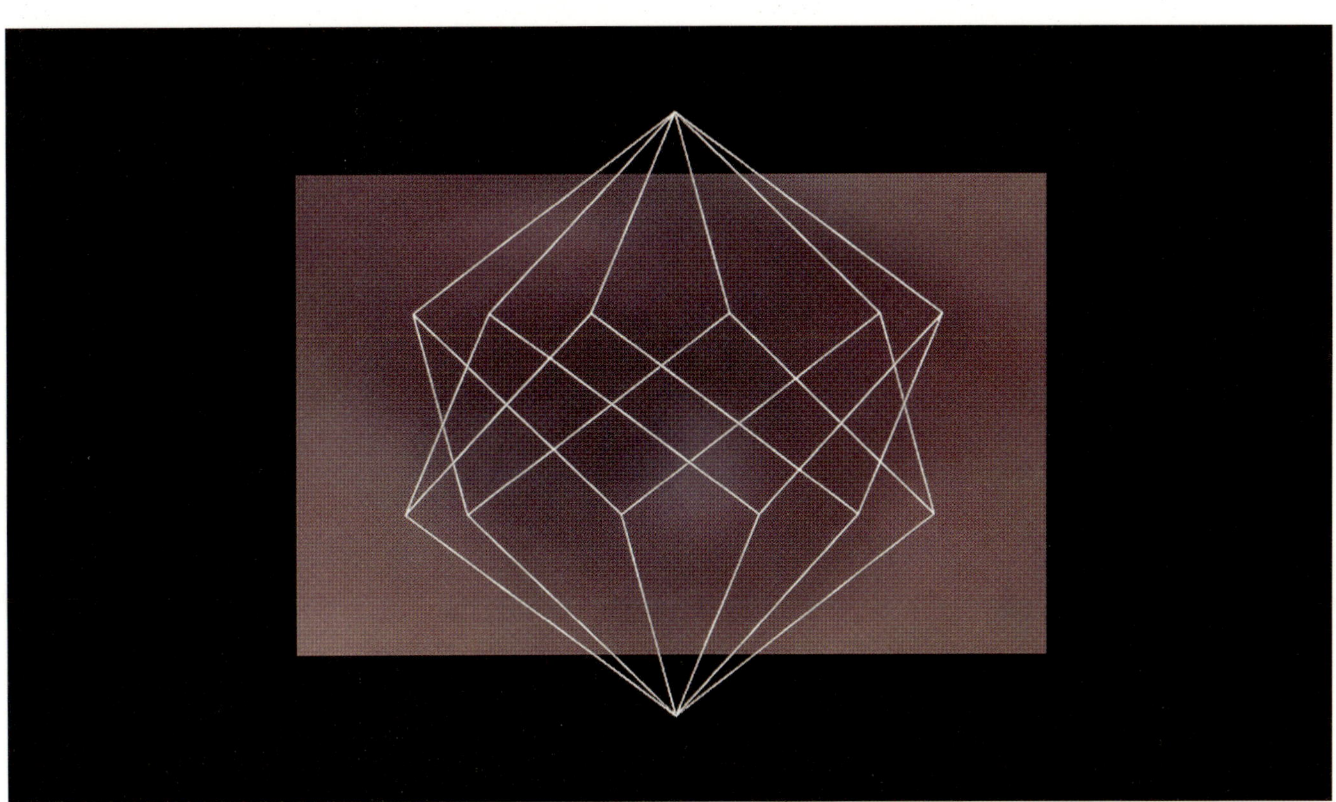

5

1. – 2. *She Was Whistling He Was Shooting*, 2016 (stills)
HD video, color, and sound, 2:15 min

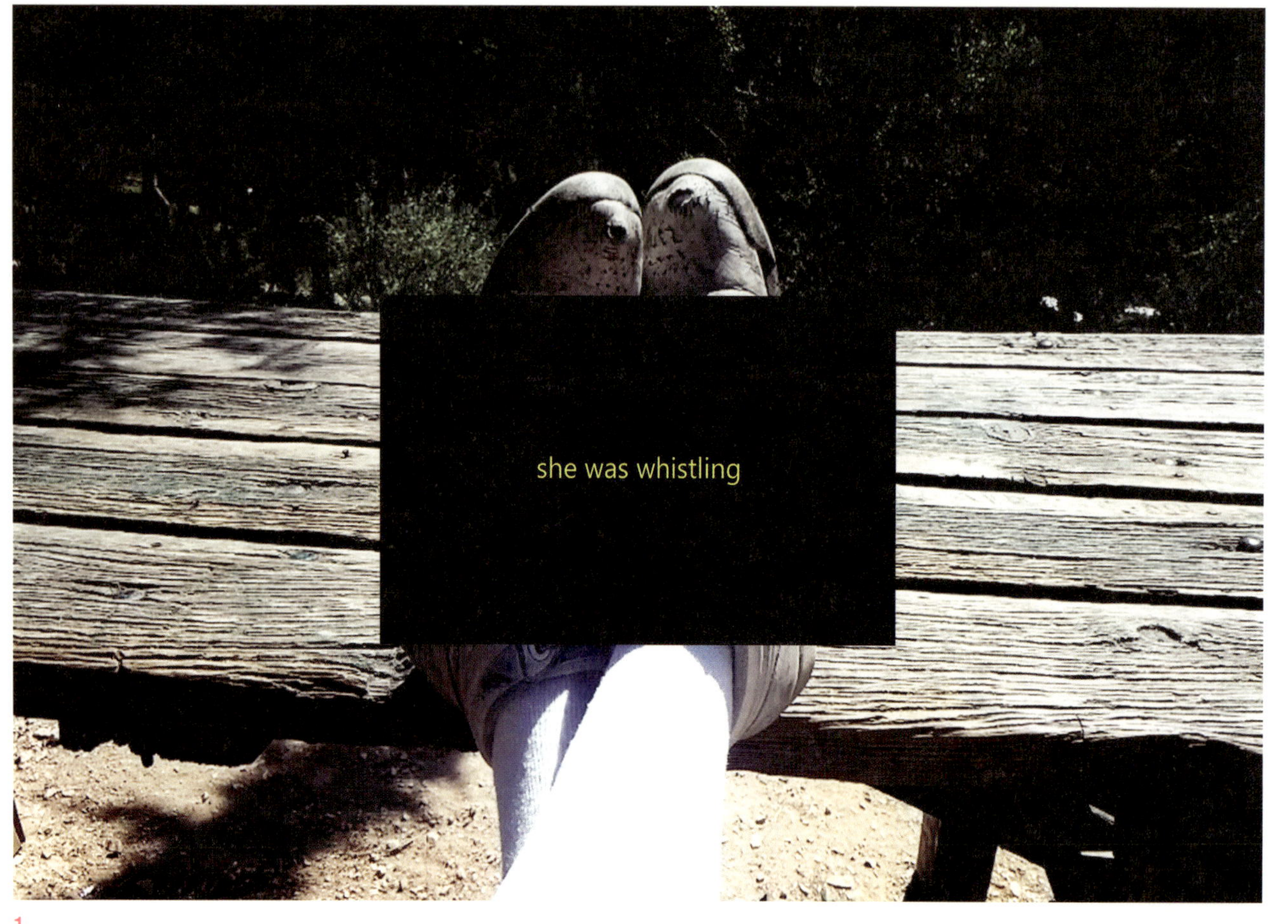

1

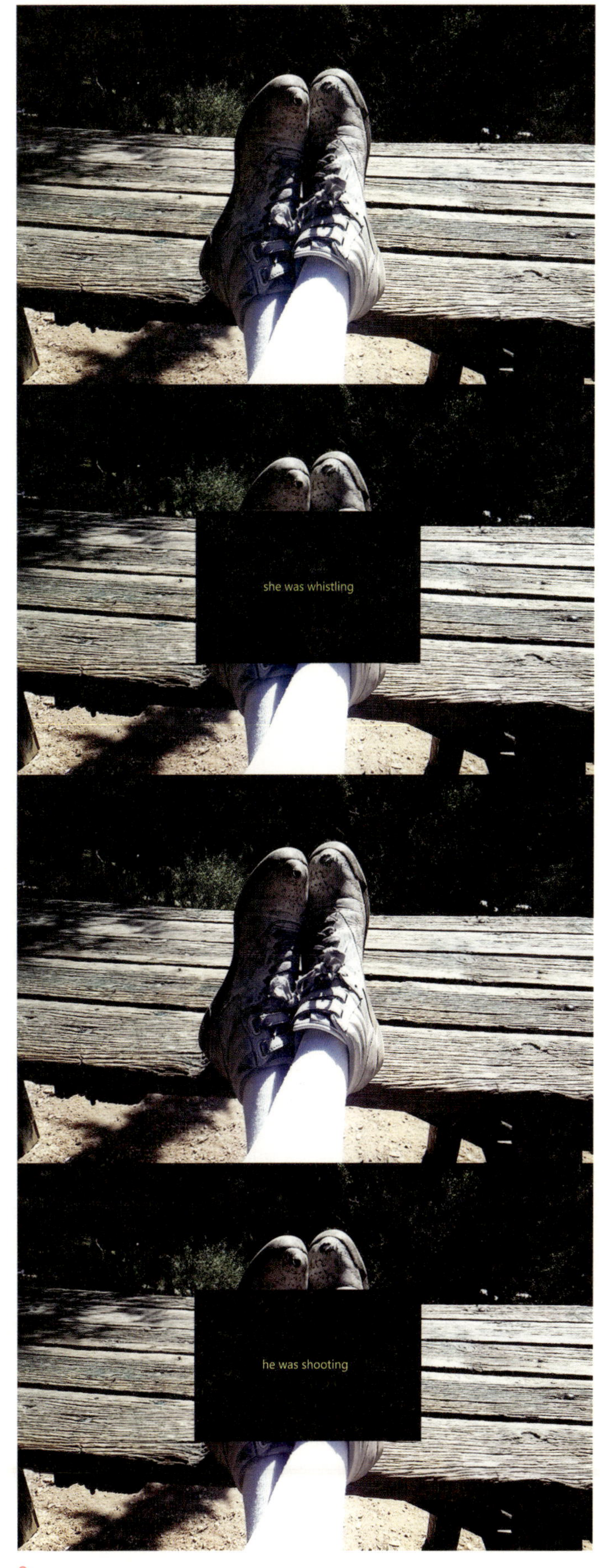
she was whistling
he was shooting

1. *Piss Off and Look in Front of You*, 2015
Sumi ink on paper, 150 x 200 cm

2. *Om*, 2015
Acrylic on canvas, 200 x 200 cm

3. *Re, Your Shadow is Bigger Than You*, 2015
Sumi ink on paper, 150 x 200 cm

4. *Seeking Individuals*, 2015
Pastel and colored pencil on colored paper, 50 x 70 cm

5. *Ce chien est à moi*, 2015
Sumi ink on paper, 150 x 200 cm

6. *I Knew I Had Something Too*, 2015
Sumi ink on paper, 150 x 200 cm

7. *West, East, North and South Meet*, 2015
Acrylic on canvas, 160 x 200 cm

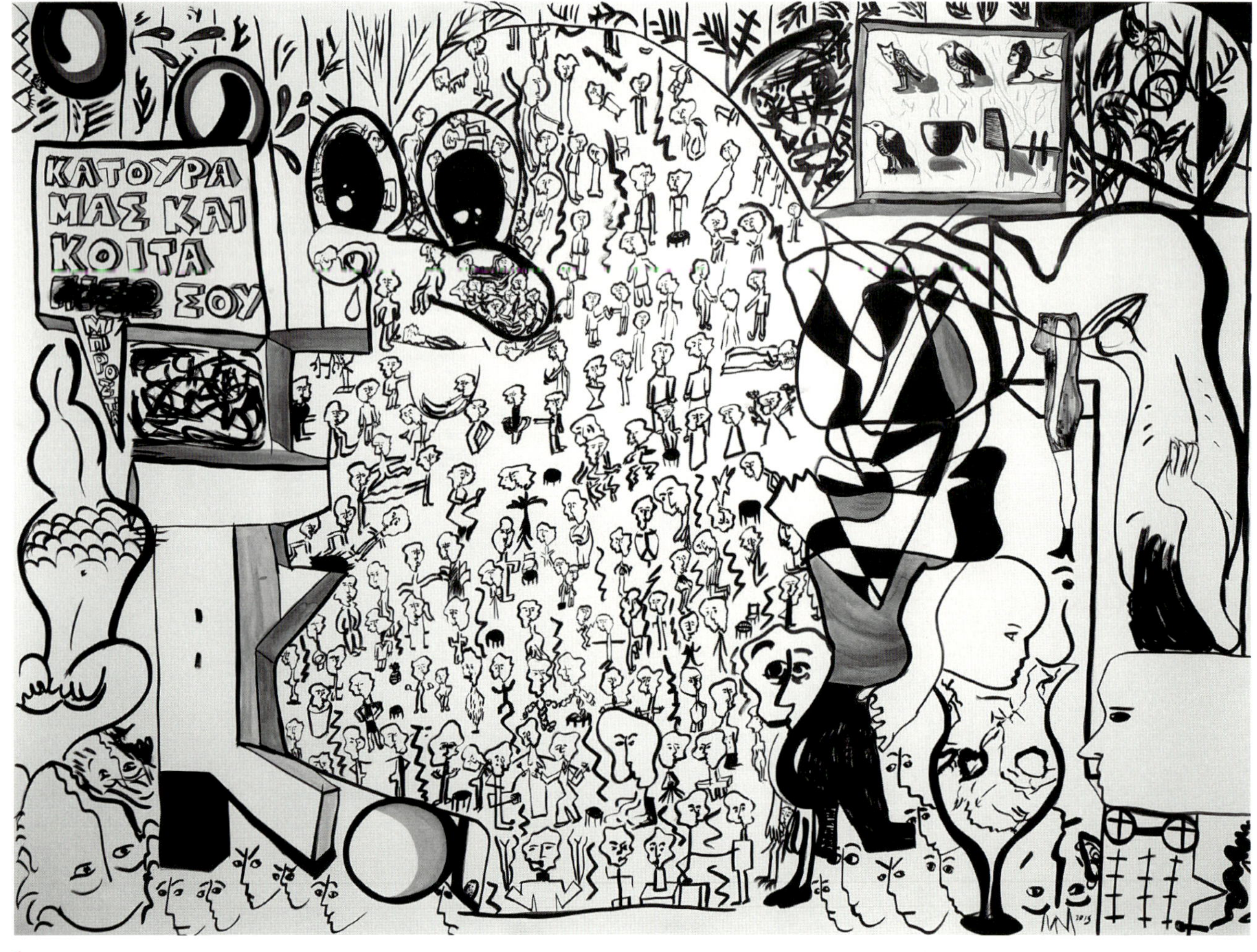

1

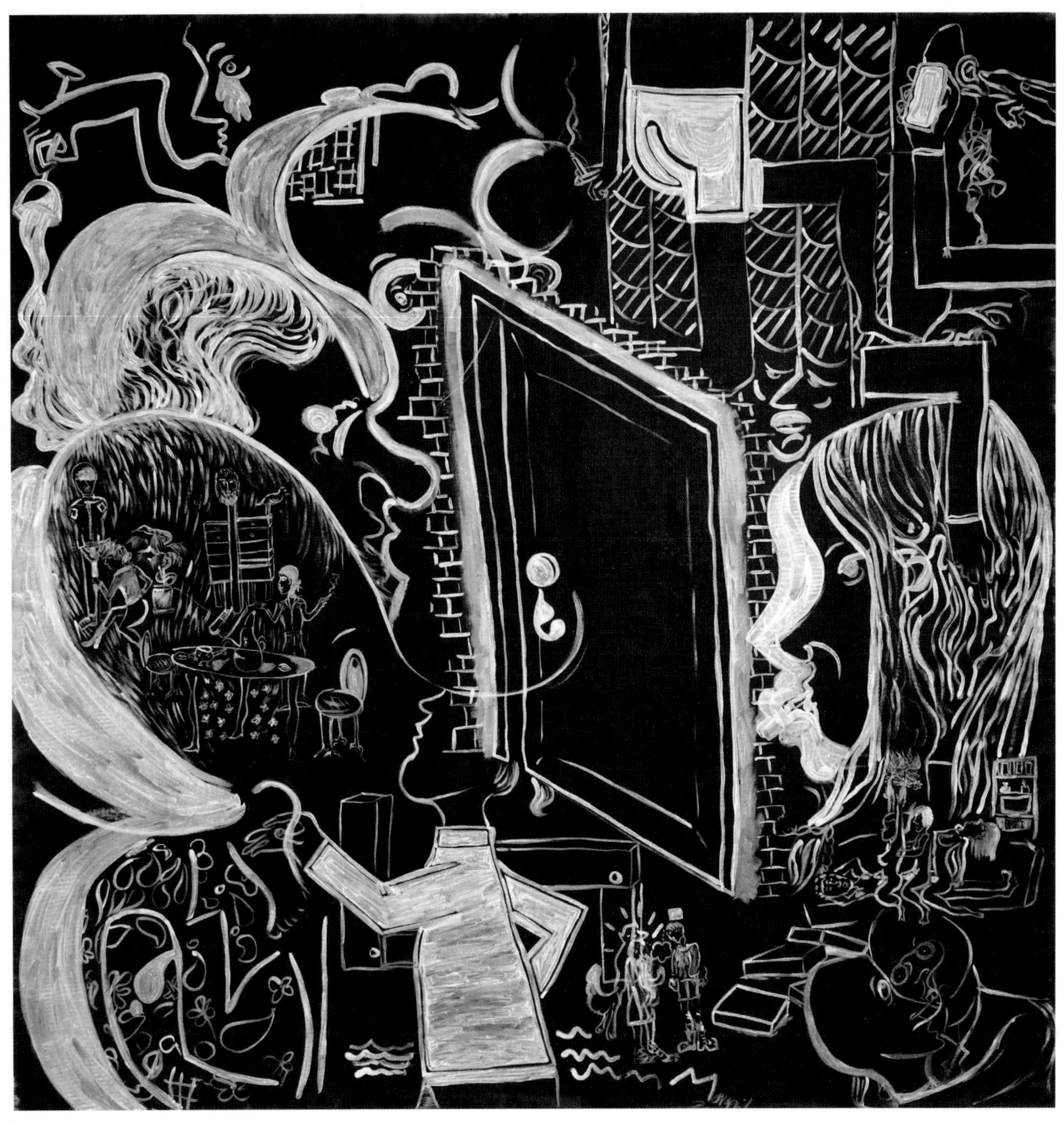

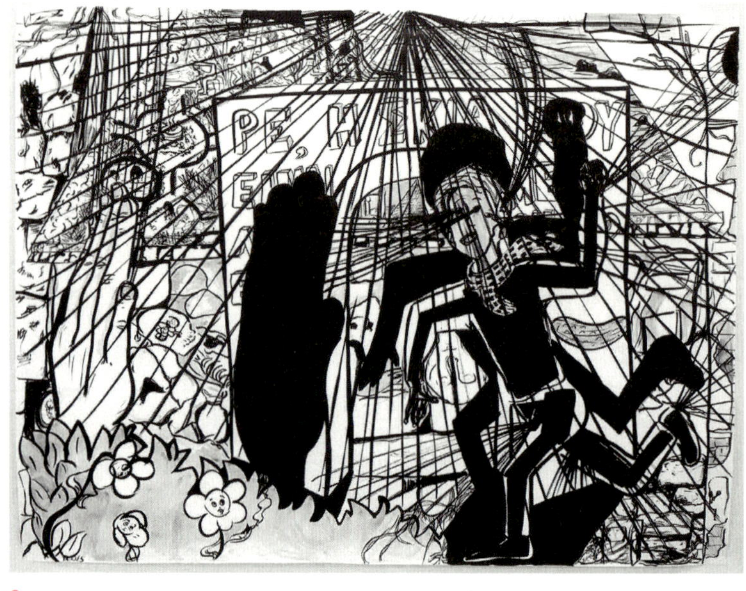

3

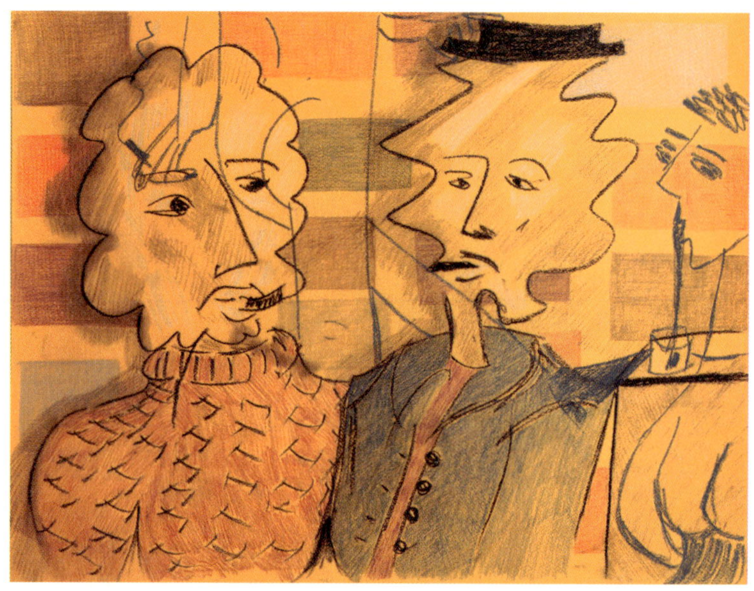

4

5

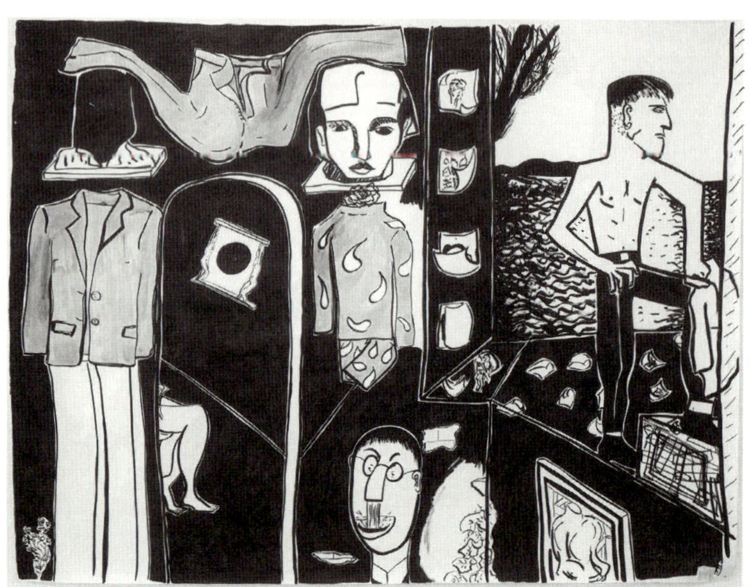

6

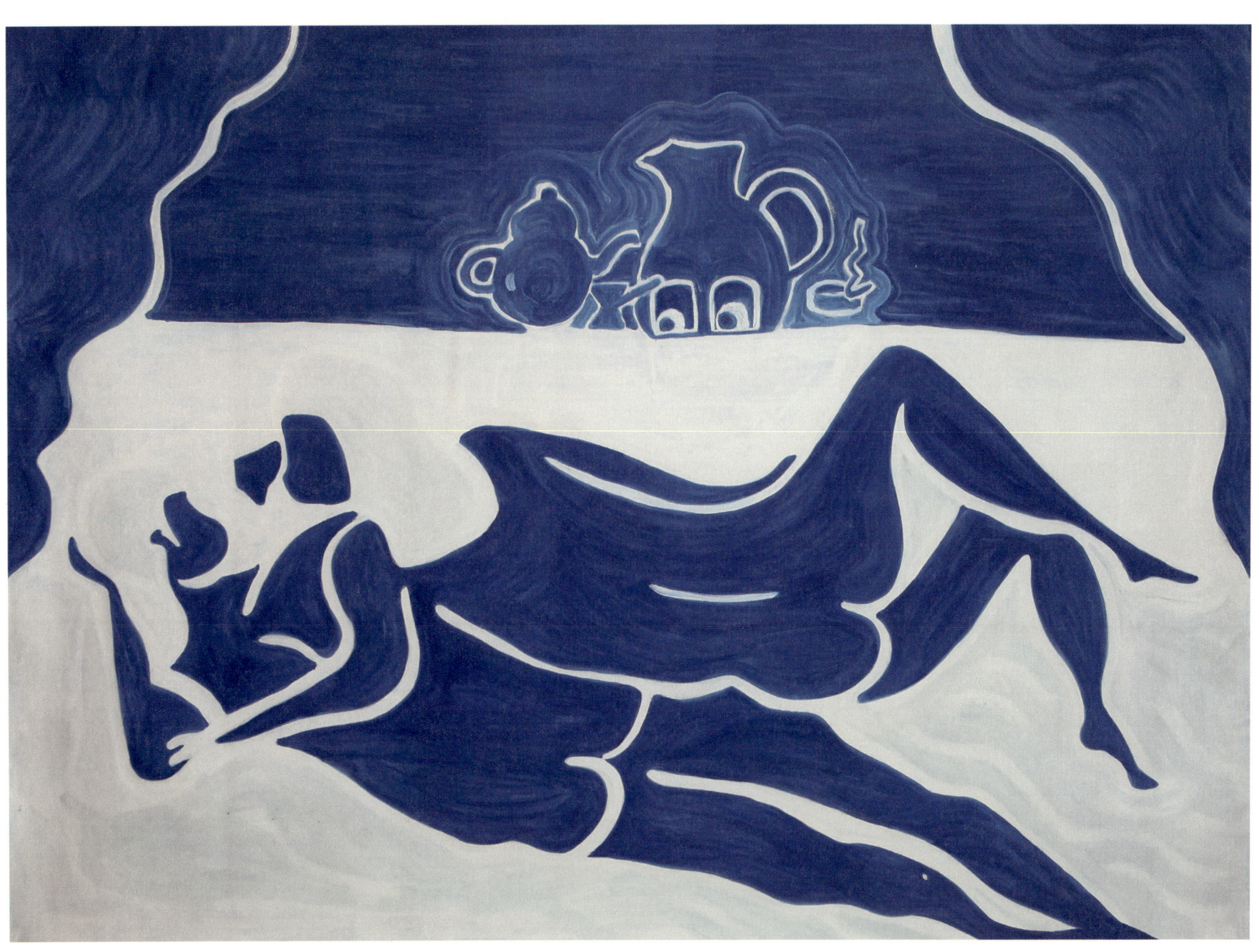

1. *A river needs banks to flow*, 2014
Two-channel HD video with color and sound, wooden telescope tripods with mini LED-projectors, screen prints and voice over audio, 55:00 min

2. *Black Mountain*, 2015
HD video, color, and sound, 10:33 min

3. *l'histoire d'histoire d'une histoire*, 2012
122 glass lantern slides transferred to 35mm, two synchronized slide projections in color and black and white, and voiceover sound, 21:30 min

4. *Shelter Cove*, 2015
Two-channel HD video, color, and sound, 13:00 min

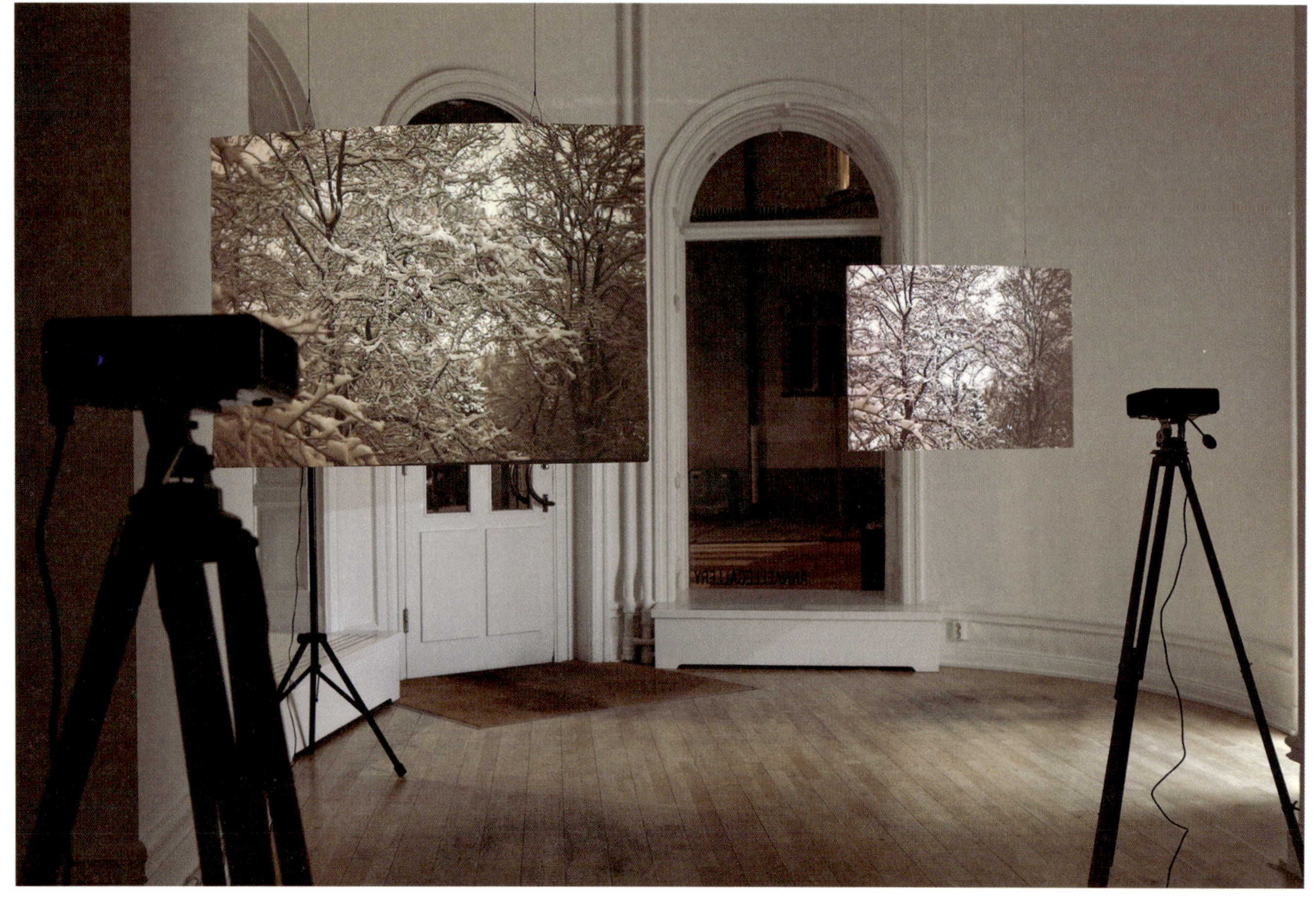

1

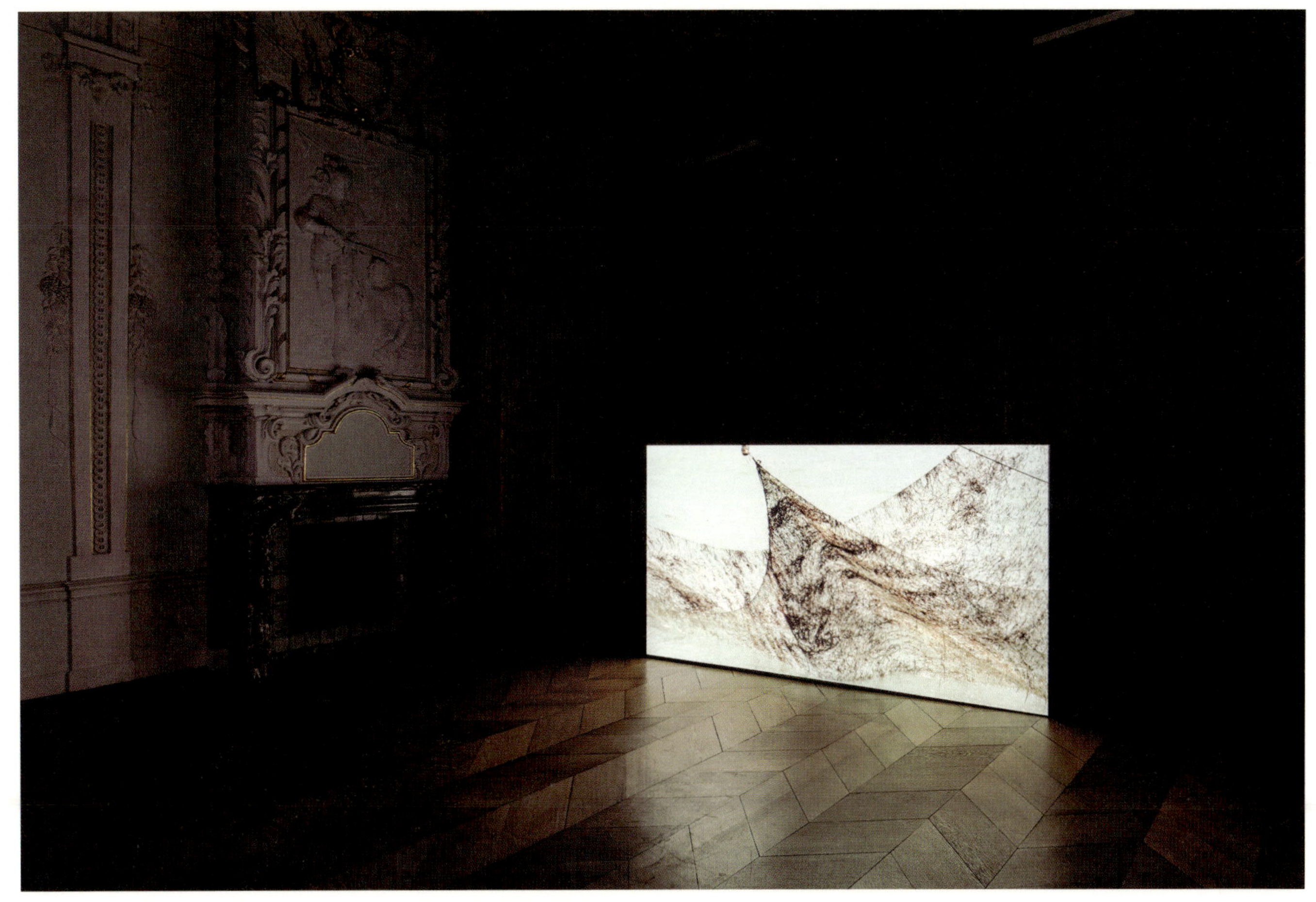

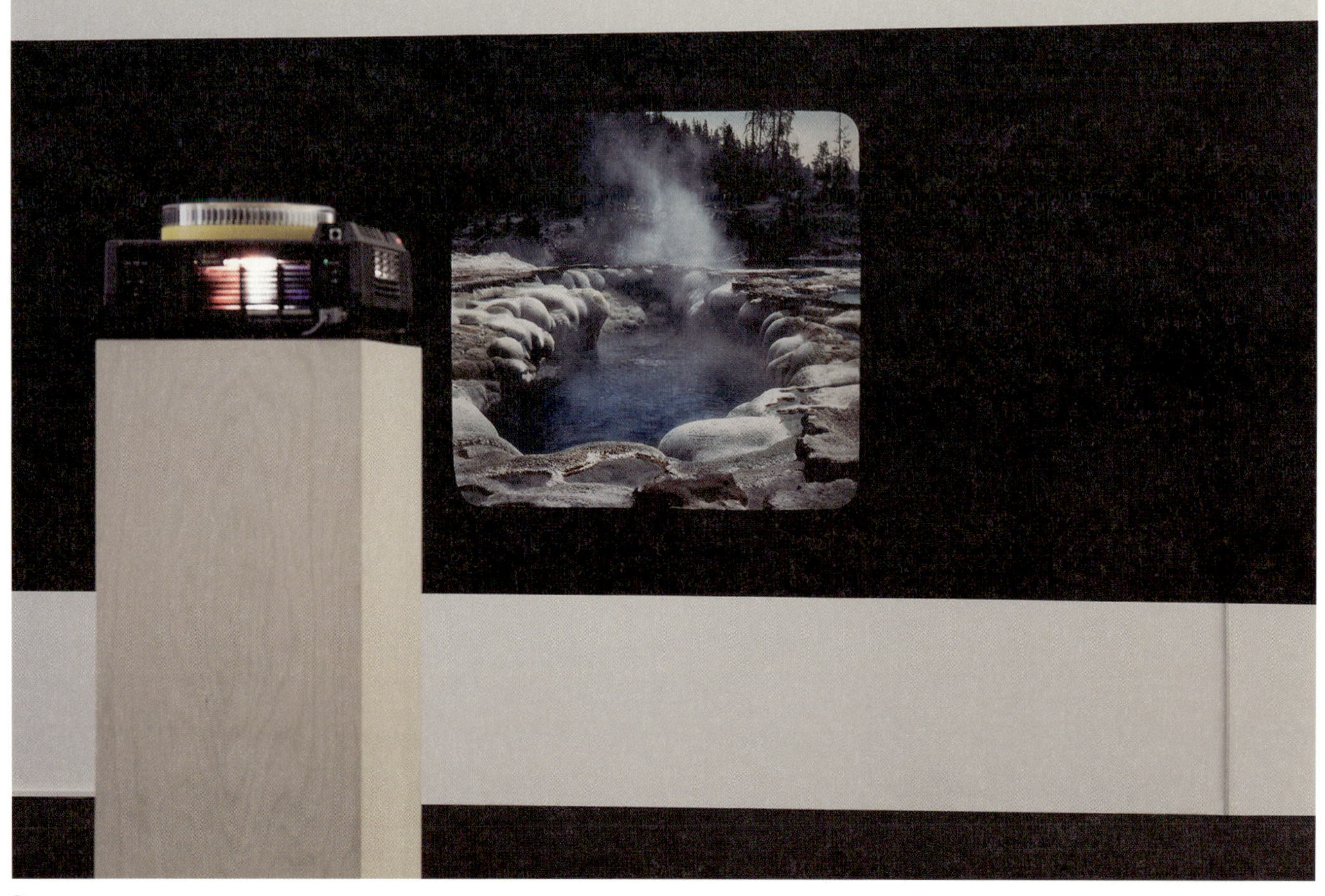

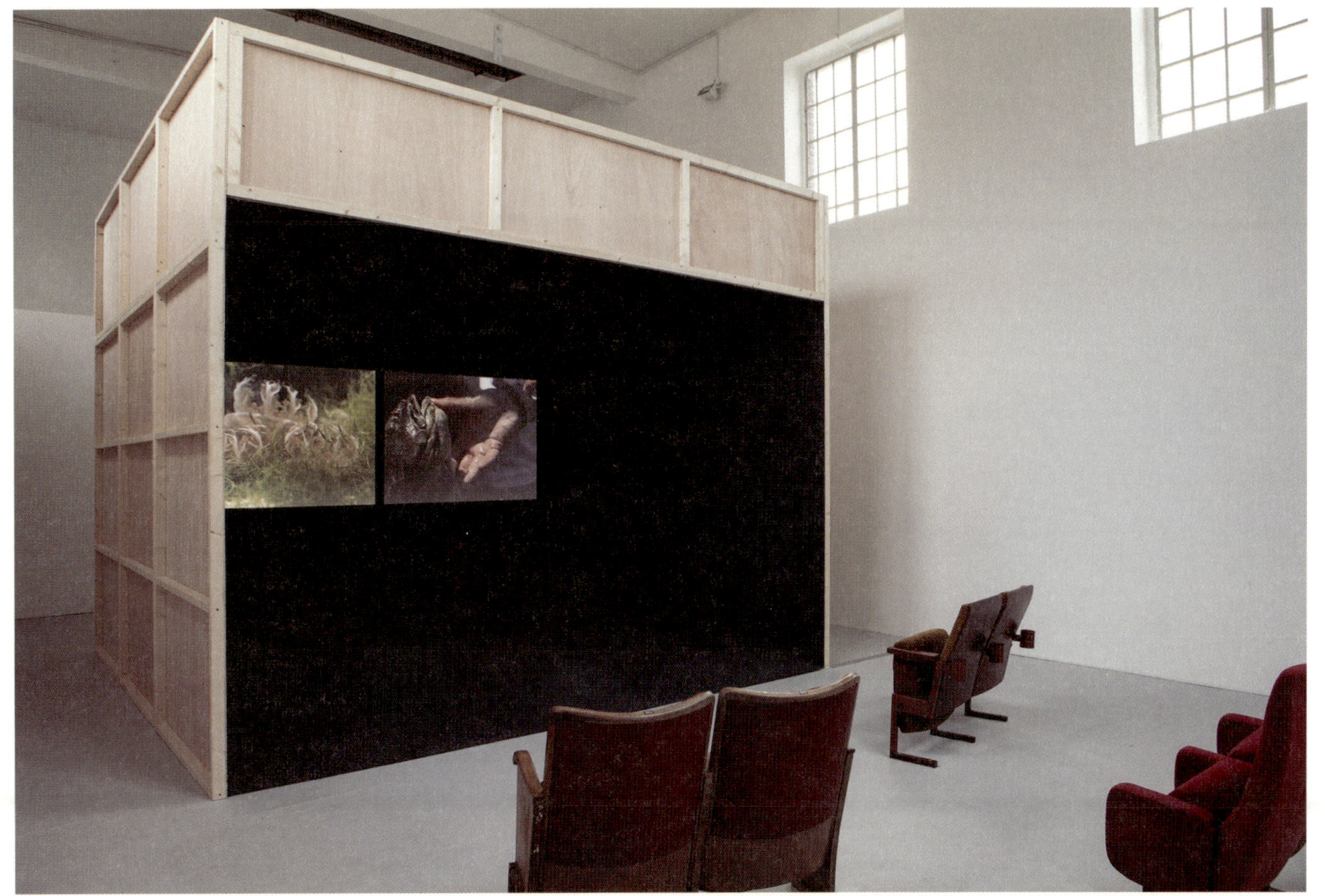

1. *Crystal Cravings*, 2015
C-prints on Fujifilm paper and liquid tar on matboard, 93.4 x 151 cm

2. – 4. *Crystal Cravings*, 2015 (details)
C-prints on Fujifilm paper and liquid tar on matboard, 93.4 x 151 cm

5. *Silent Hysteria*, 2015
Petroleum and water in iron tanks, dimensions variable

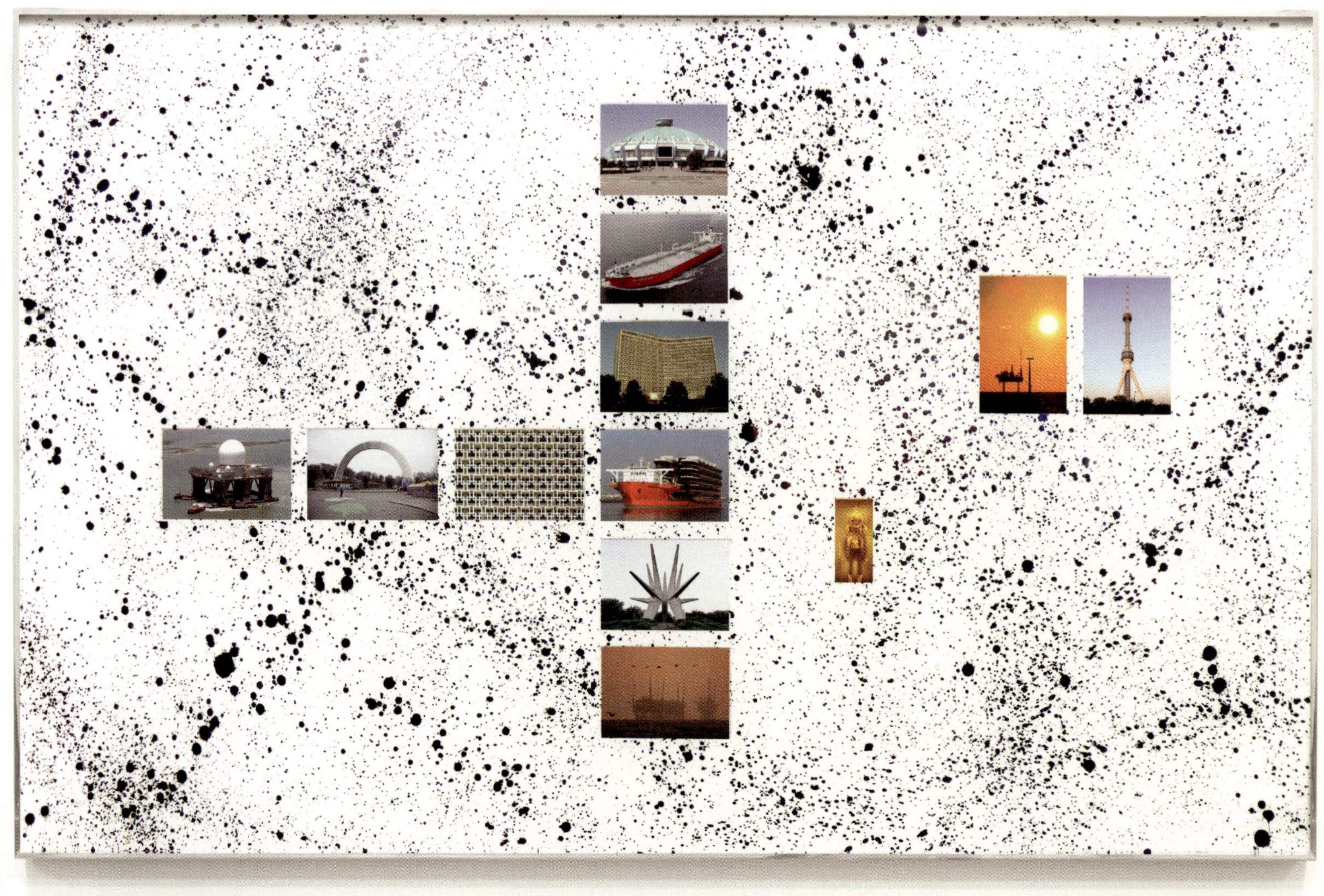

1

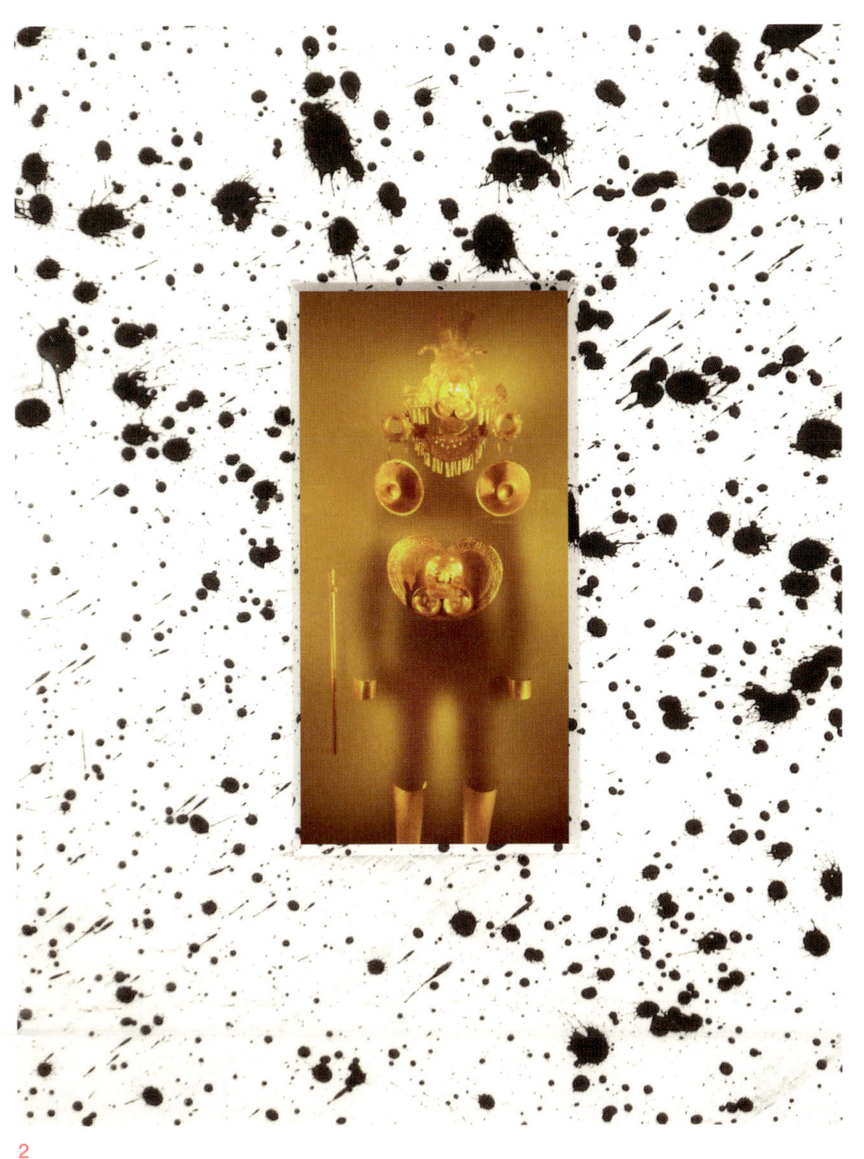

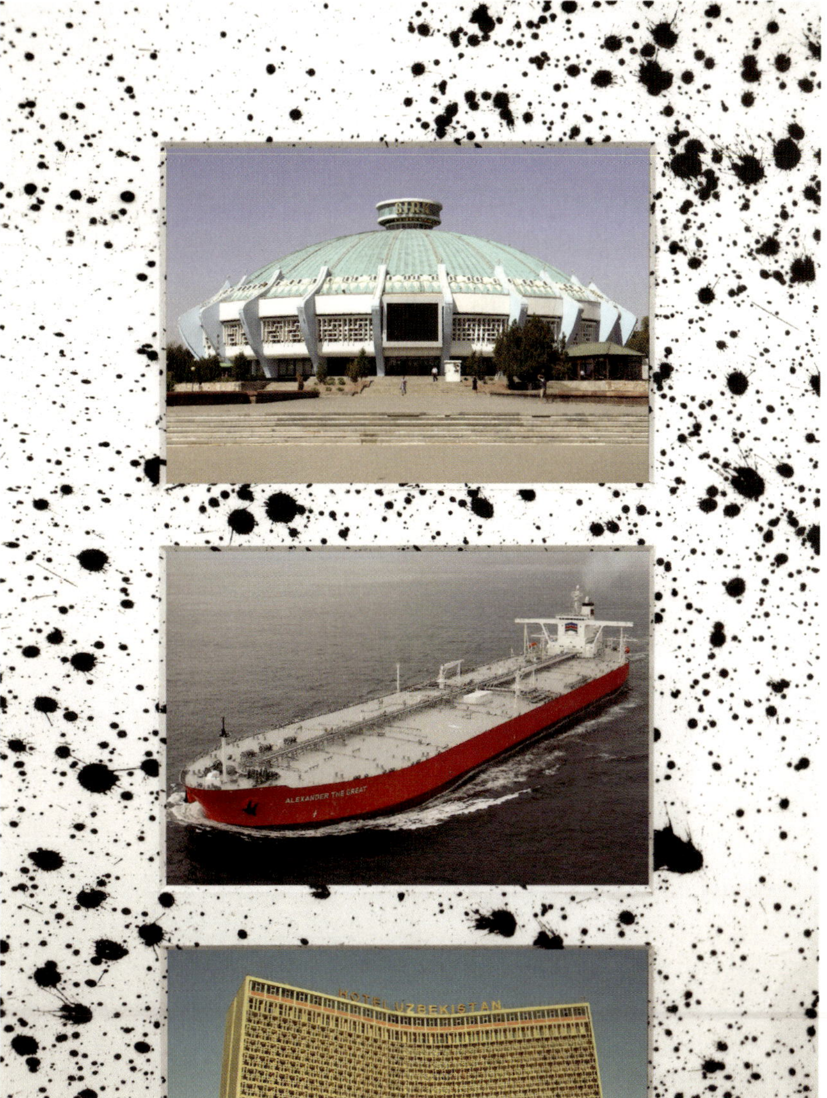
ALEXANDER THE GREAT
HOTEL UZBEKISTAN

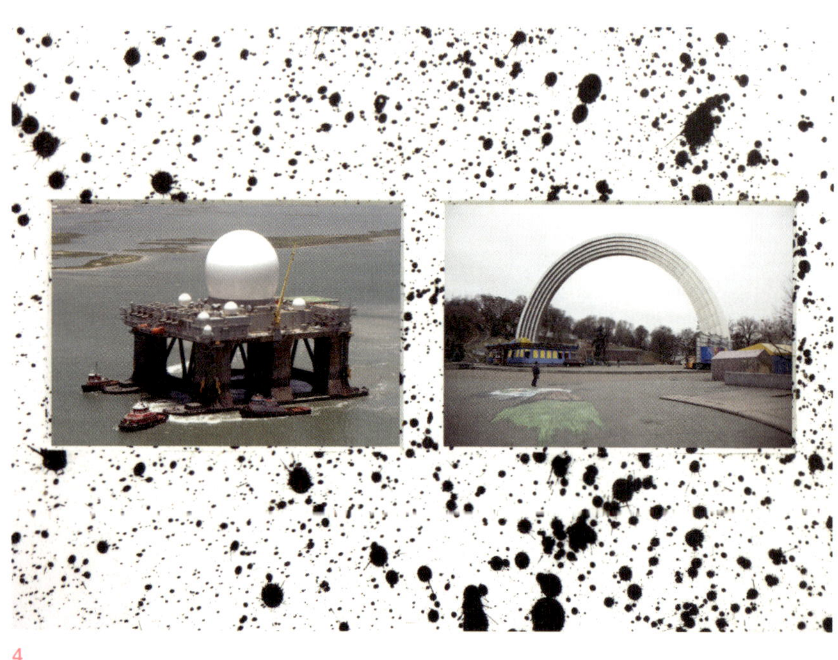

4

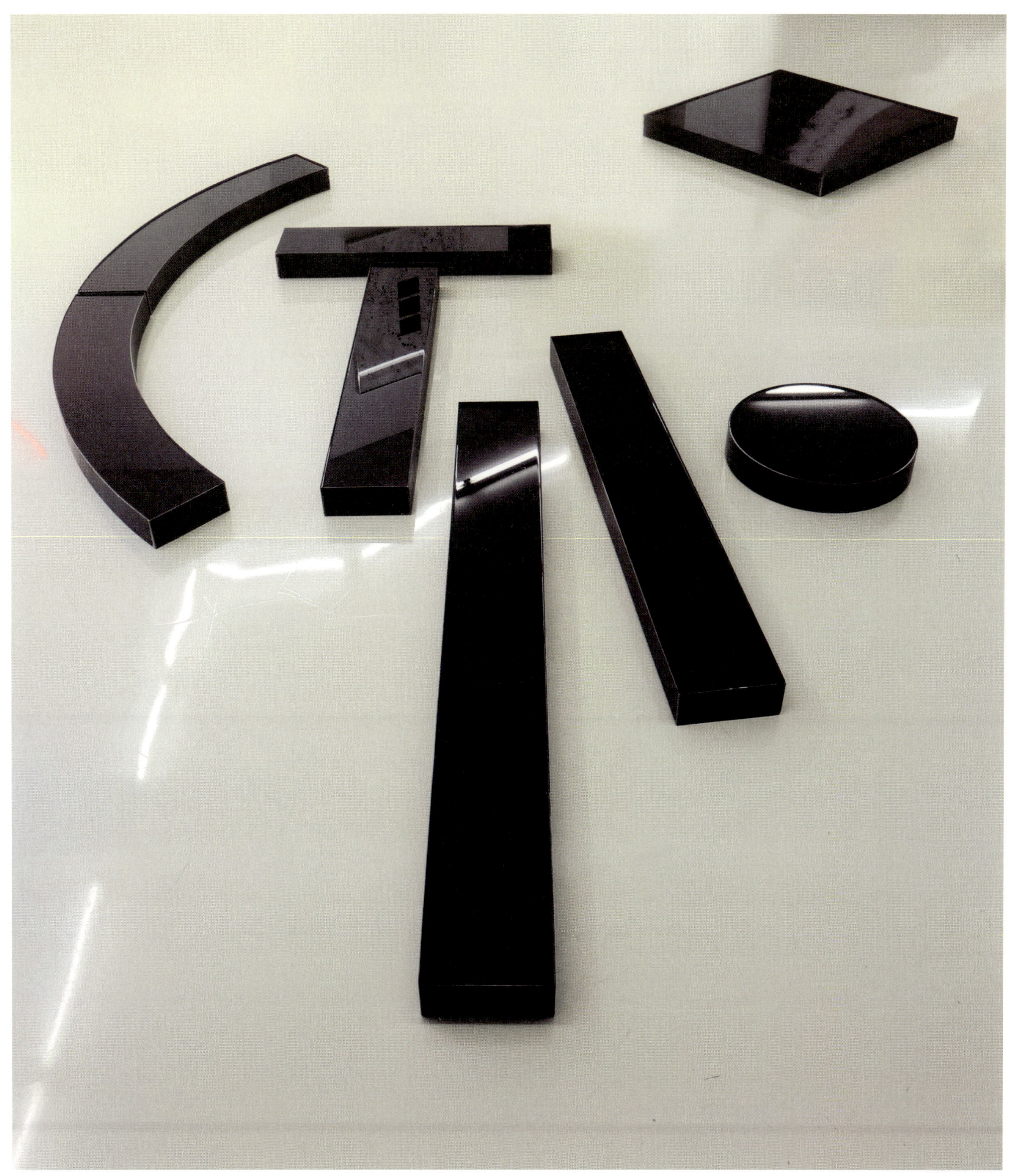

1. *Bridge* from the series *Gold Rush*, 2016
Inkjet print on paper, 82 x 110 cm

2. *Interception Corner* from the series *Gold Rush*, 2016
Inkjet print on paper, 110 x 82 cm

3. *Lucky Numbers* from the series *Gold Rush*, 2016
Inkjet print on paper, 82 x 110 cm

4. *Town Council* from the series *Gold Rush*, 2016
Inkjet print on paper, 82 x 110 cm

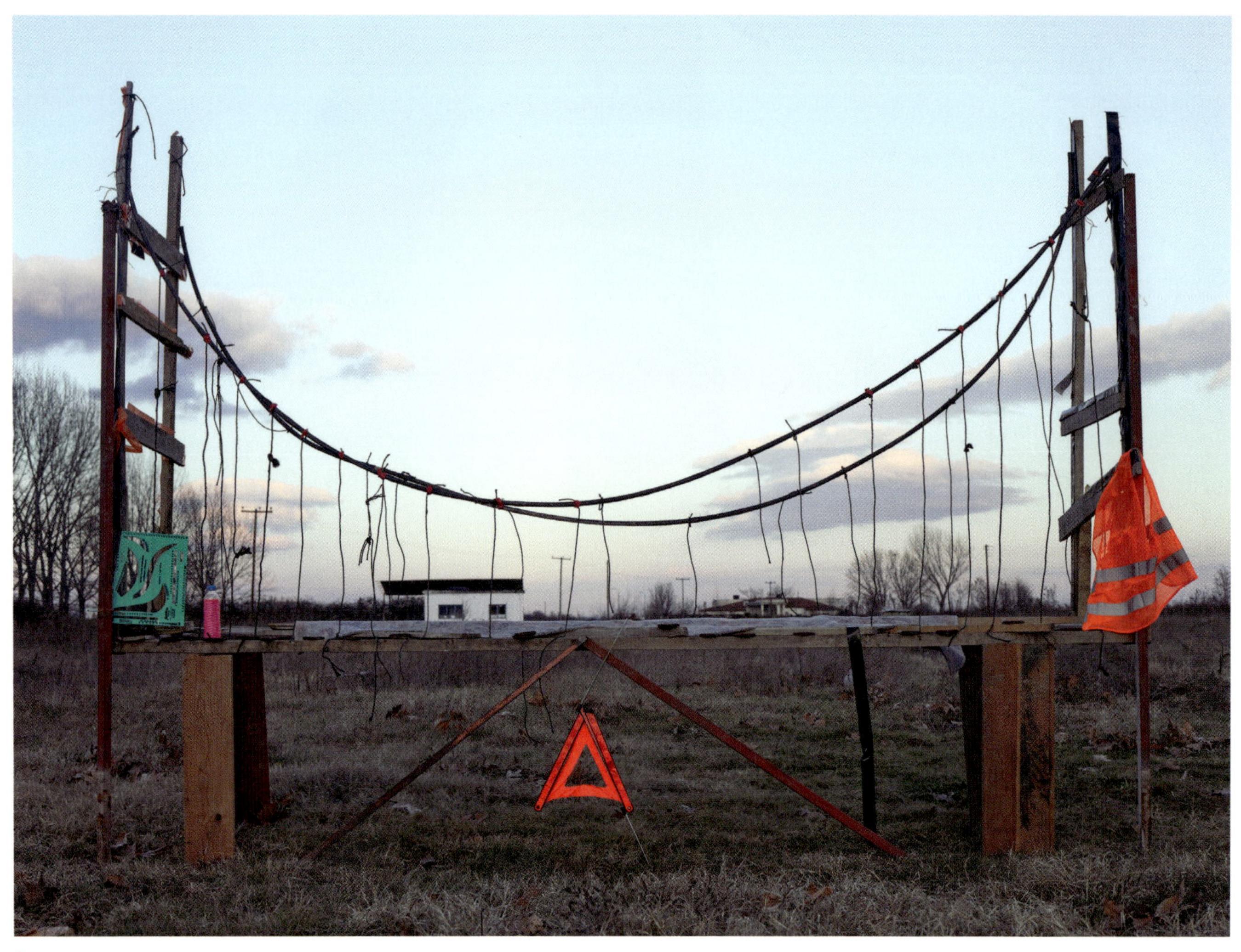

1

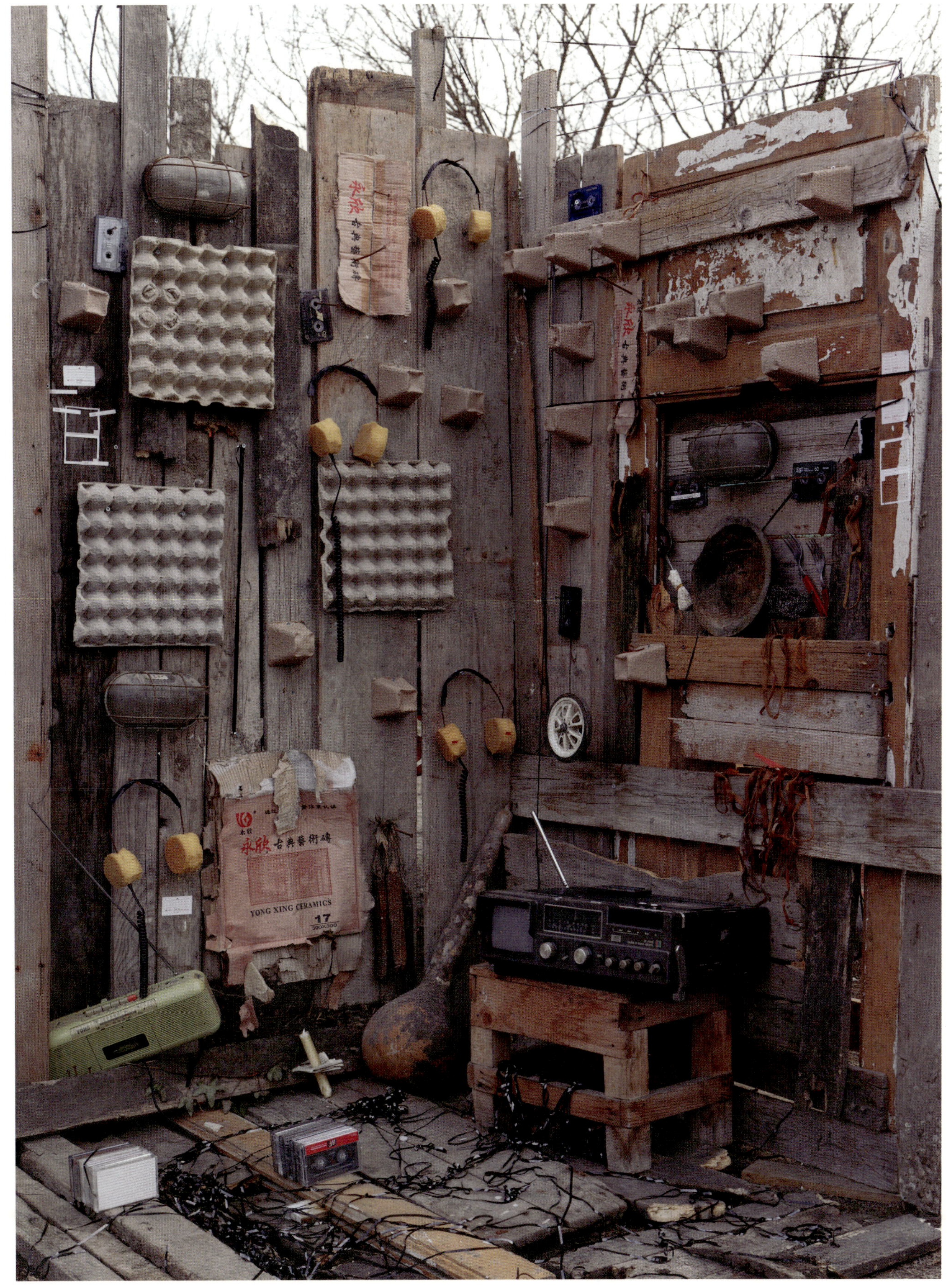
YONG XING CERAMICS
17
200X300

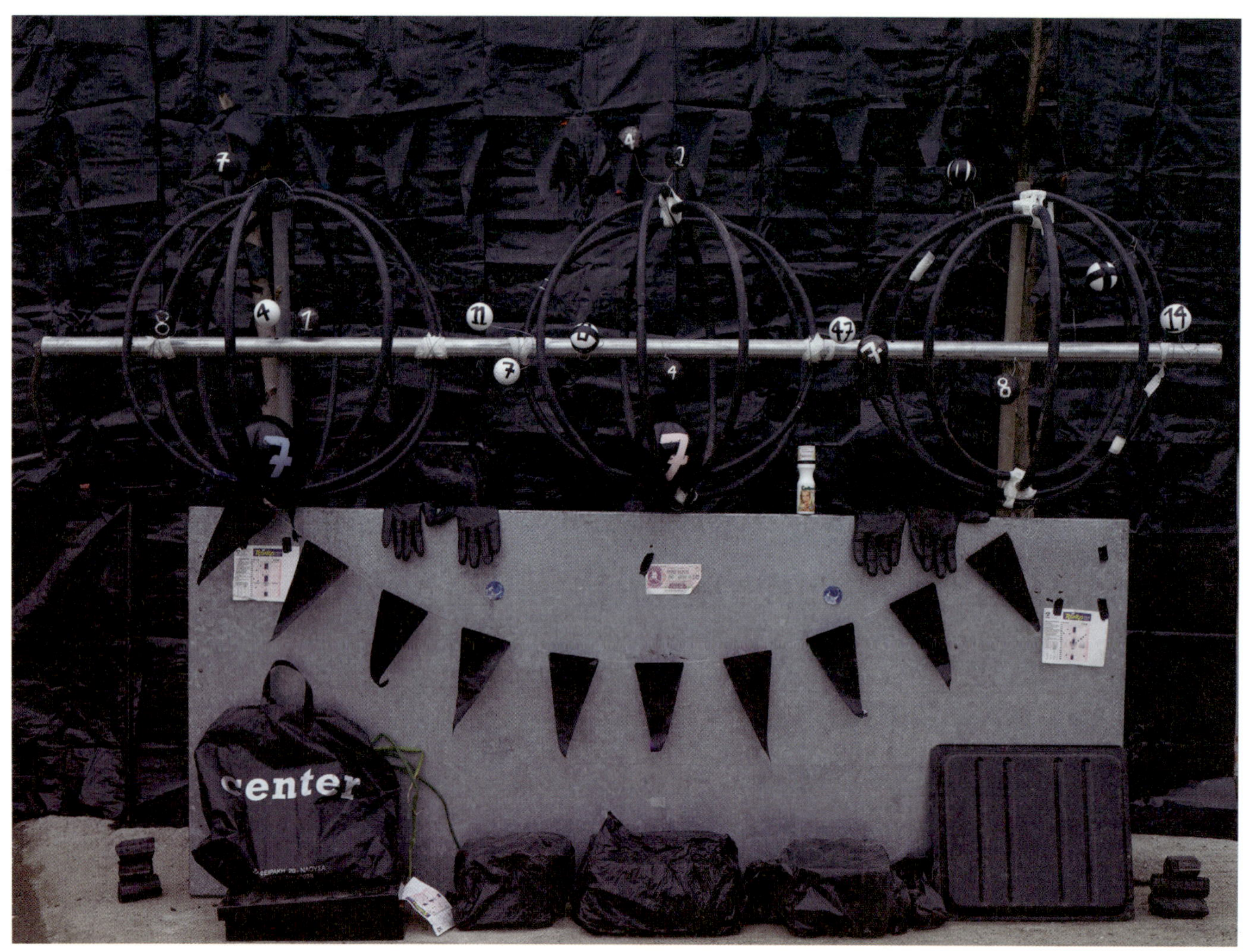
center

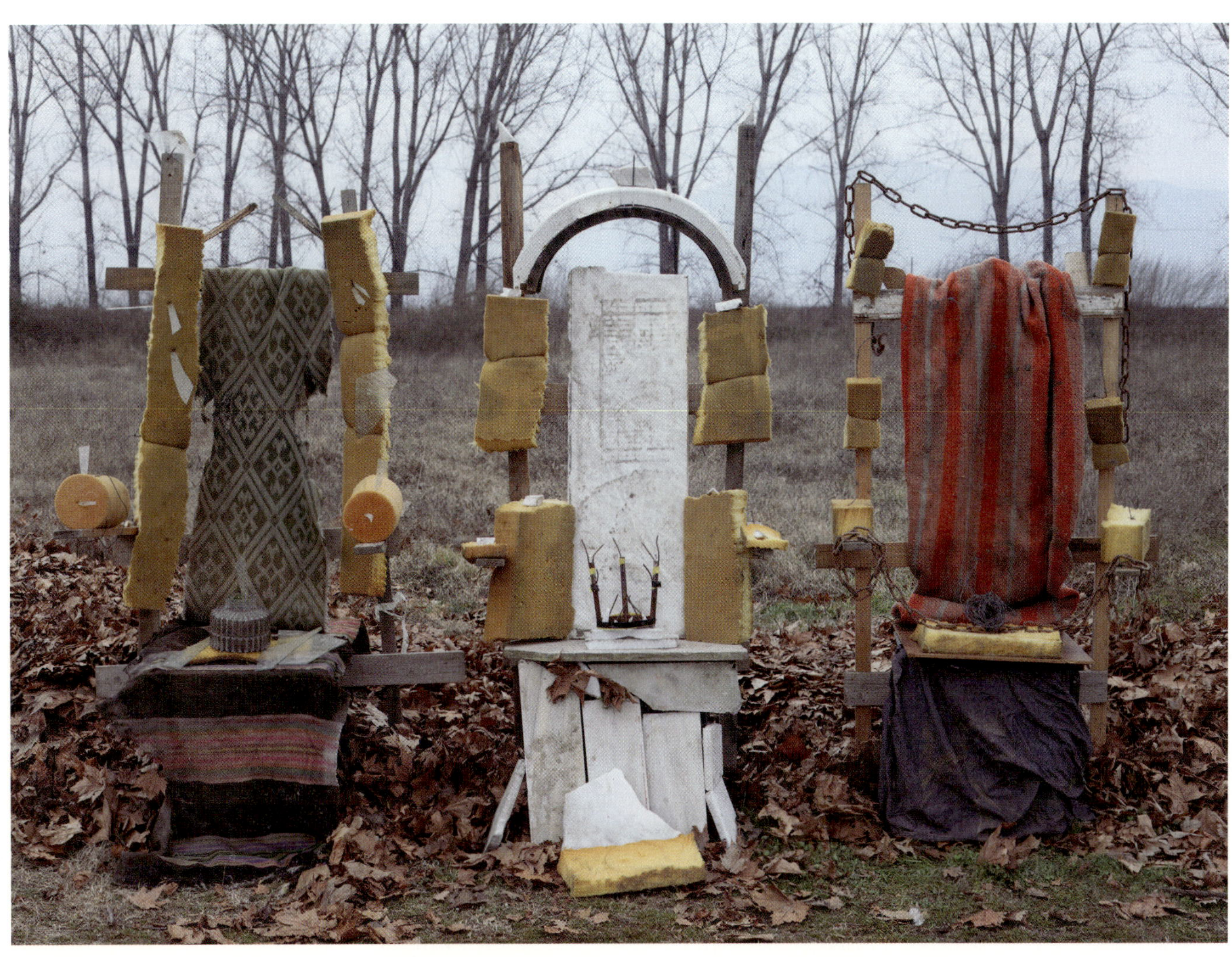

1. *Other Things Happen in December Besides Christmas 1*, 2015–16
Oil and screen print on paper mounted on aluminum, three panels: 33 x 33 cm each

2. *Other Things Happen in December Besides Christmas 2*, 2015–16
Oil and screen print on paper mounted on aluminum, two panels: 33 x 33 cm each

3. *Other Things Happen in December Besides Christmas 3*, 2015–16
Oil and screen print on paper mounted on aluminum, two panels: 33 x 33 cm each

4. *Other Things Happen in December Besides Christmas 4*, 2015–16
Oil and screen print on paper mounted on aluminum, three panels: 33 x 33 cm each

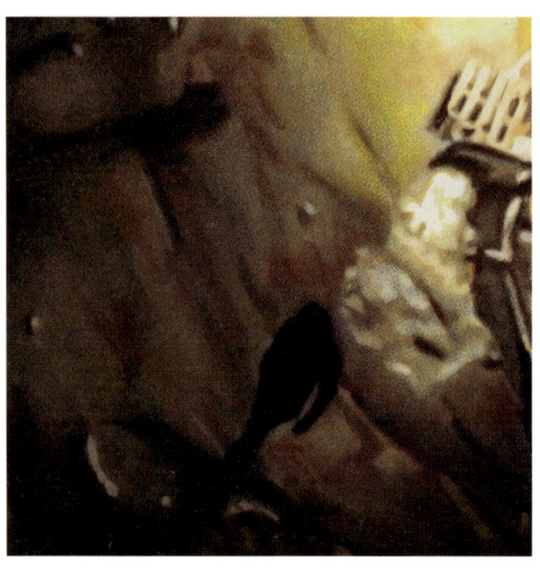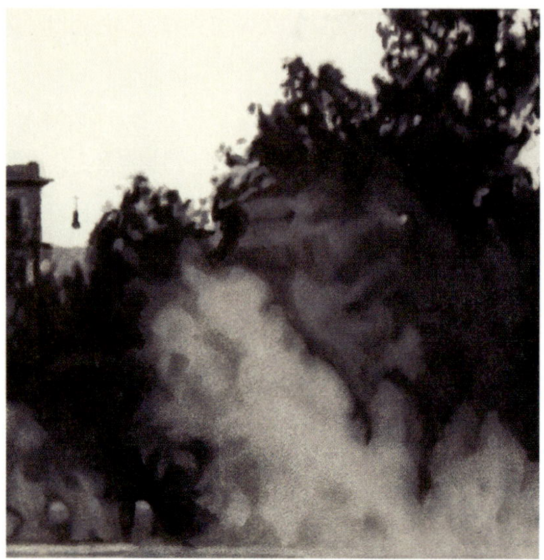

1

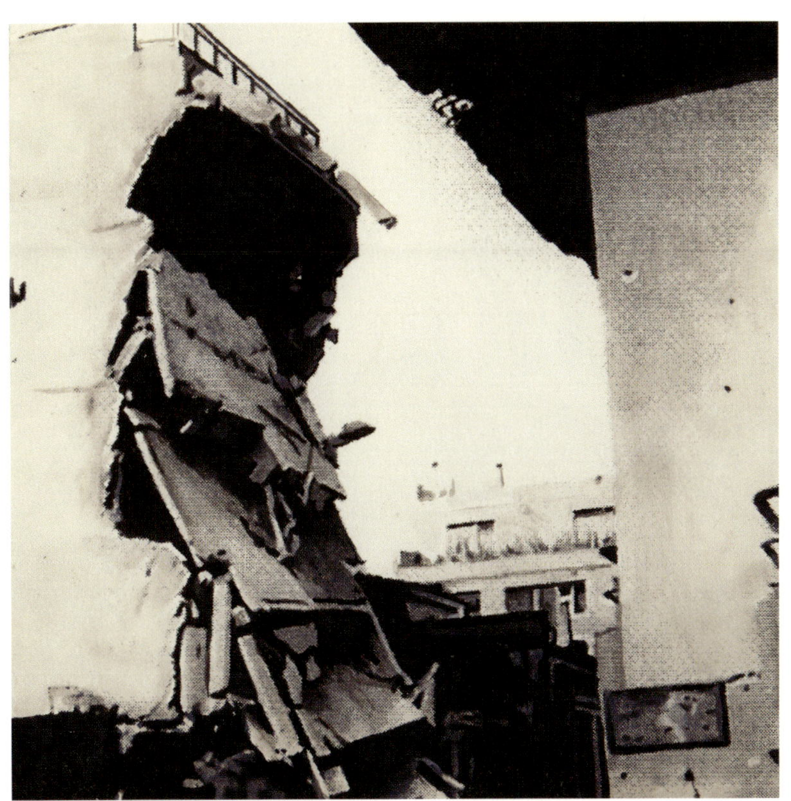

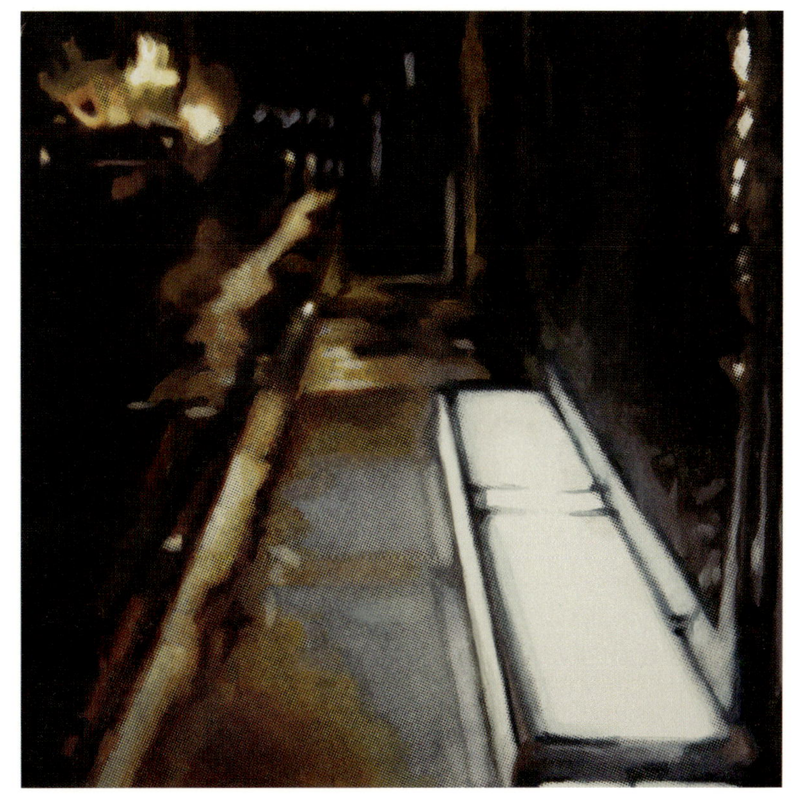

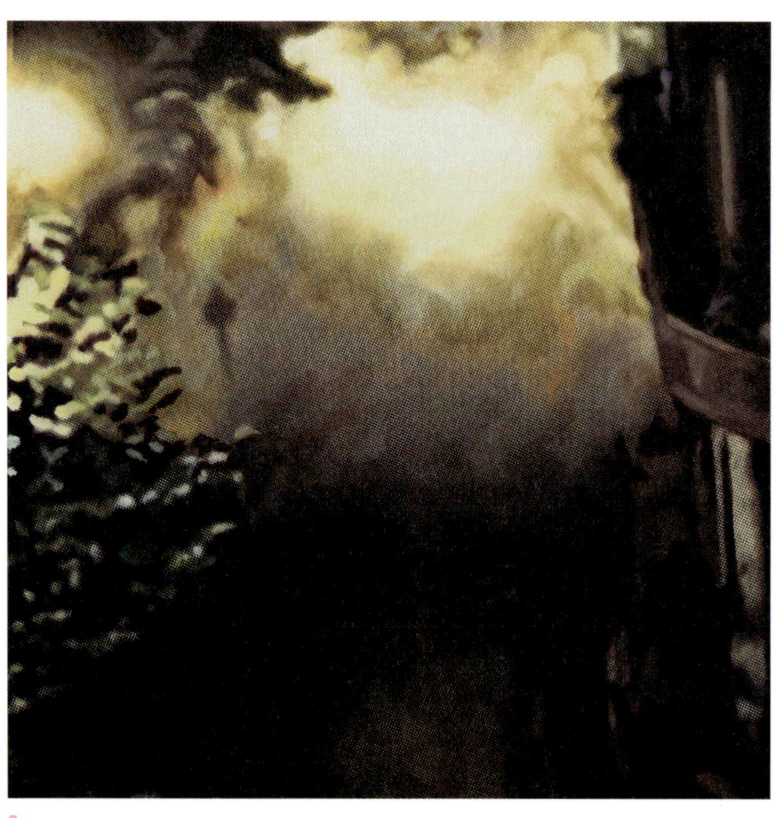

3

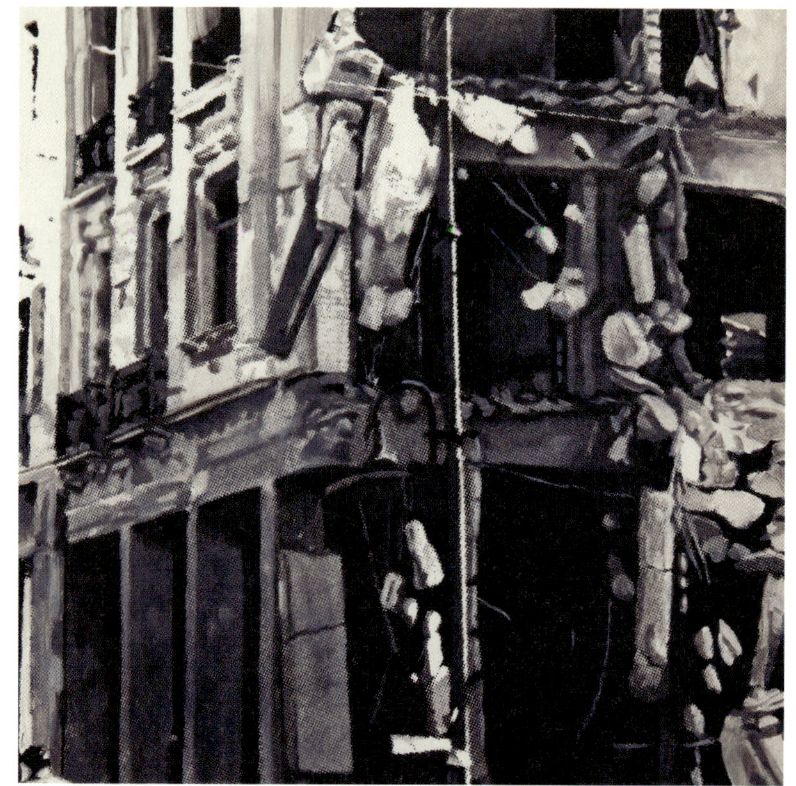

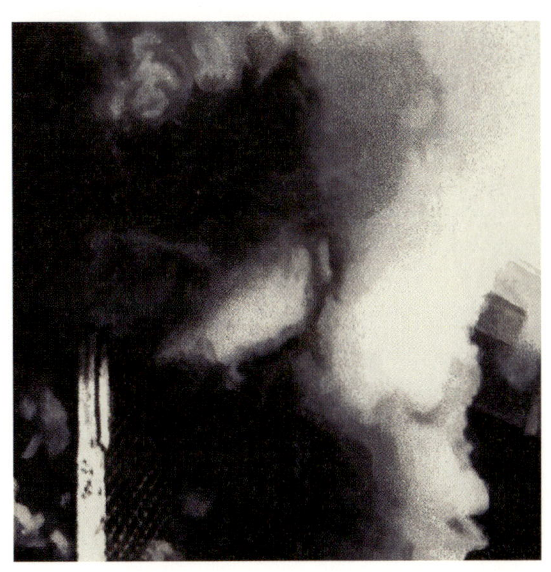
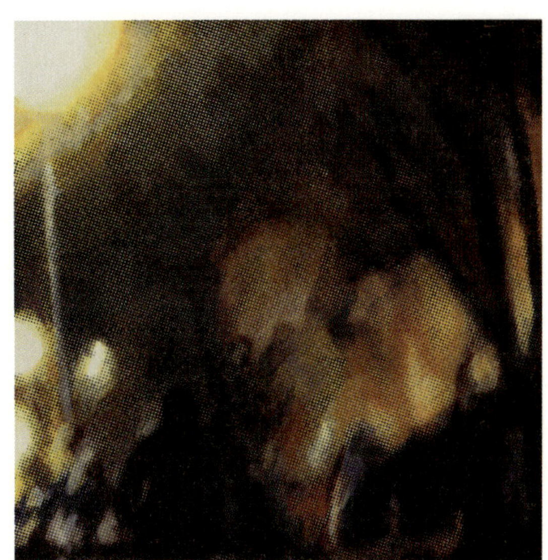
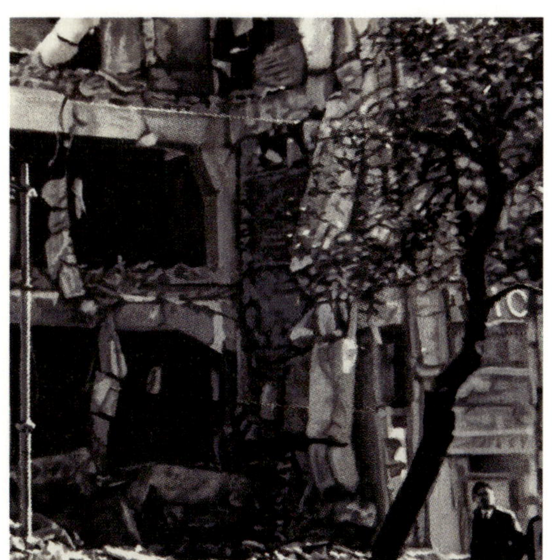

4

1. *Ritual*, 2016
Acrylic and thread on canvas, 115 x 200 cm

2. *Passage*, 2016
Acrylic and thread on canvas, 240 x 135 cm

3. *Betwixt*, 2015
Acrylic and thread on canvas, 135 x 188 cm

4. *Guardian*, 2016
Acrylic and thread on canvas, 152 x 79 cm

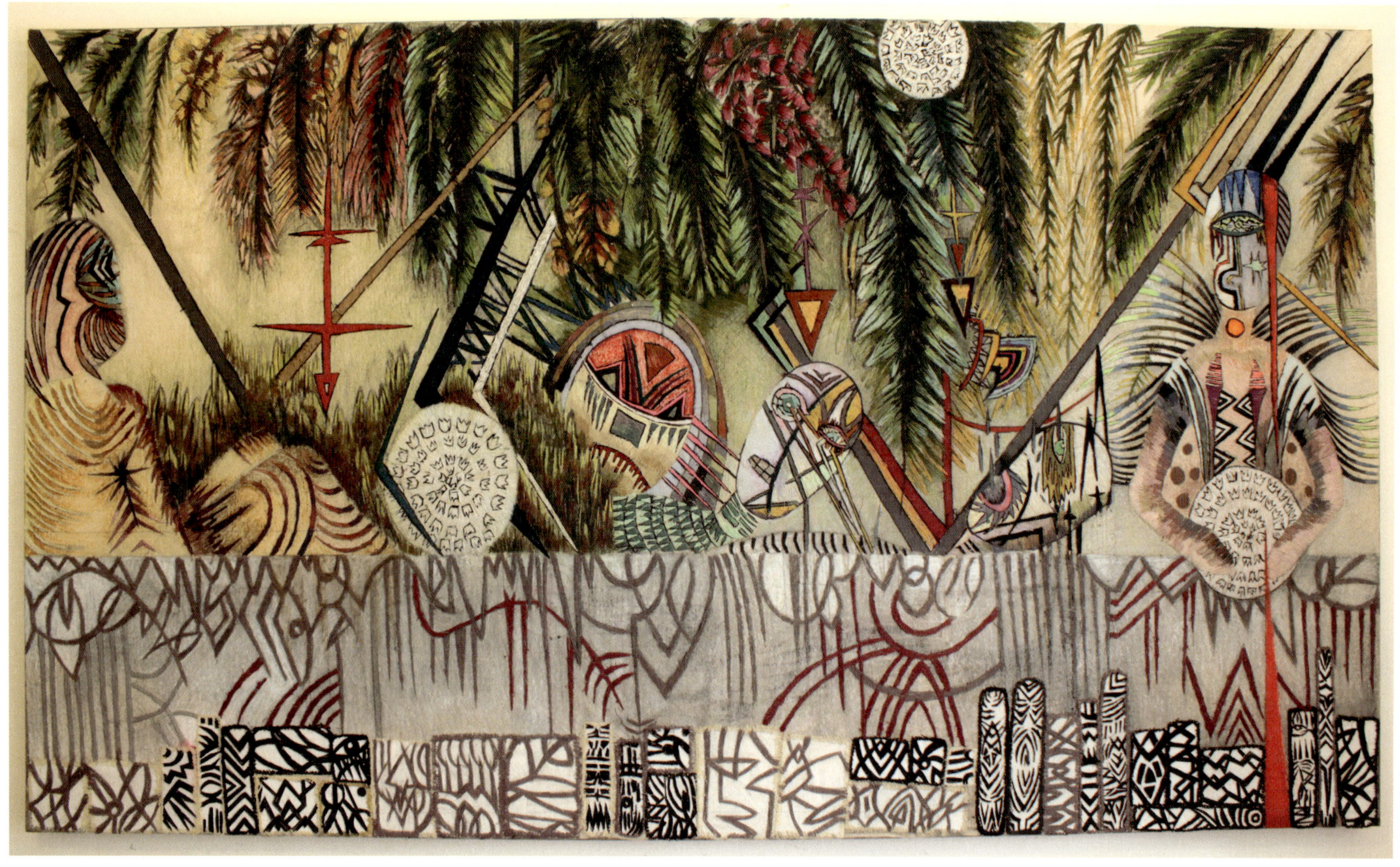

1

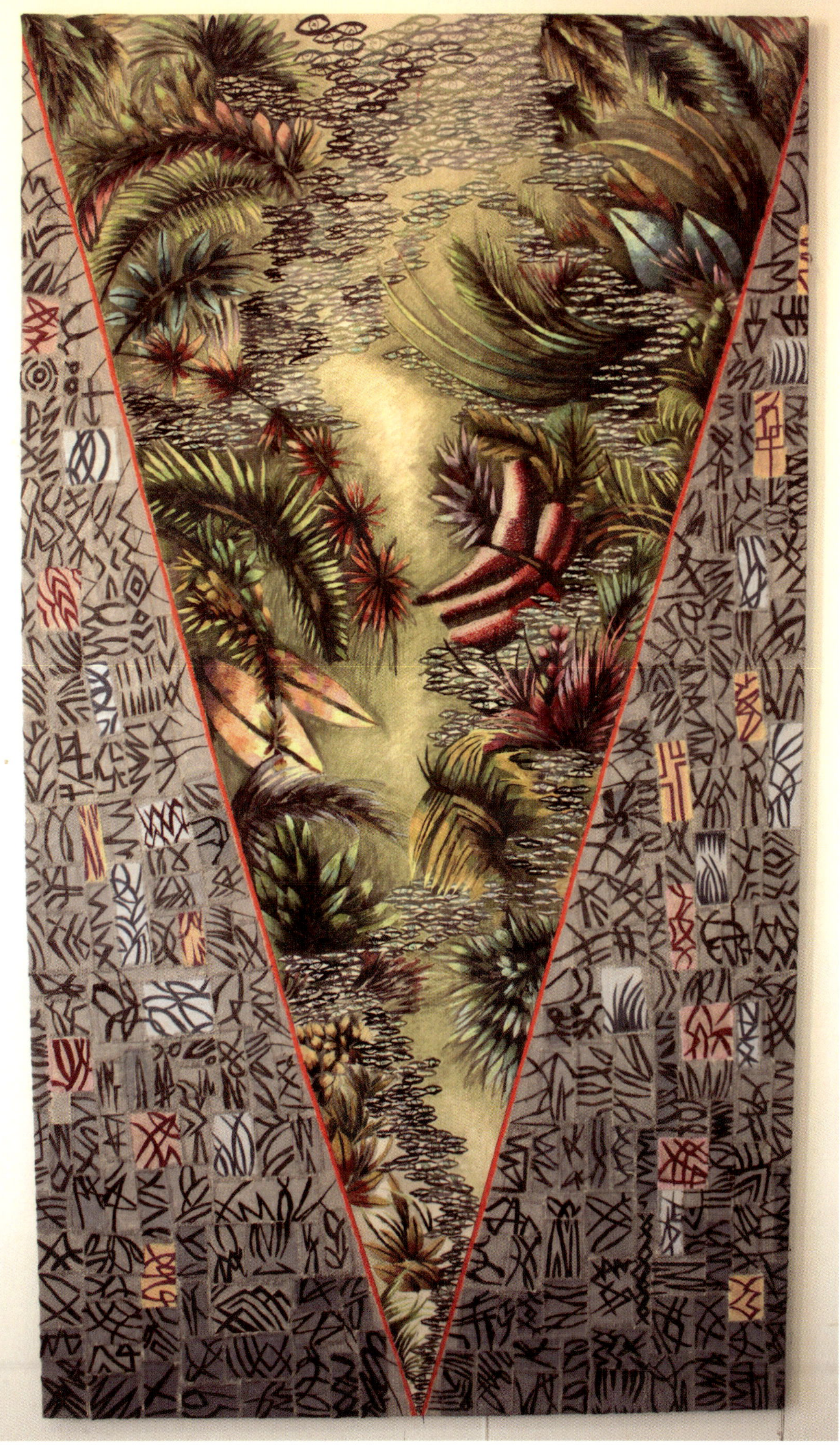

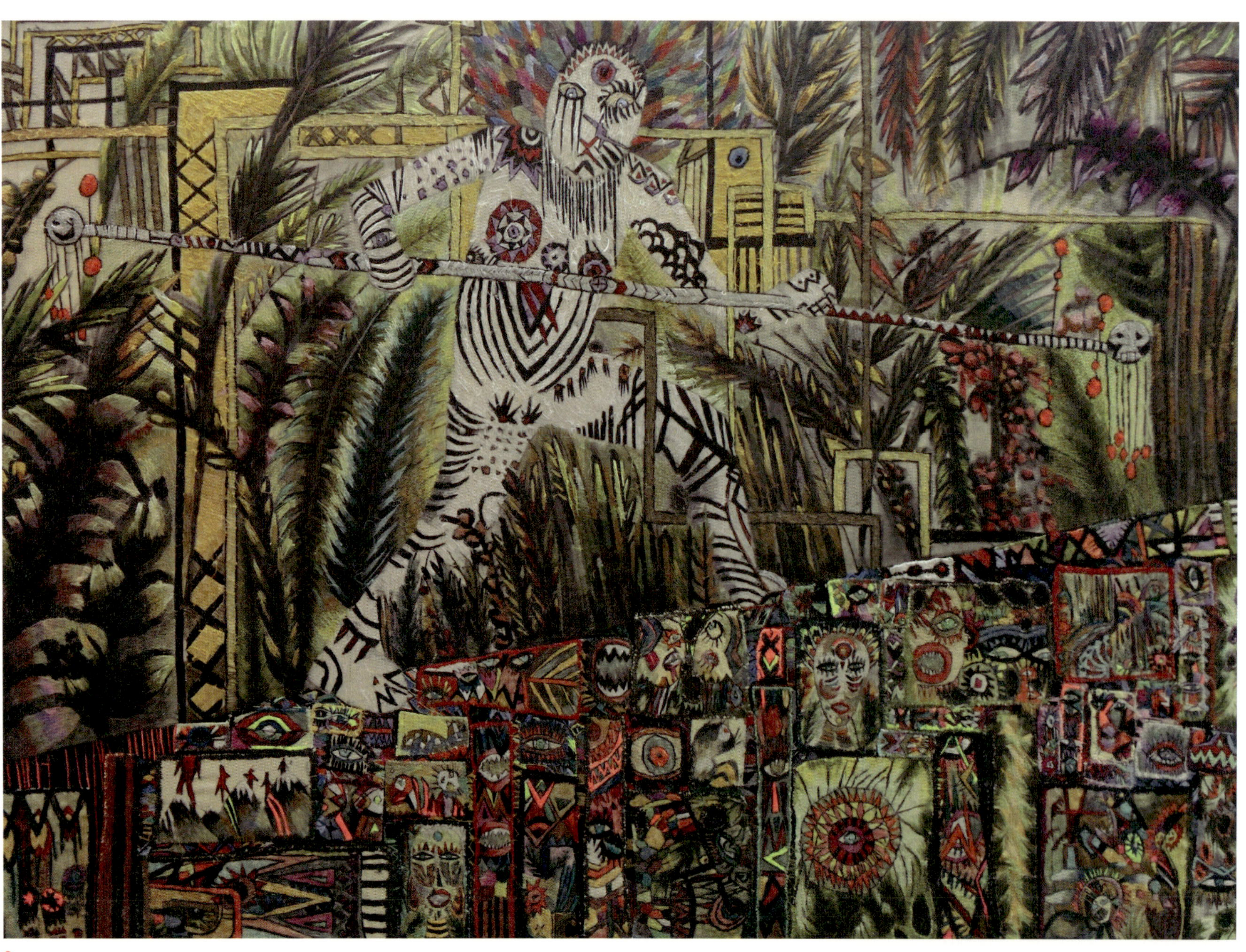

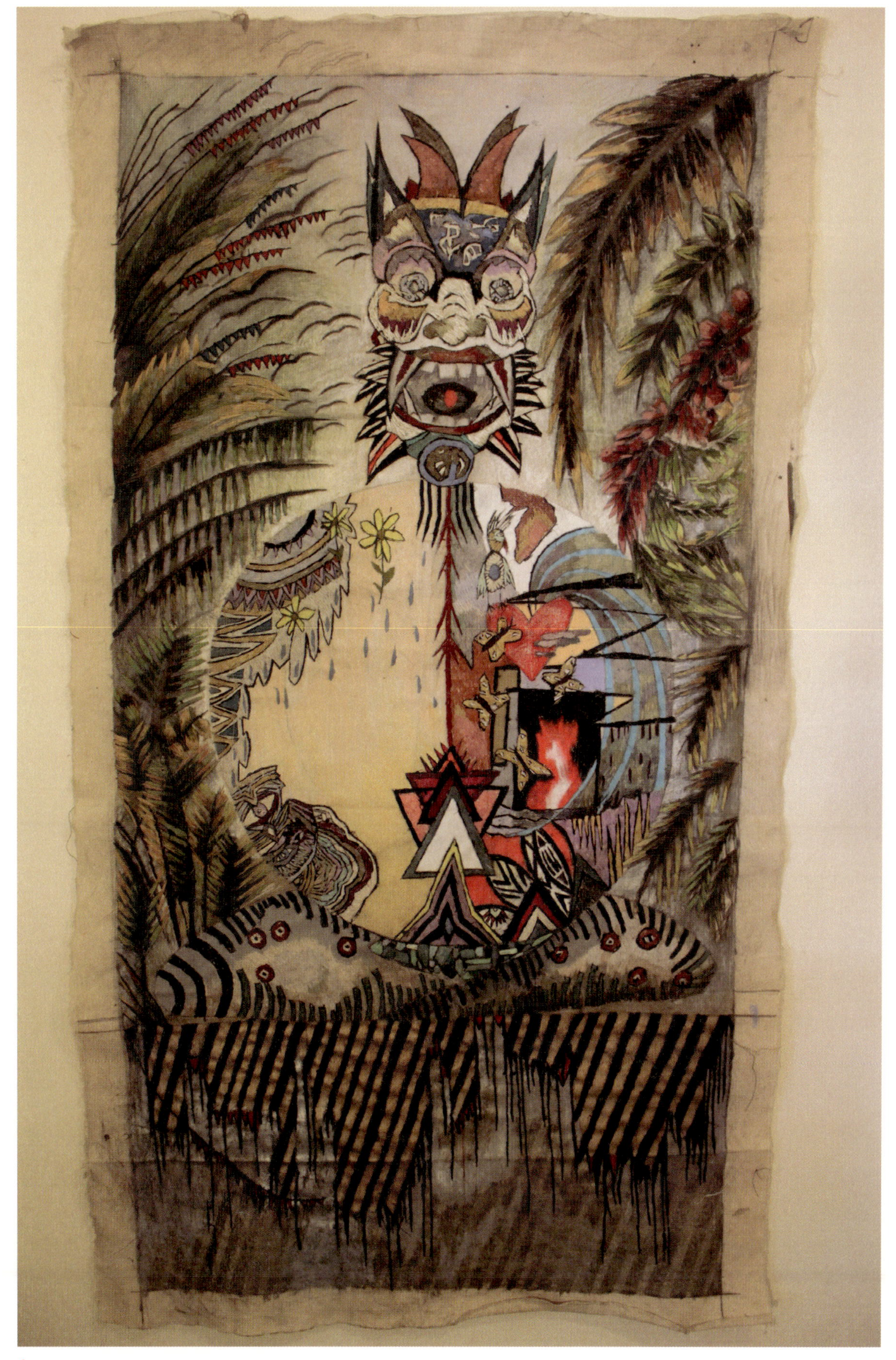

1. *Pieces of a Clash,* 2016
Colored dust on paper, 70 x 50 cm

2. *Pieces of a Clash,* 2016
Colored dust on paper, 70 x 50 cm

3. *Pieces of a Clash – Suggestions
for a Kinetic Sculpture, 2016*
Colored dust on paper, 50 x 70 cm

4. *Pieces of a Clash – Kinetic Sculpture,* 2016
Hammer, fan head and parts, matches, rubber glove, ceramic vase,
stones, and bronze, dimensions variable

5. *Pieces of a Clash,* 2016 (detail)
Colored dust on paper, 70 x 100 cm

6. *Pieces of a Clash,* 2016
Colored dust on paper, 100 x 70 cm

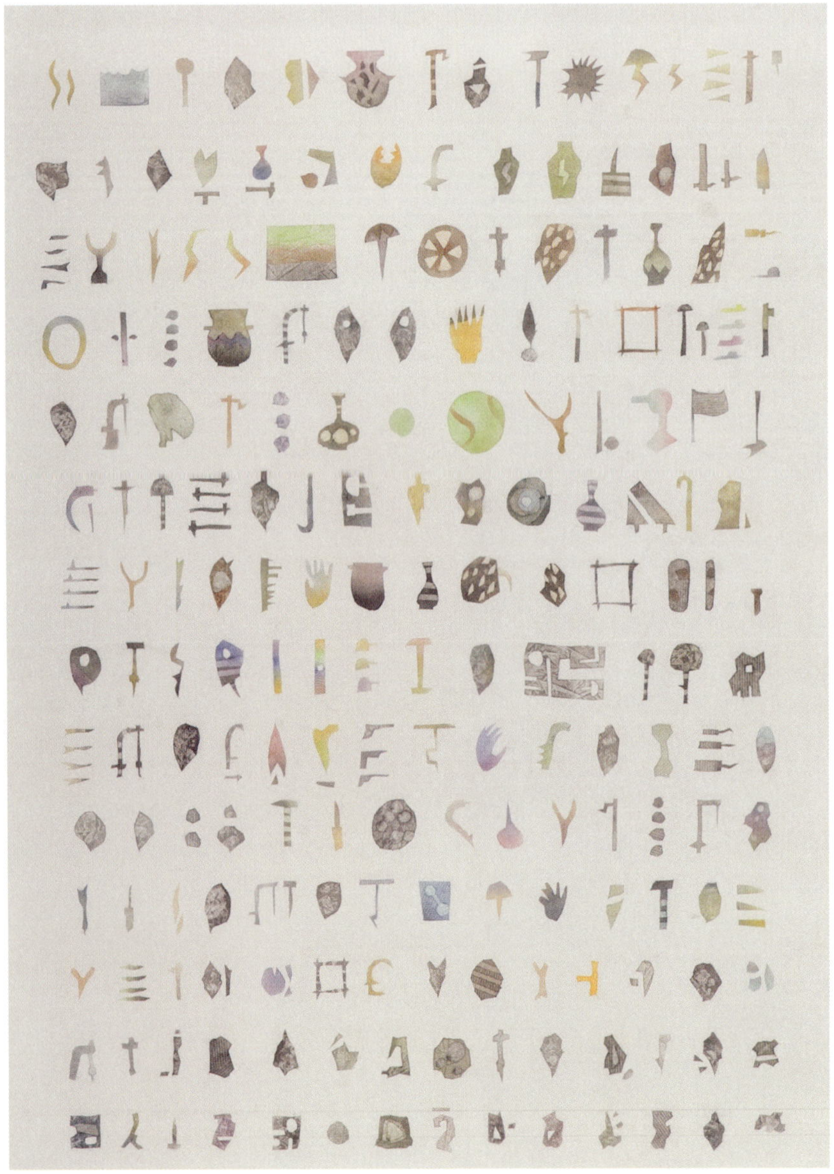

1

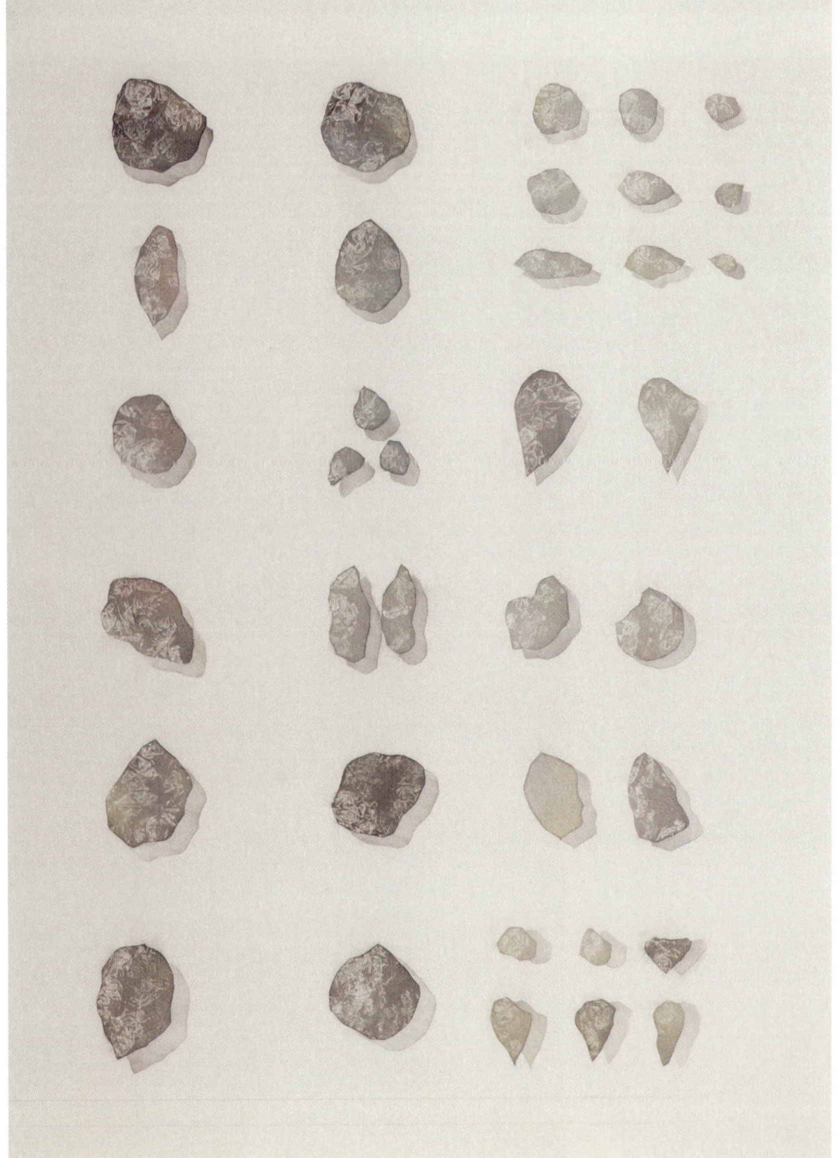

2

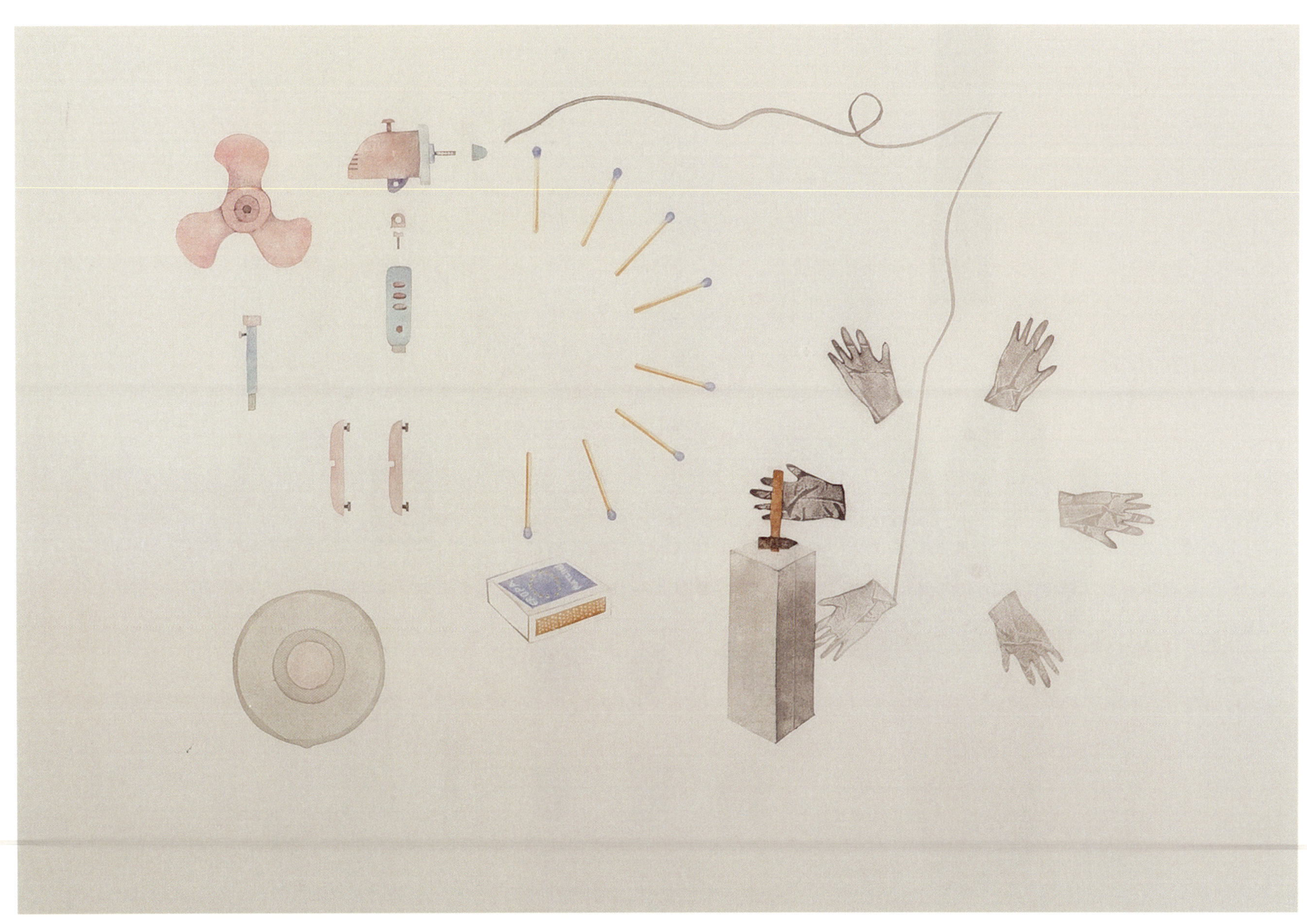

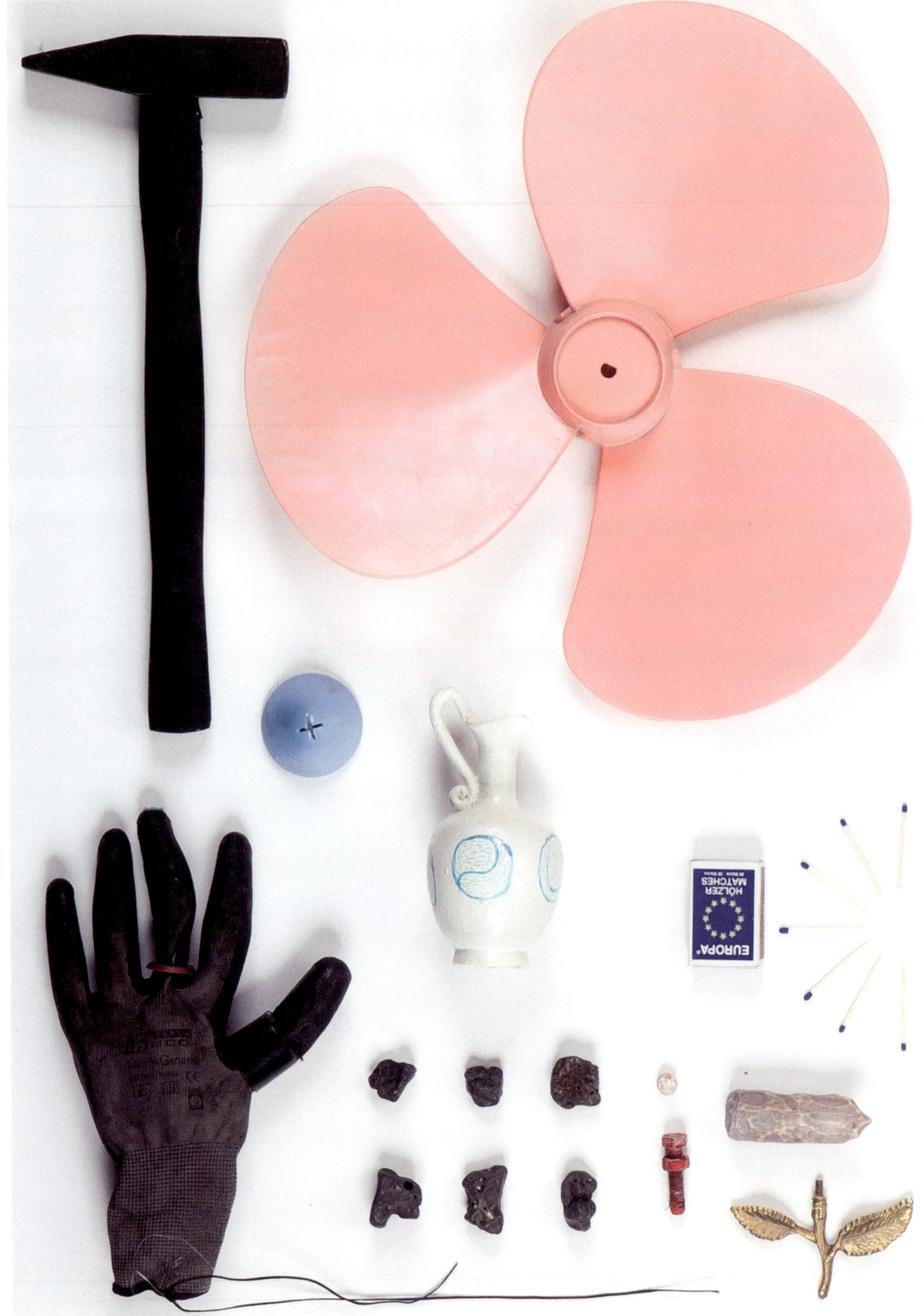

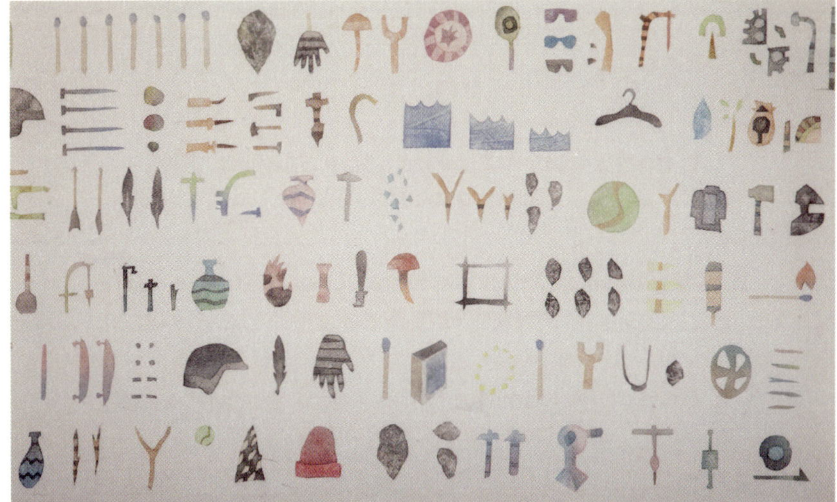

5

6

1. *Bricks* from the series *Local Studies*, 2015
Pigment print, 87 x 130 cm

2. *Bougainvillea* from the series *Local Studies*, 2015
Pigment print, 40 x 60 cm

3. *Ghost City* from the series *Local Studies*, 2016
Pigment print, 66 x 100 cm

4. *Skeleton* from the series *Local Studies*, 2015
Pigment print, 130 x 87 cm

5. *Stage* from the series *Local Studies*, 2015
Pigment print, 30 x 20 cm

6. *Pink House* from the series *Local Studies*, 2015
Pigment print, 60 x 40 cm

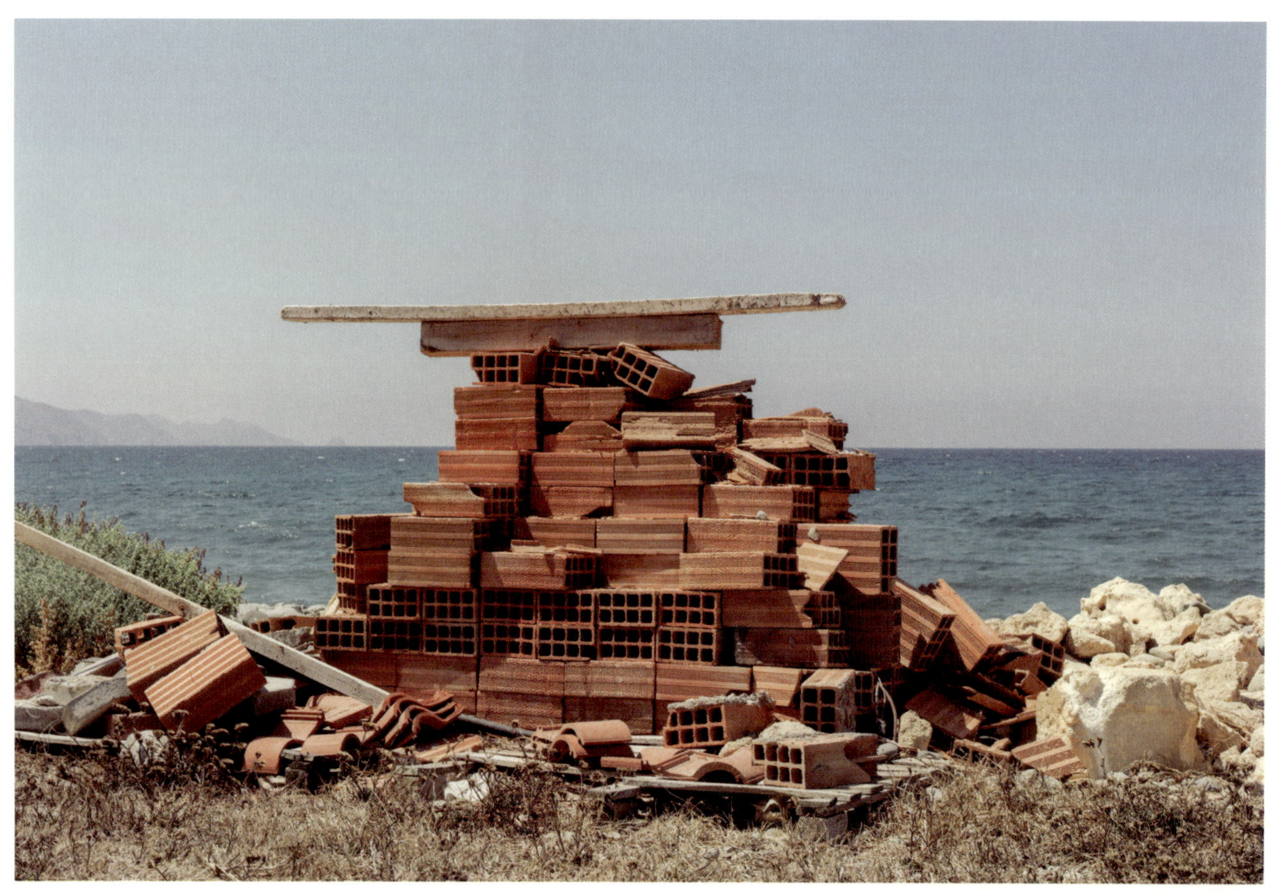

1

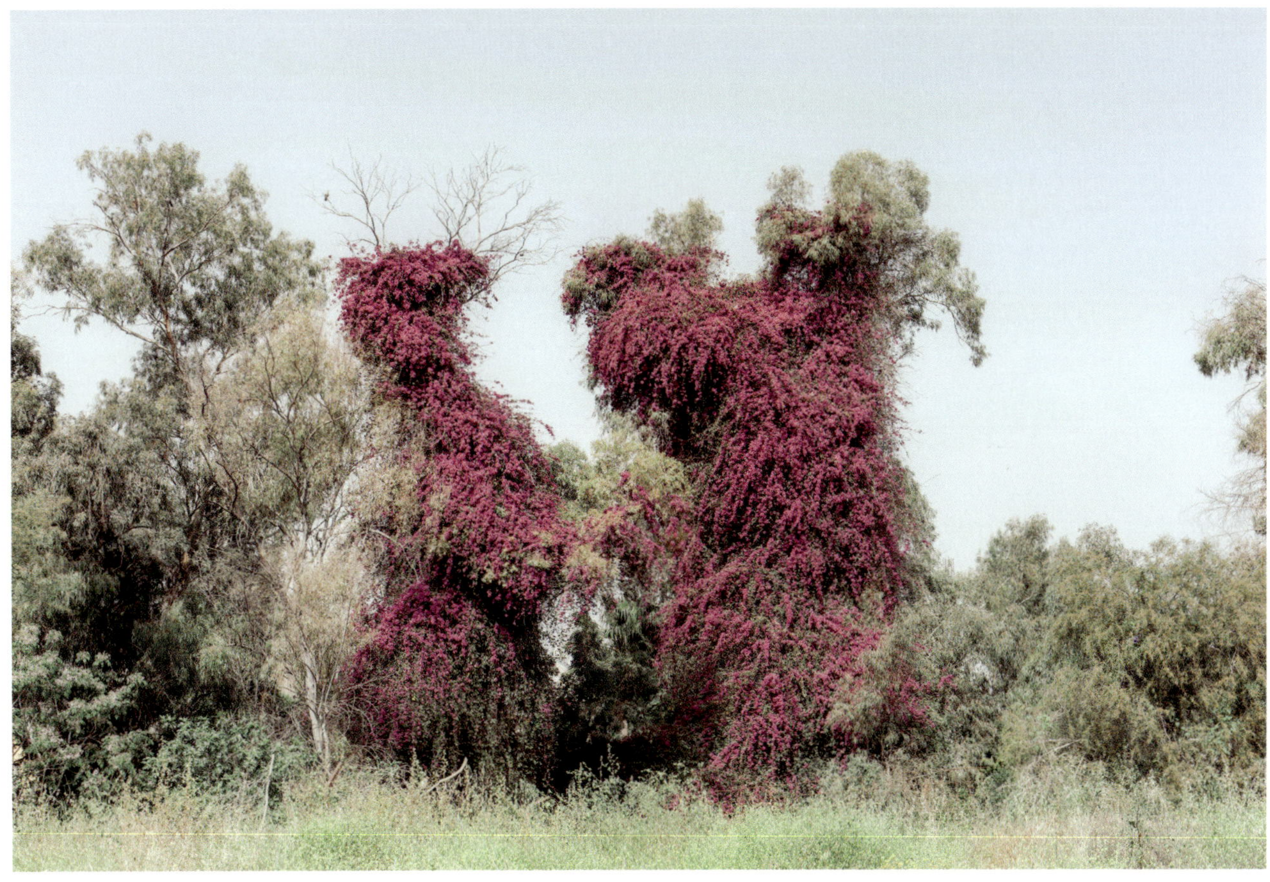

2

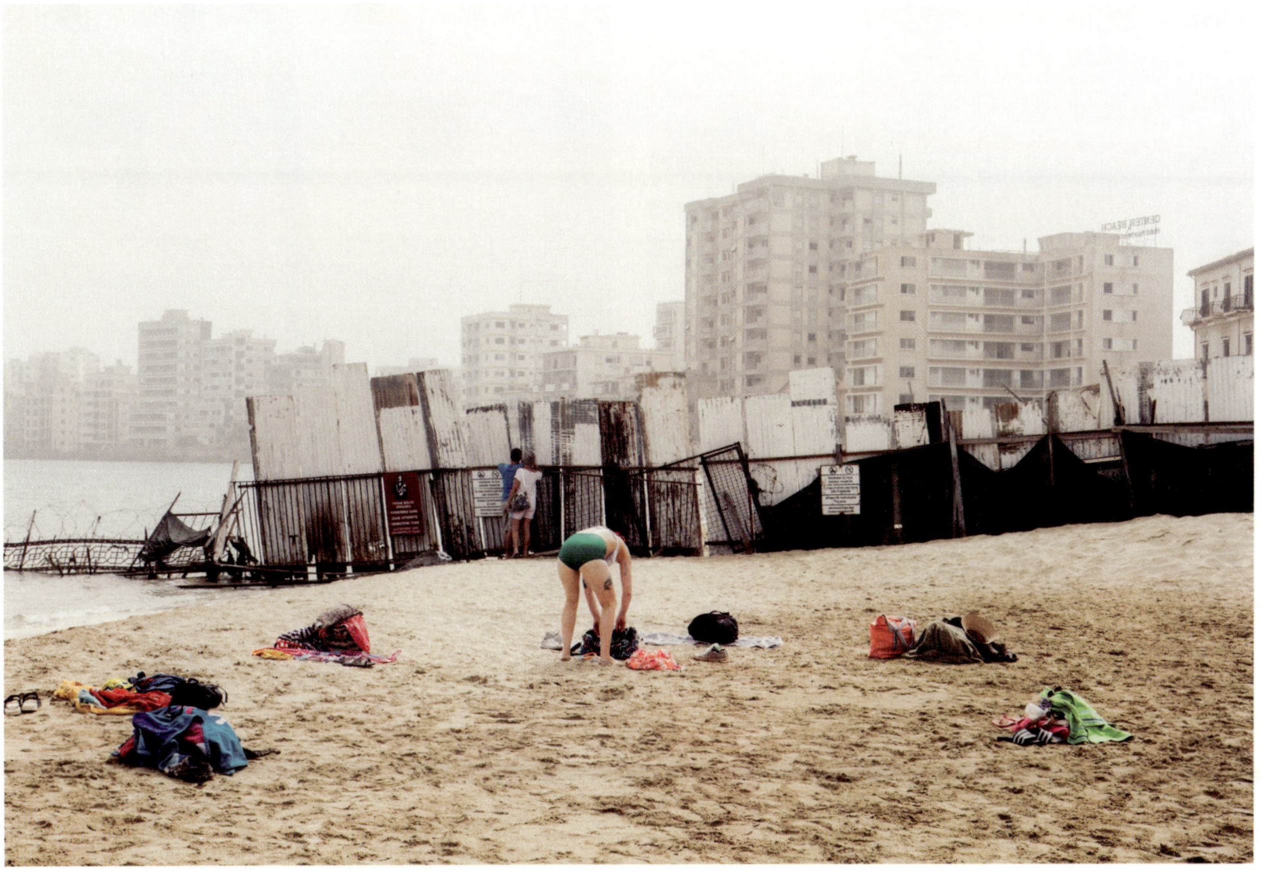

3

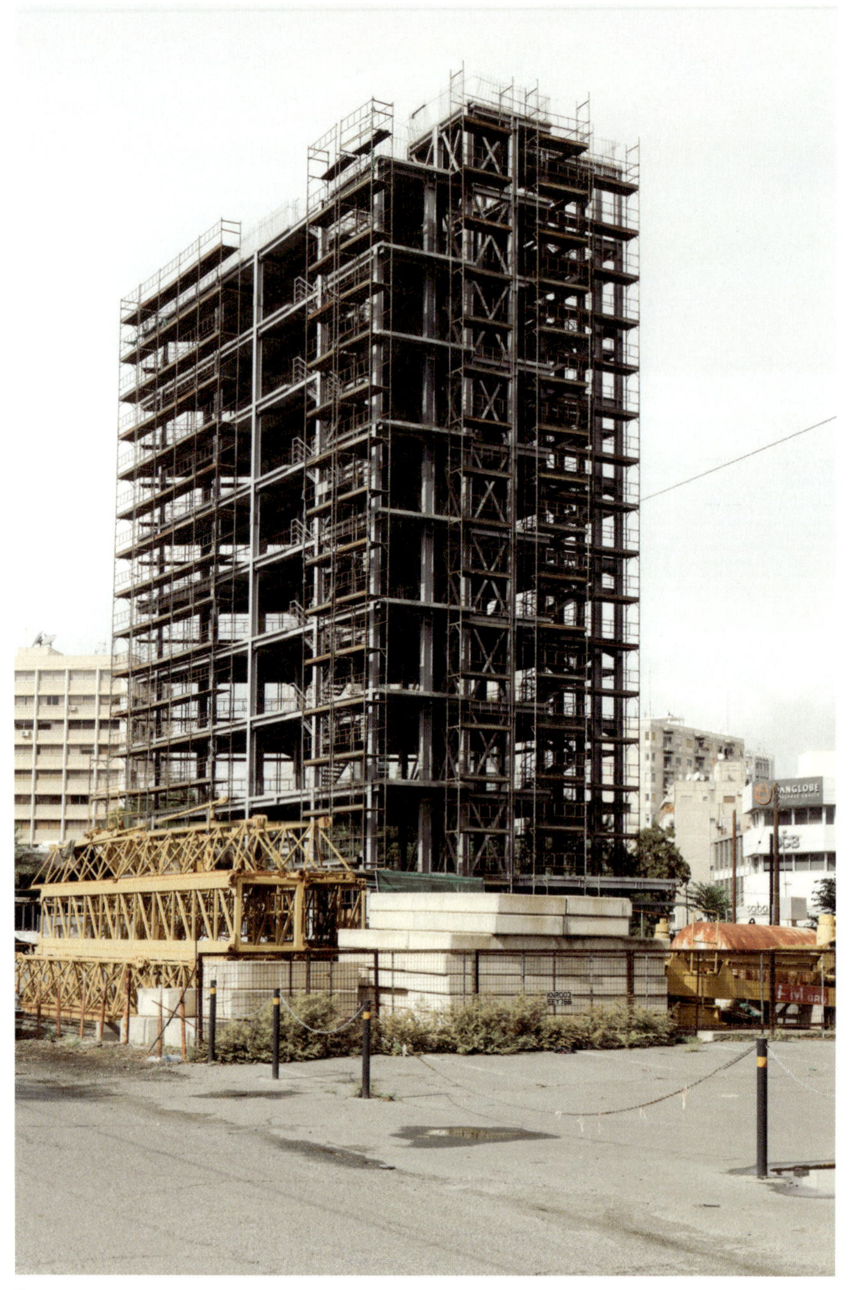

4

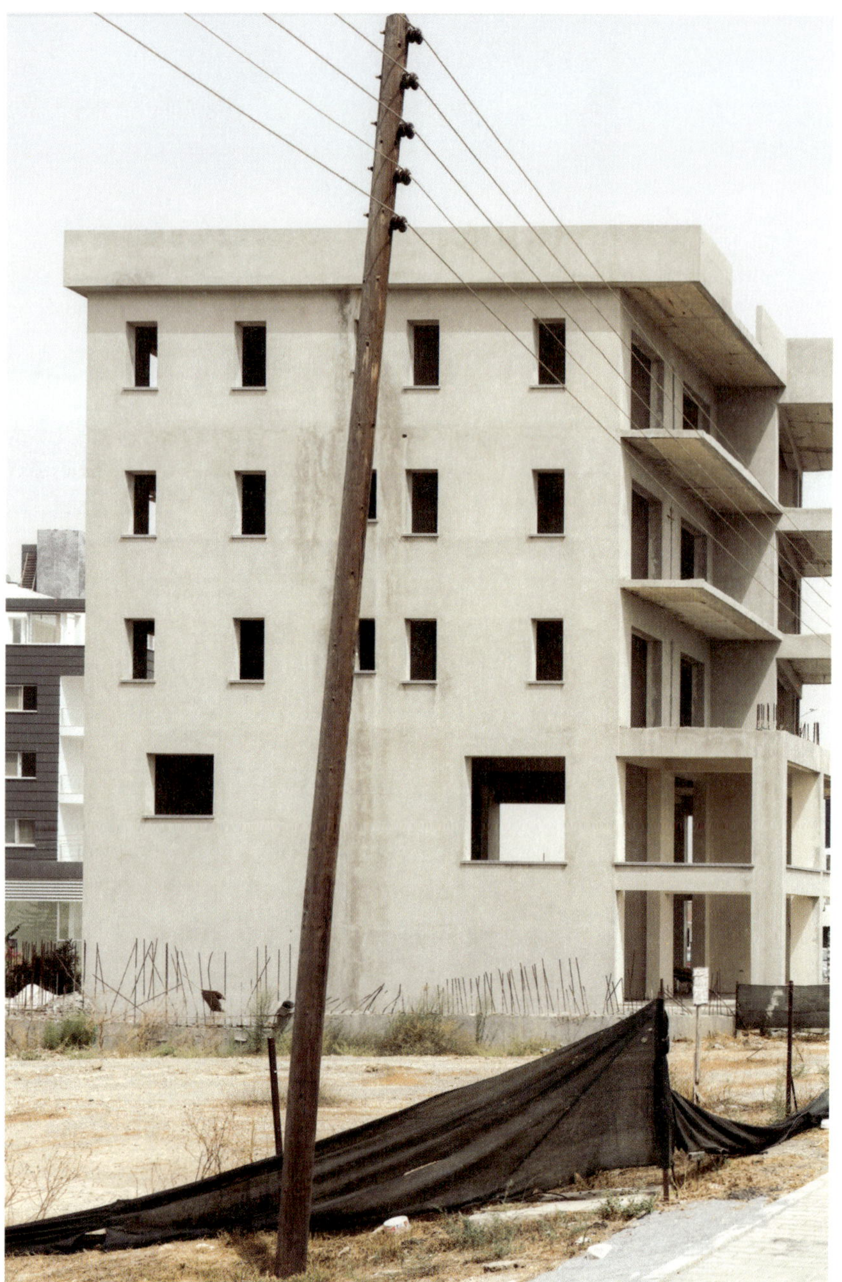

5

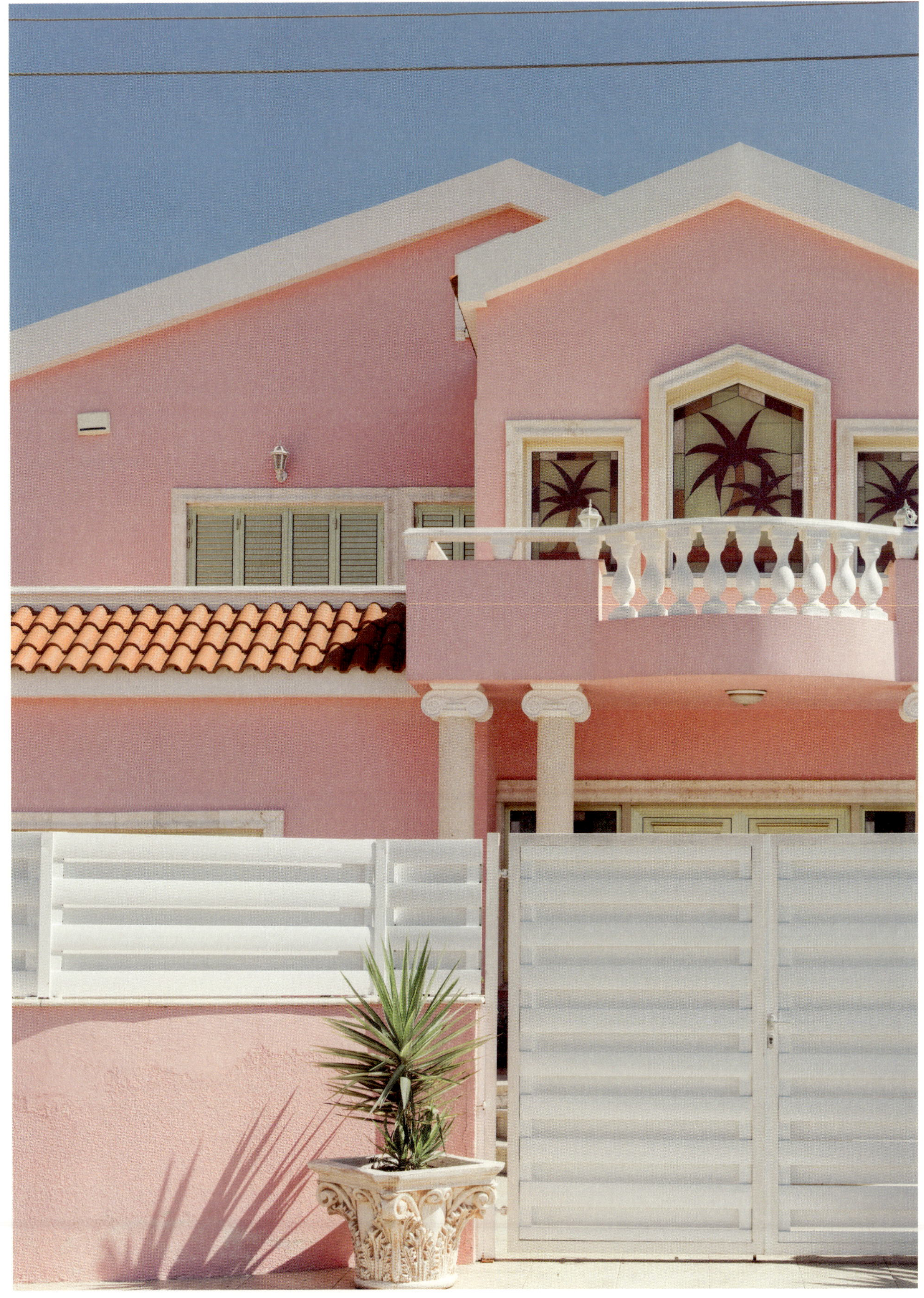

1. *During Athens*, 2014
C-print, 150 x 150 cm

2. *Self-Proclaimed Artist*, 2015
C-print, 100 x 100 cm

3. *Soldier Returning Home*, 2015
C-print, 150 x 150 cm

4. *Photographs*, 2016
C-print, 150 x 150 cm

5. *Building Without Windows*, 2011
C-print, 100 x 100 cm

6. *Ancient Soldiers Wrapped in Cellophane*, 2016
C-print, 150 x 150 cm

7. *The Lake*, 2014
C-print, 100 x 100 cm

8. *Empty Advertising Board*, 2012
C-print, 100 x 100 cm

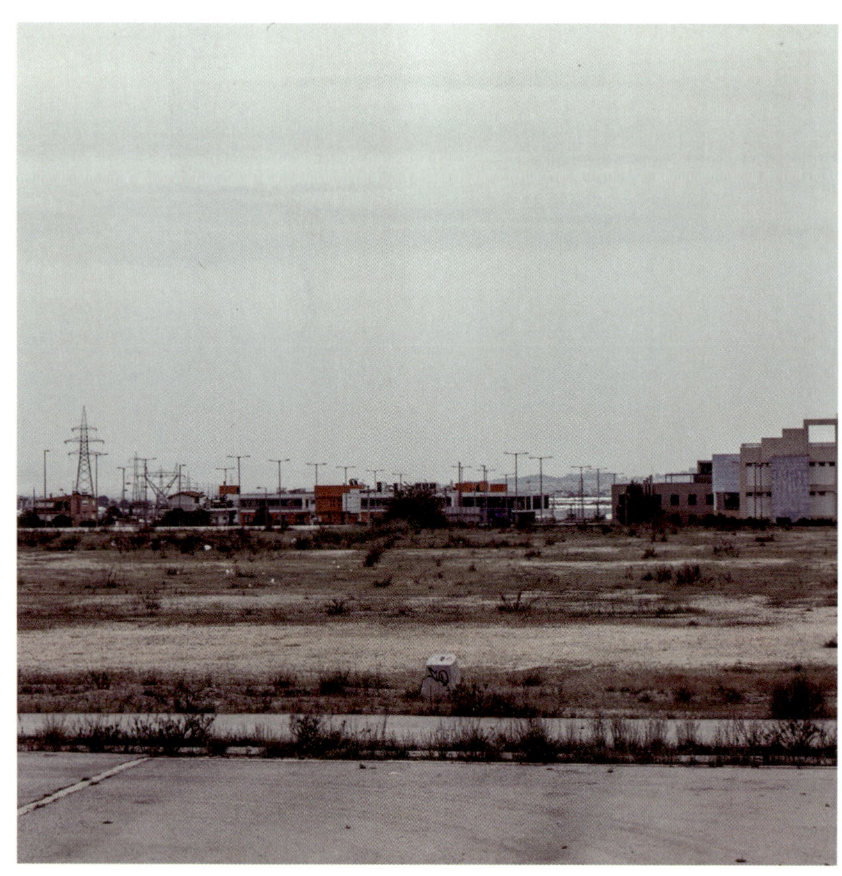

1

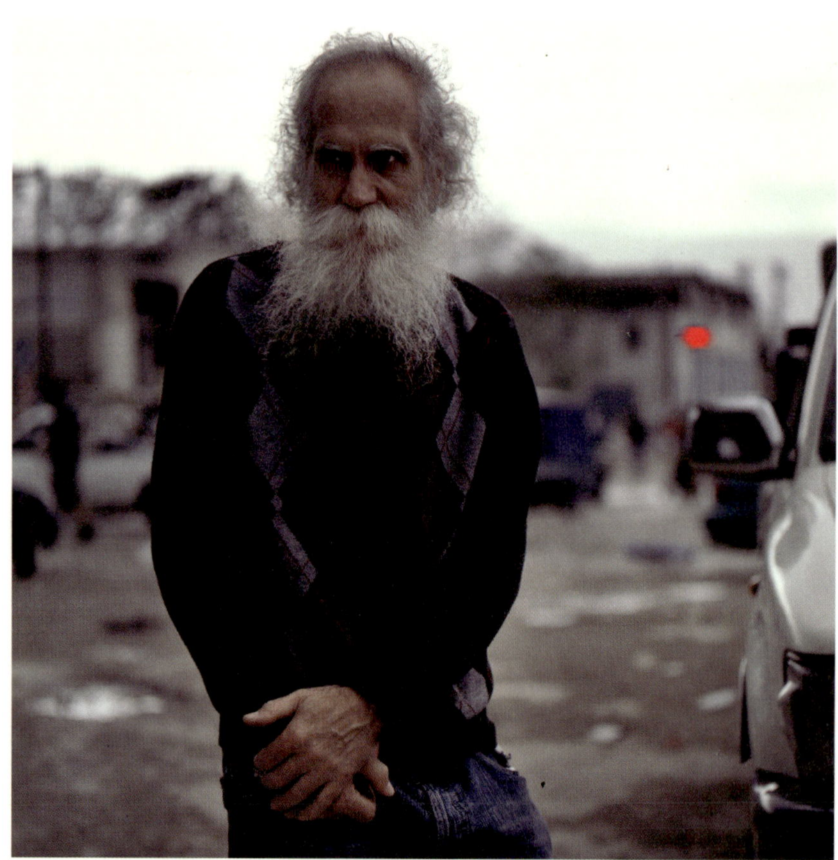

2

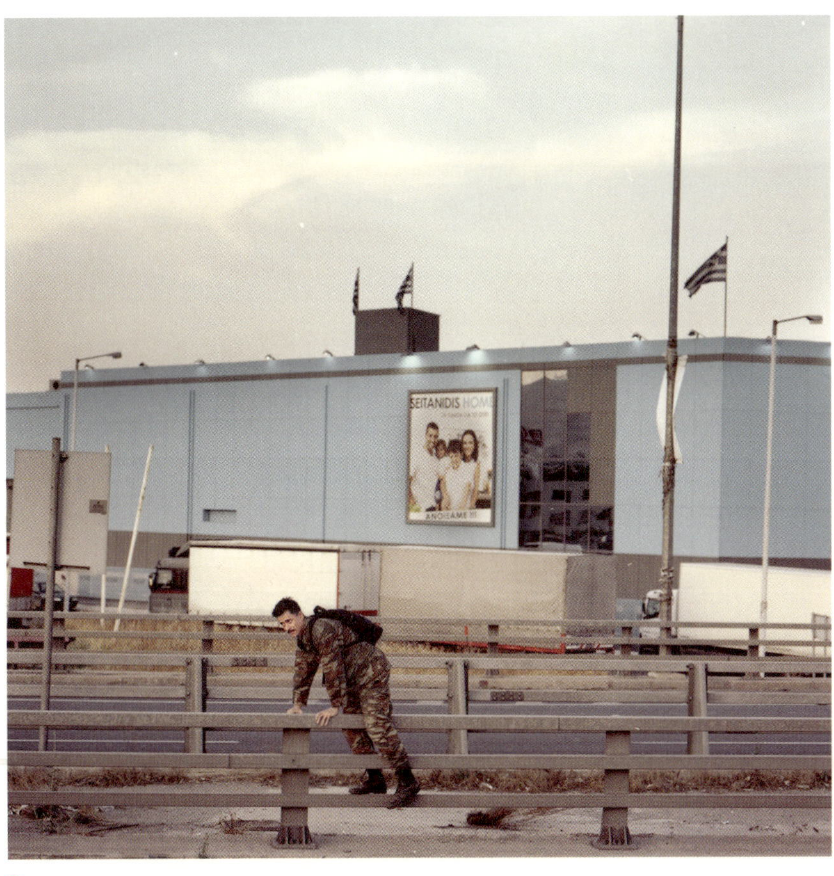

3

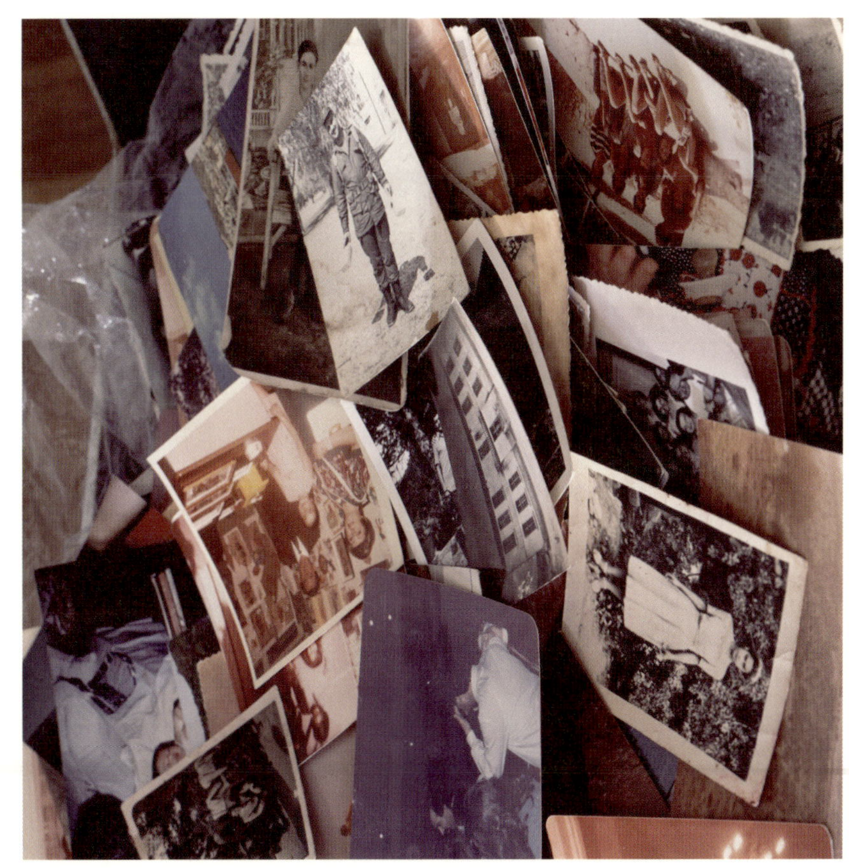

4

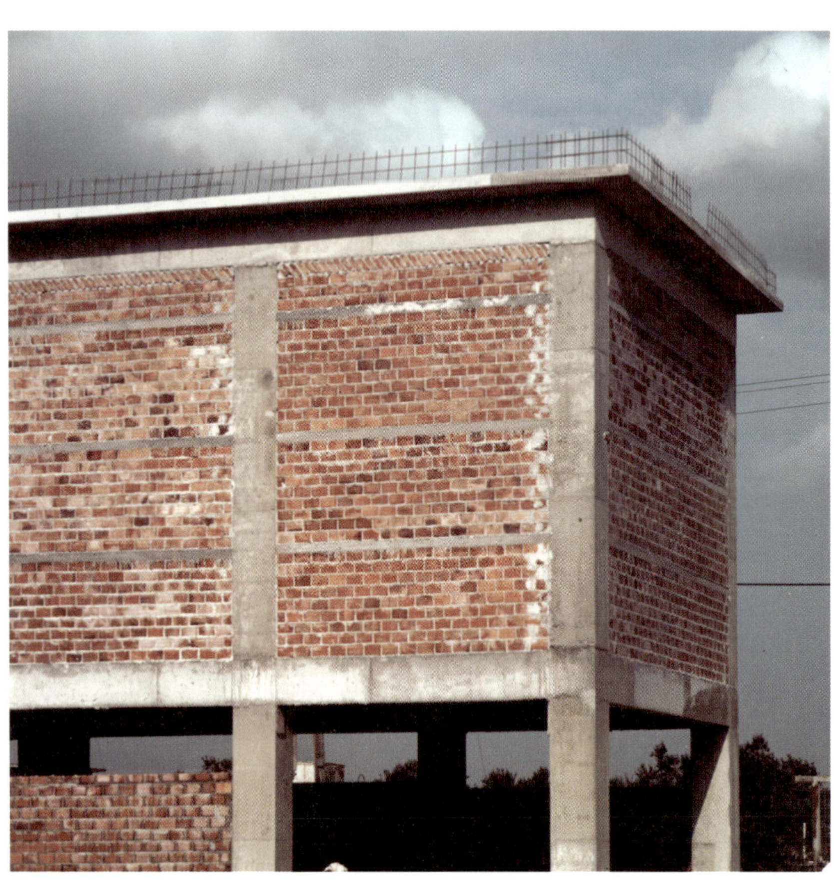

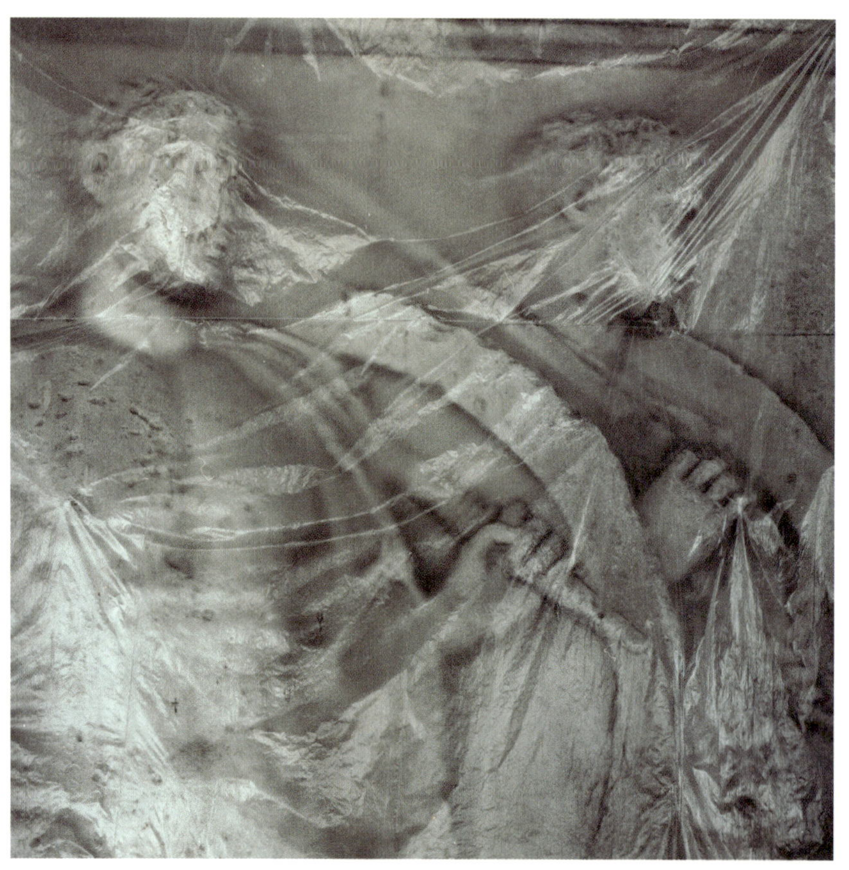

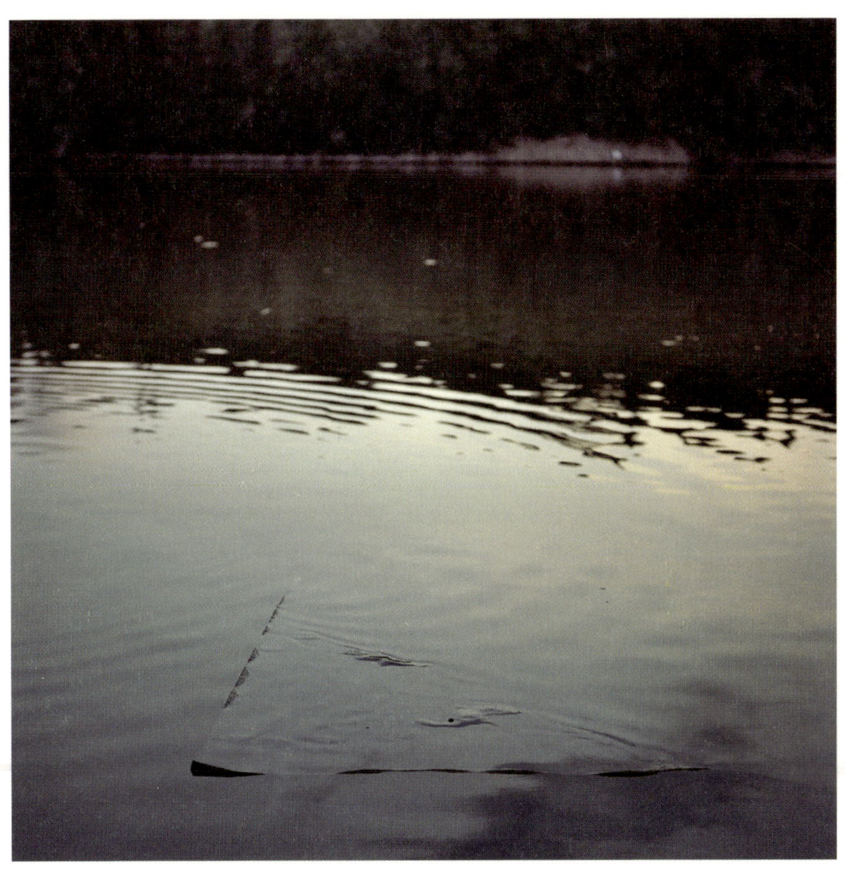

7

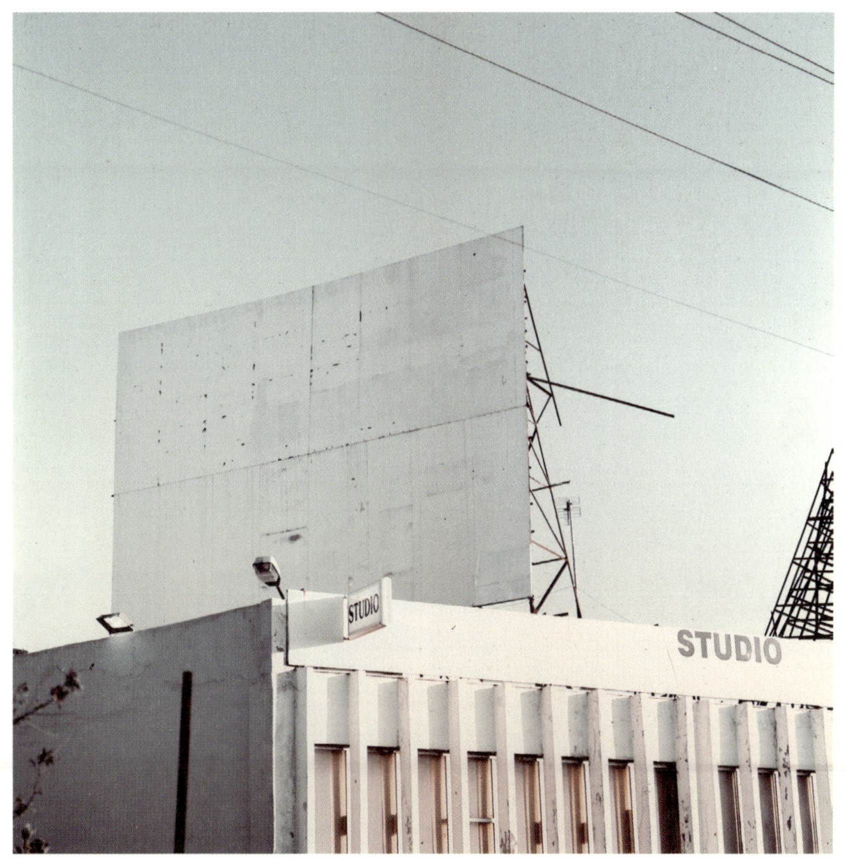

8

1. *Solar Love for the Rapid Felines Vol. 1: Them, their planets, their sun, the shadow*, 2016 (detail)
Copper, bronze, brass, digital embroidery on Lycra, and plastic mannequin, dimensions variable

2. *Solar Love for the Rapid Felines Vol. 1: Them, their planets, their sun, the shadow*, 2016
Copper, bronze, brass, digital embroidery on Lycra, and plastic mannequin, dimensions variable

3. *Solar Love for the Rapid Felines Vol. 3: Weapons, rays, trophies*, 2016 (detail)
Steel, copper, bronze, and HD video, 3:22 min, dimensions variable

4. *Solar Love for the Rapid Felines Vol. 1: Them, their planets, their sun, the shadow*, 2016 (detail)
Copper, bronze, brass, digital embroidery on Lycra, and plastic mannequin, dimensions variable

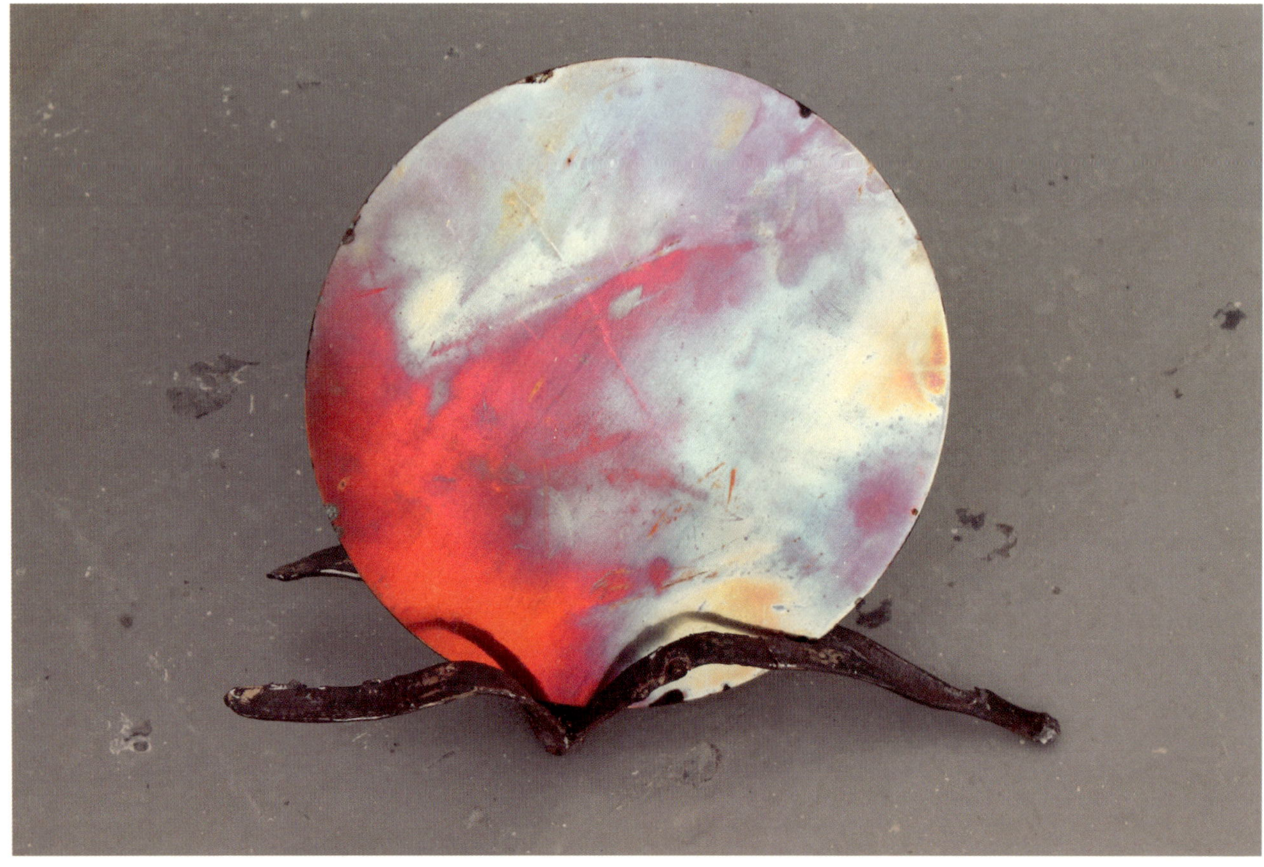

1

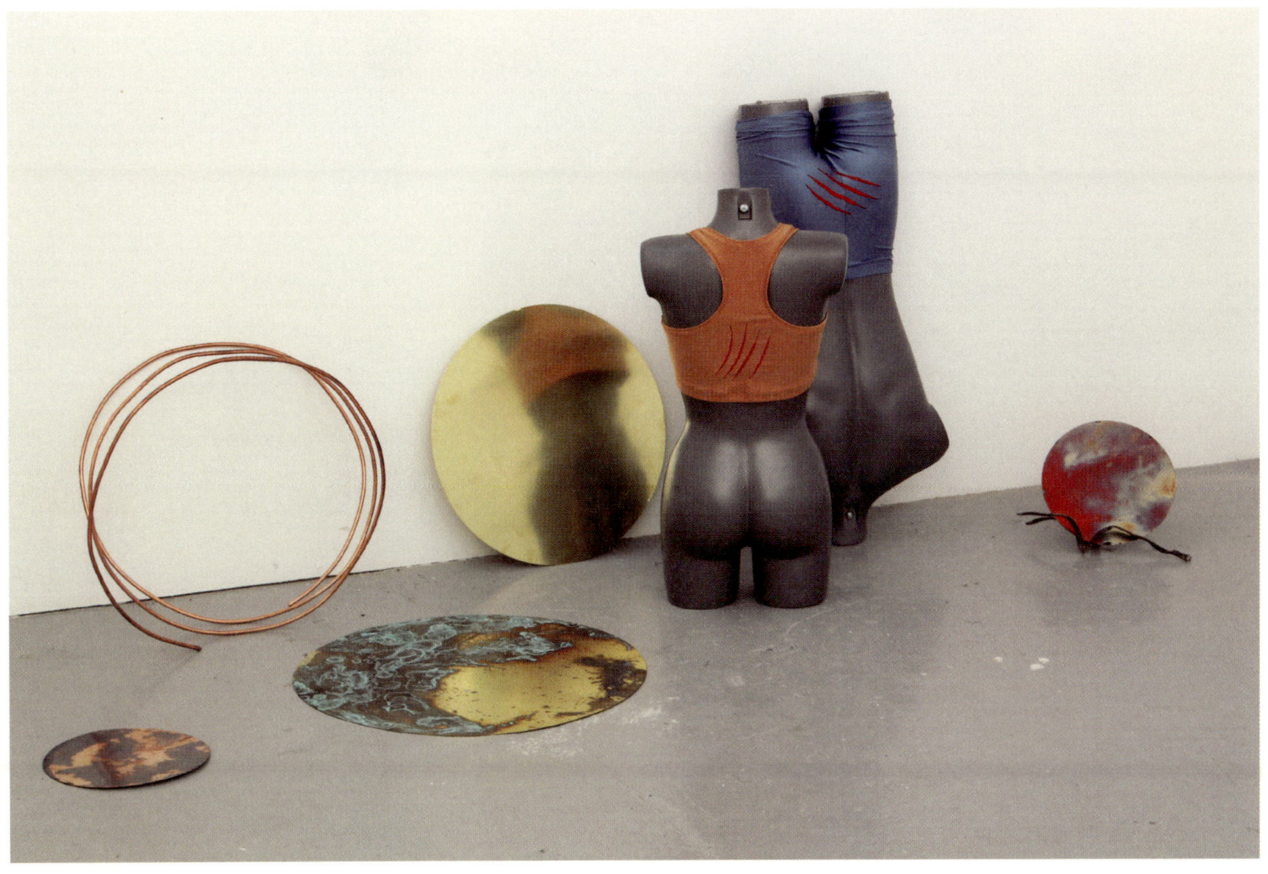

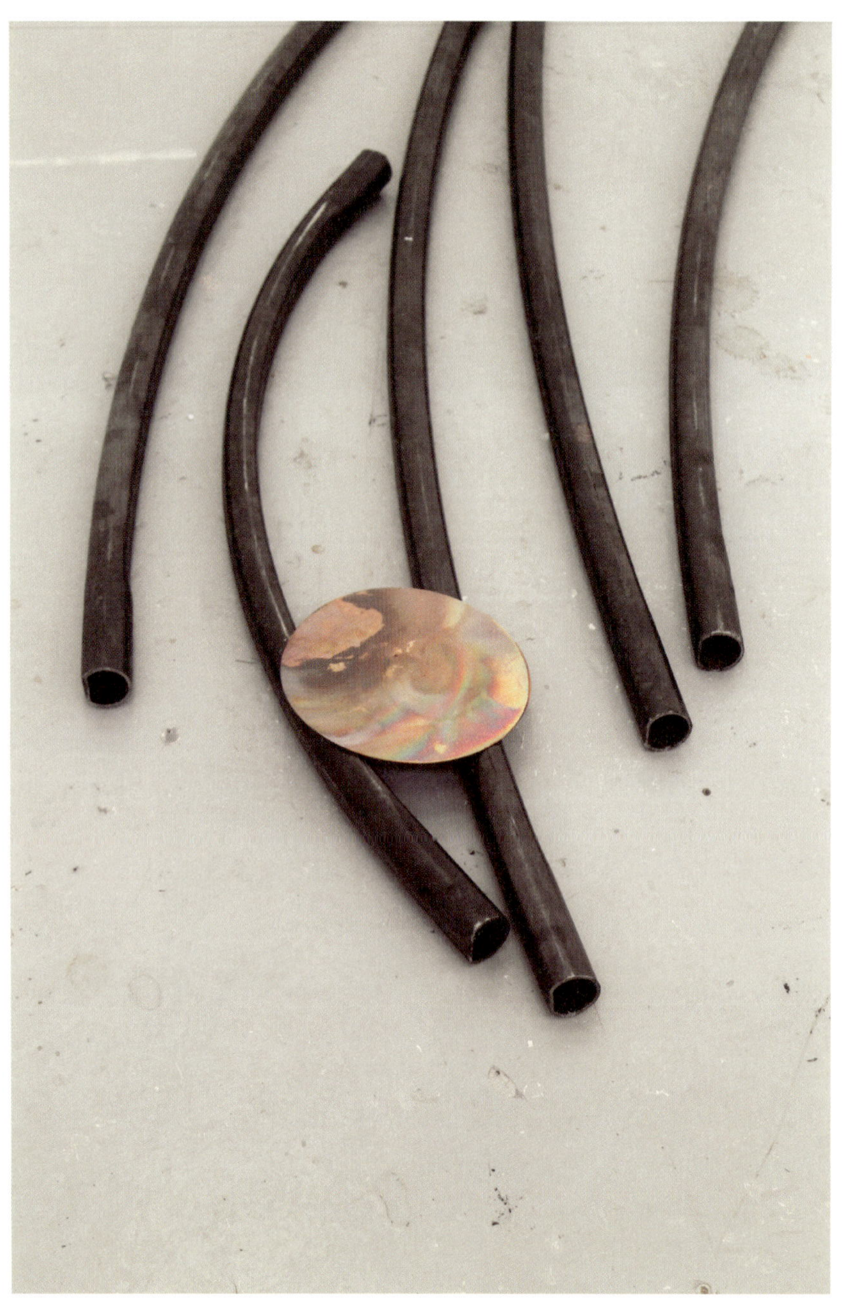

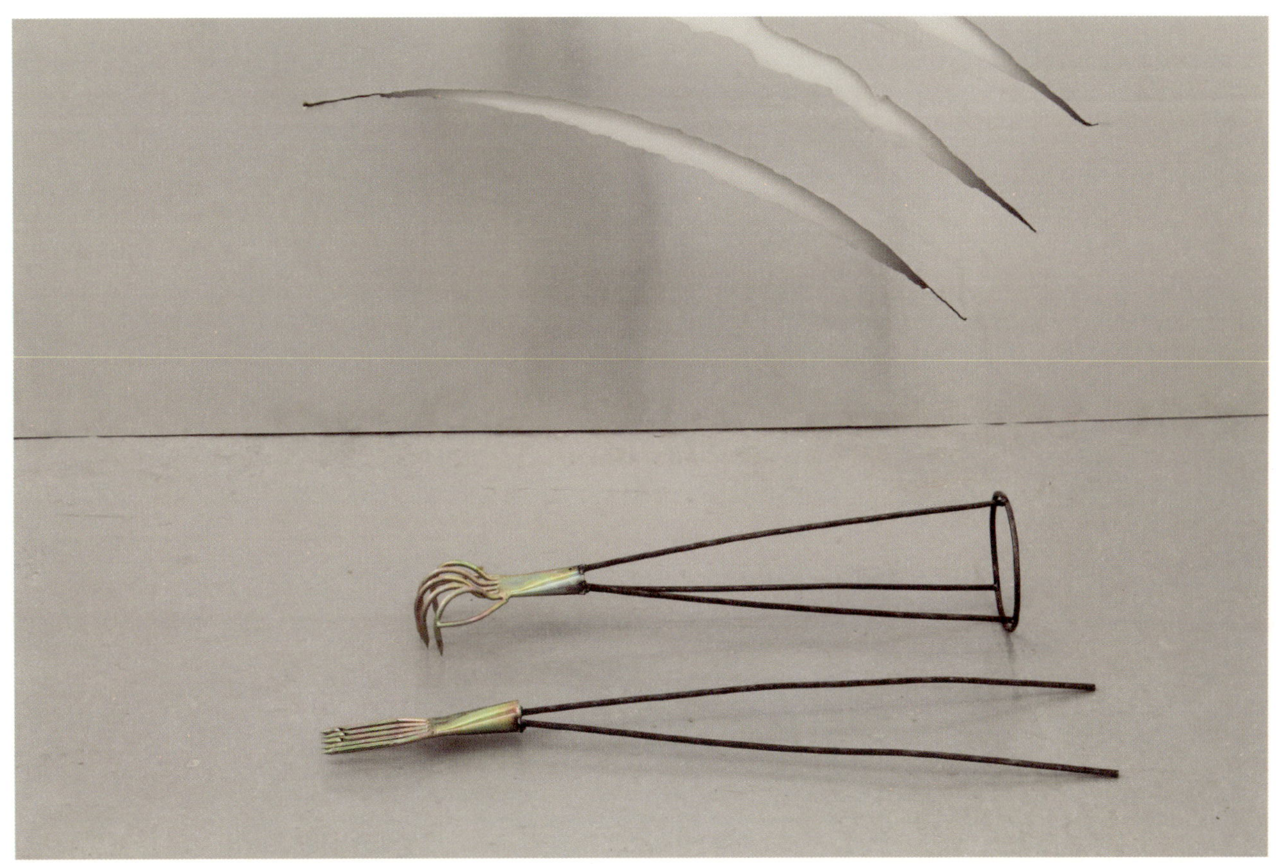

4

1. *Impact 1*, 2015
Grade A scrap copper, 70 x 120 cm

2. *Bridge (OFK)*, 2015
Vinyl print, 222 x 348 cm

3. *Raw Rate (NSK)*, 2015 (still)
HD video, color, and sound, 11:26 min

4. *Raw Rate*, 2012 (still)
HD video, color, and sound, 8:59 min

5. *Cascade (Inputs, Loops and Anchors)*, 2013 (detail)
Polypropylene safety netting and custom-designed aluminum hardware parts, dimensions variable

6. *Mirrors (Scale 021, 027)*, 2012
19"/45u server rack steel frames, rackmount server computer, and digitally printed silk, dimensions variable

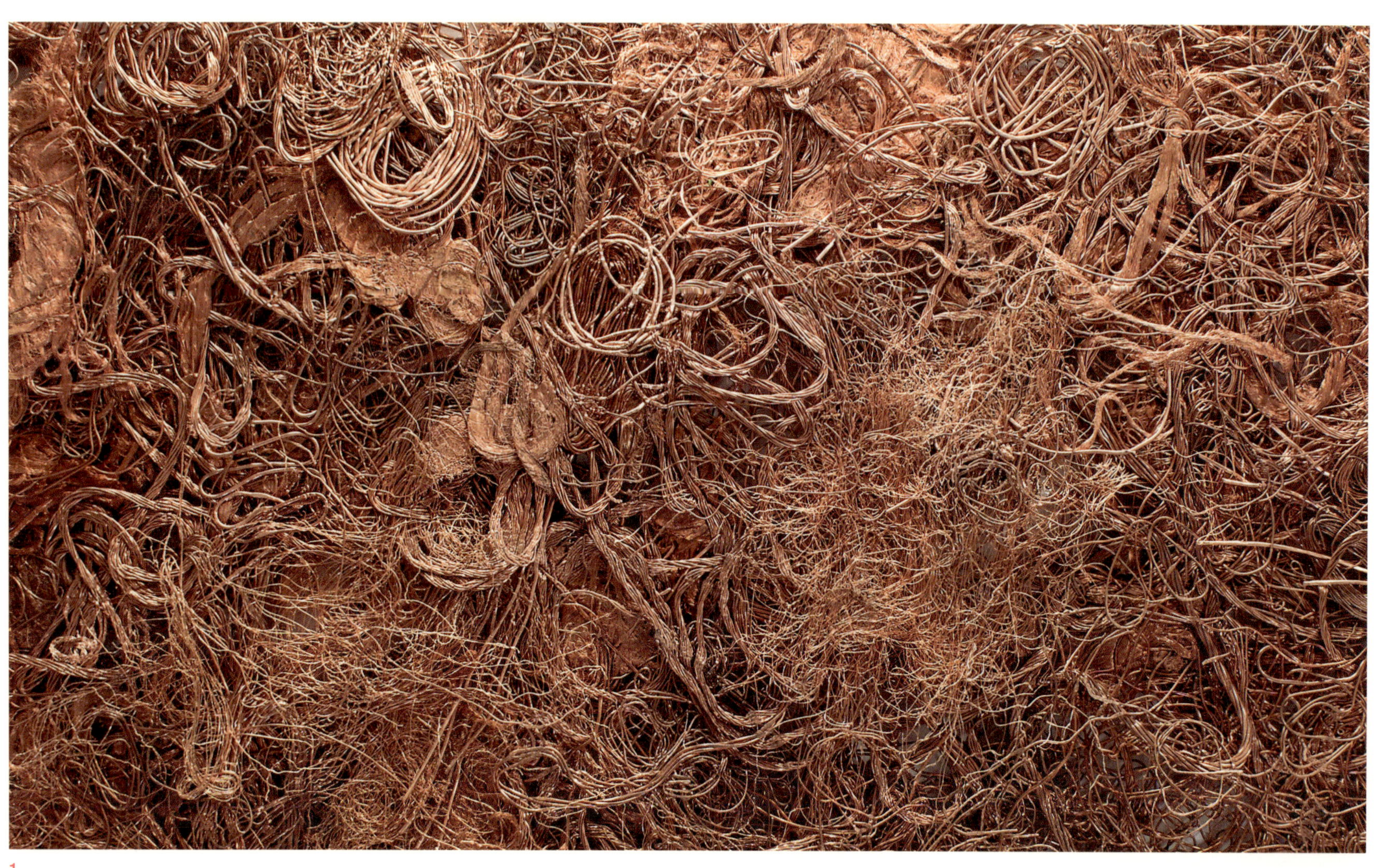

1

2

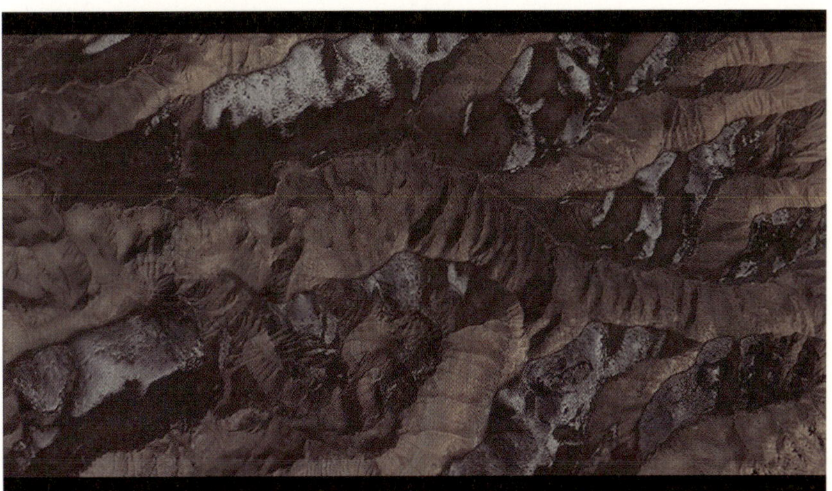

3

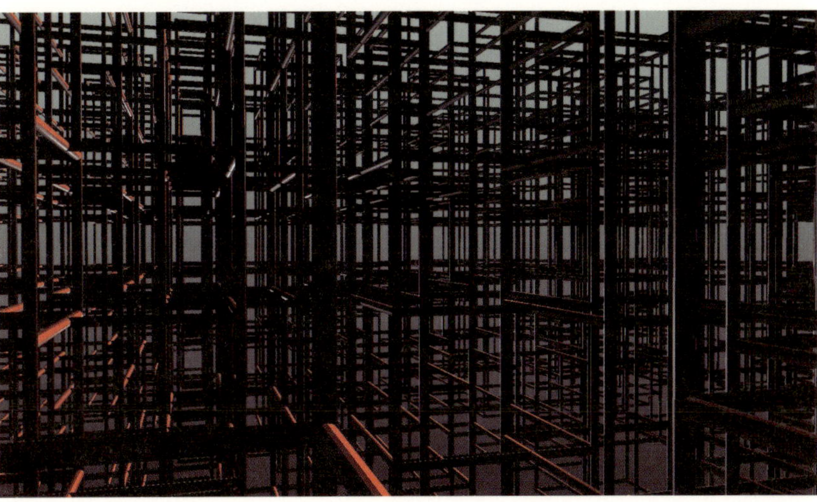

4

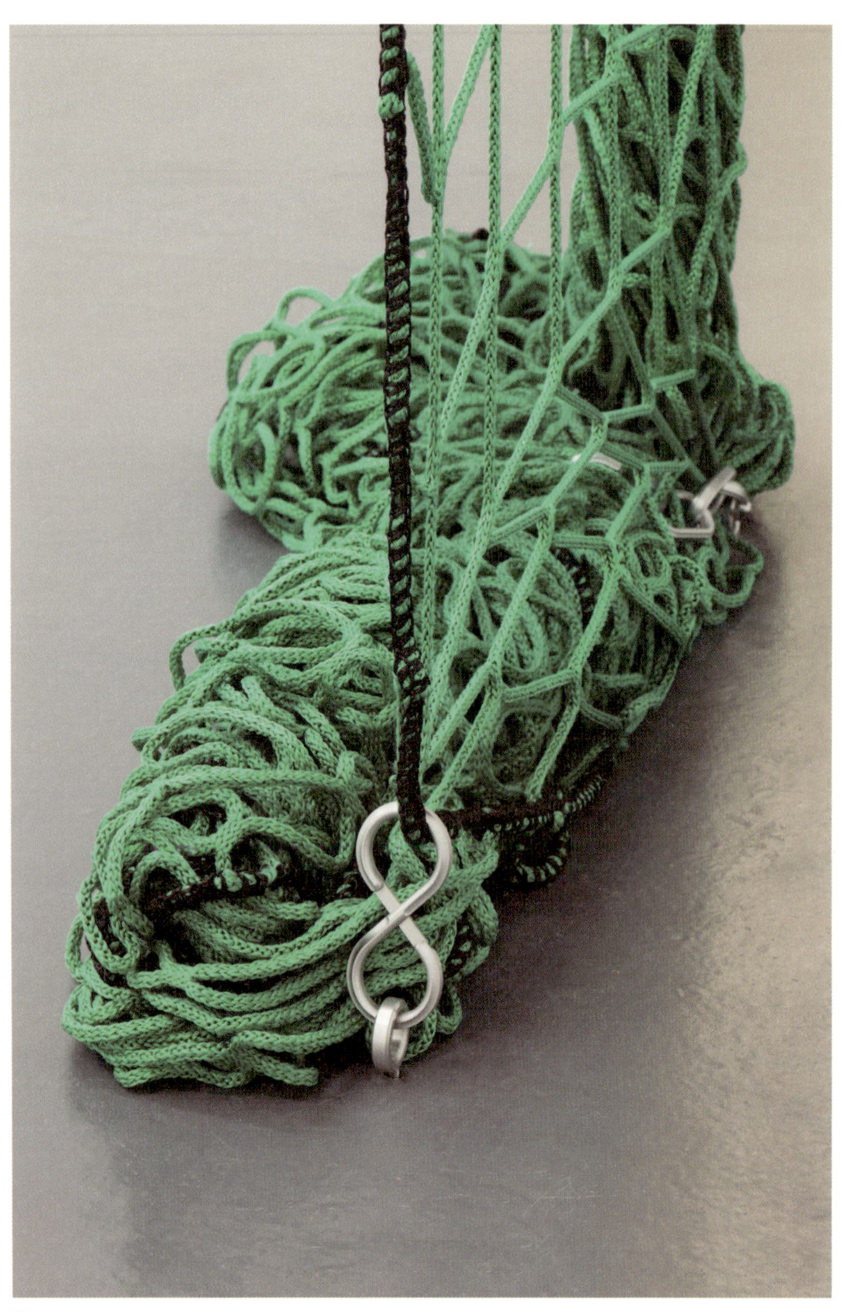

5

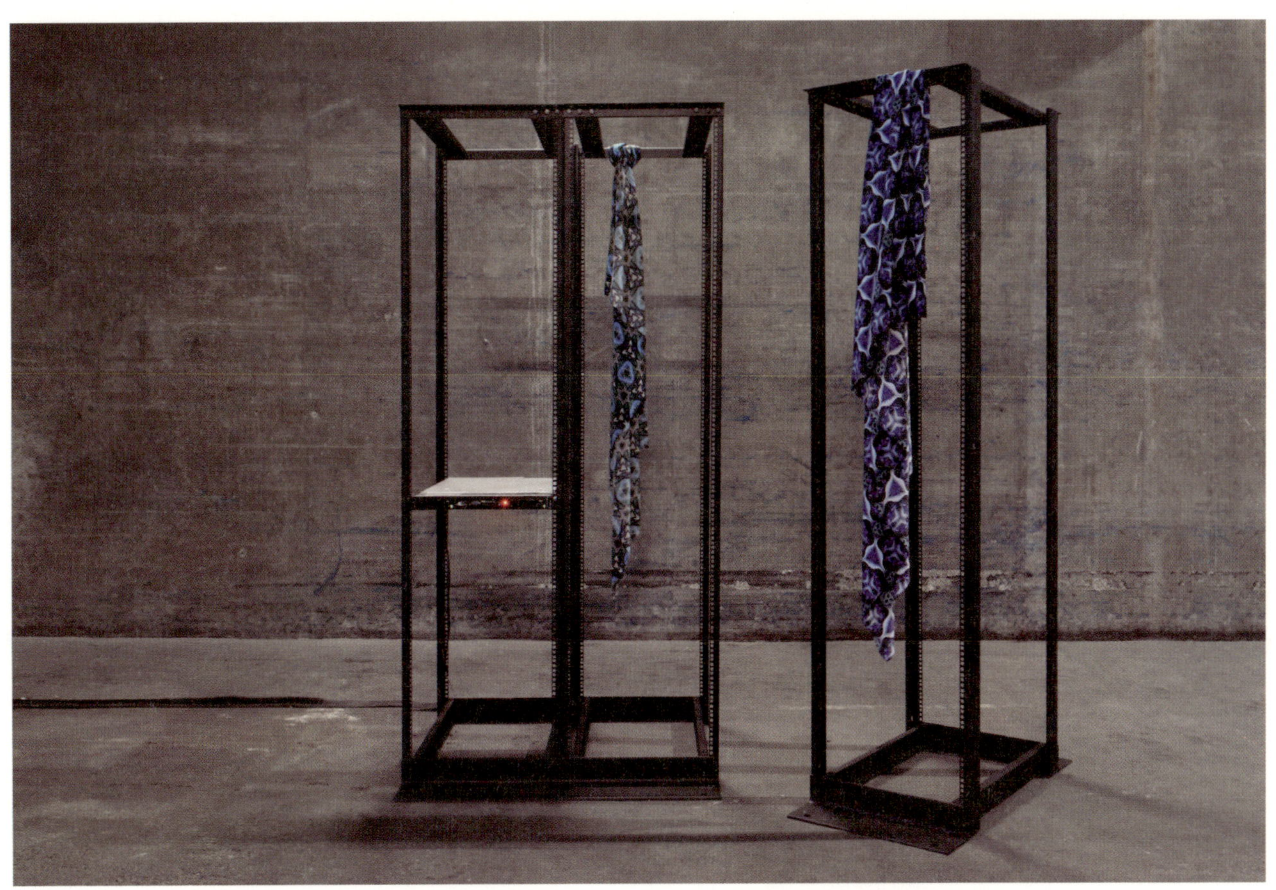

1. *Blood by Numbers* from the series *Primal Objectivities*, 2015
Lambda C-print, inkjet print, postcard, graphite and coffee stains on book cover, and ink and oil on paper, 124 x 174 cm

2. *Partial Flag* from the series *Primal Objectivities*, 2015
Lambda C-print, ink, paper burns, embroidery, textile, and canvas on paper, 124 x 144 cm

3. *Post Immigrant* from the series *Primal Objectivities*, 2016
Lambda C-print, silver gelatin print, and wood block print on paper, 154 x 164 cm

4. *Televised Embrace is Erotic Embrace of the Nation* from the series *Primal Objectivities*, 2015
Lambda C-print, collage on paper, paper burns, and ink and gouache on paper, 124 x 174 cm

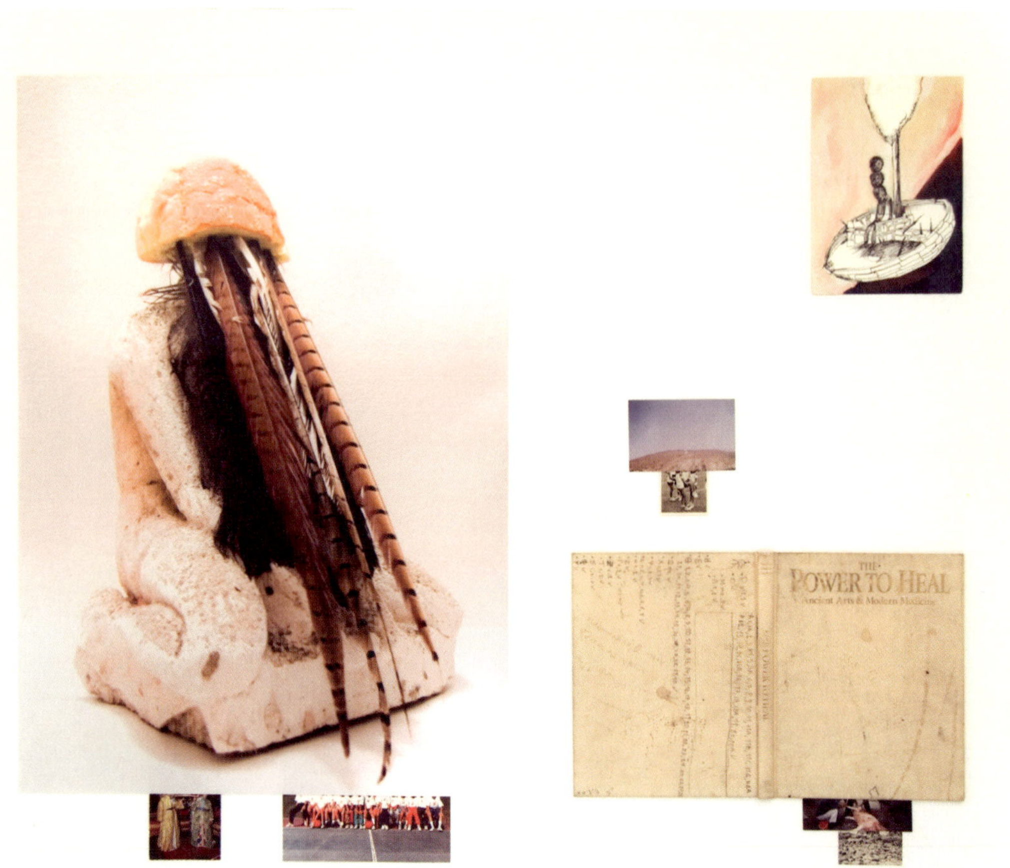

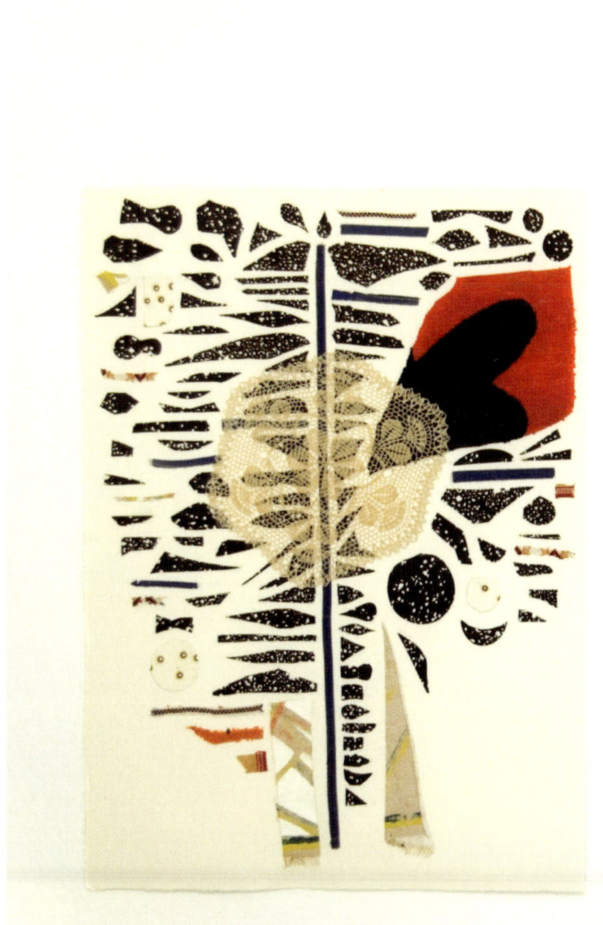

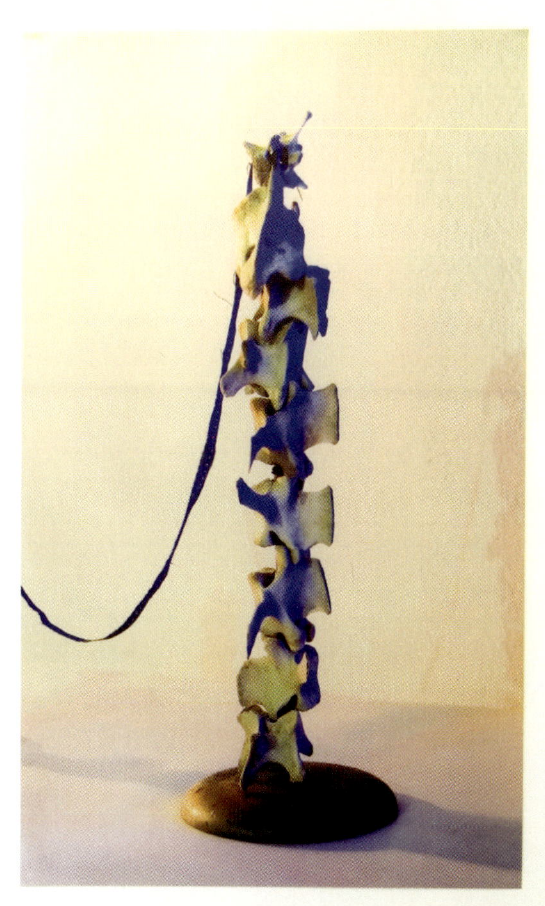

HALF TRUTH · PARTIAL TRUTH
HALF FLAG · PARTIAL FLAG
HALF BODY · PARTIAL BODY
HALF GENDER · PARTIAL GENDER
HALF TRUTH · PARTIAL TRUTH
HALF IDENTITY P · ARTIAL IDENTITY
HALF POLITICS · PARTIAL POLITICS
A PILE OF · POLITICS
HALF RELIGION · PARTIAL RELIGION
FADE
HALF TRUTH · NON TRUTH
HALF FAMILY · PARTIAL FAMILY
HALF EGO · PARTIAL EGO
HALF TRUTH · PARTIAL TRUTH
HALF TOAST · PARTIAL TOAST

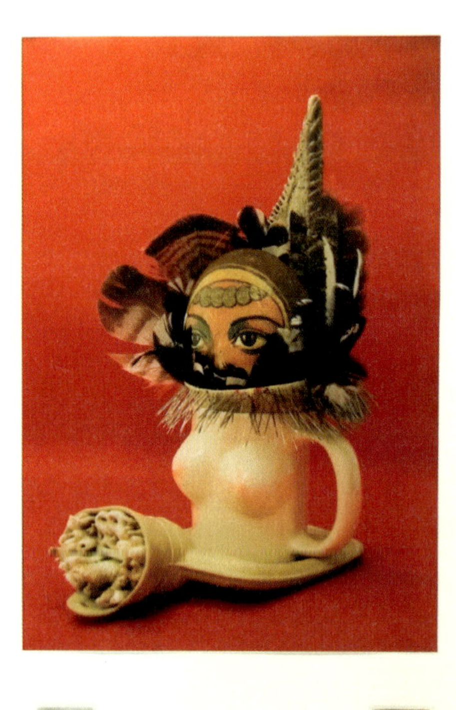

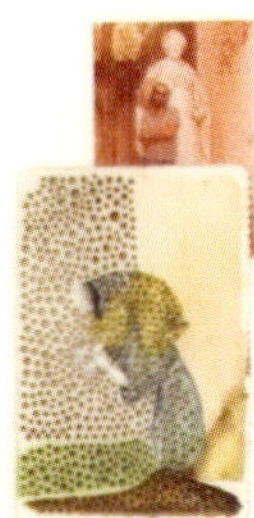

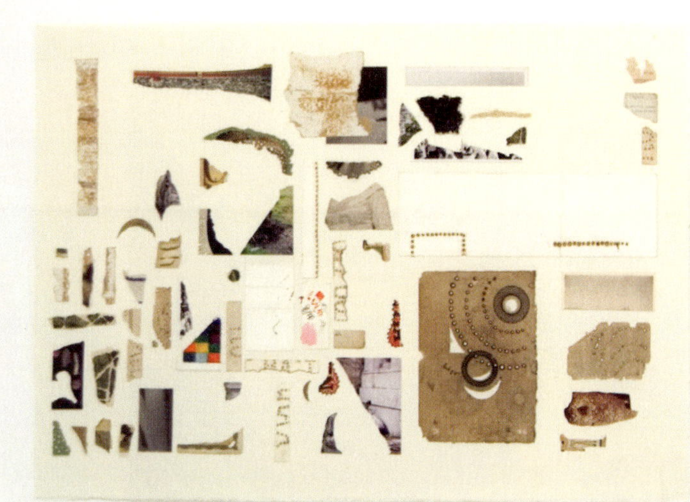

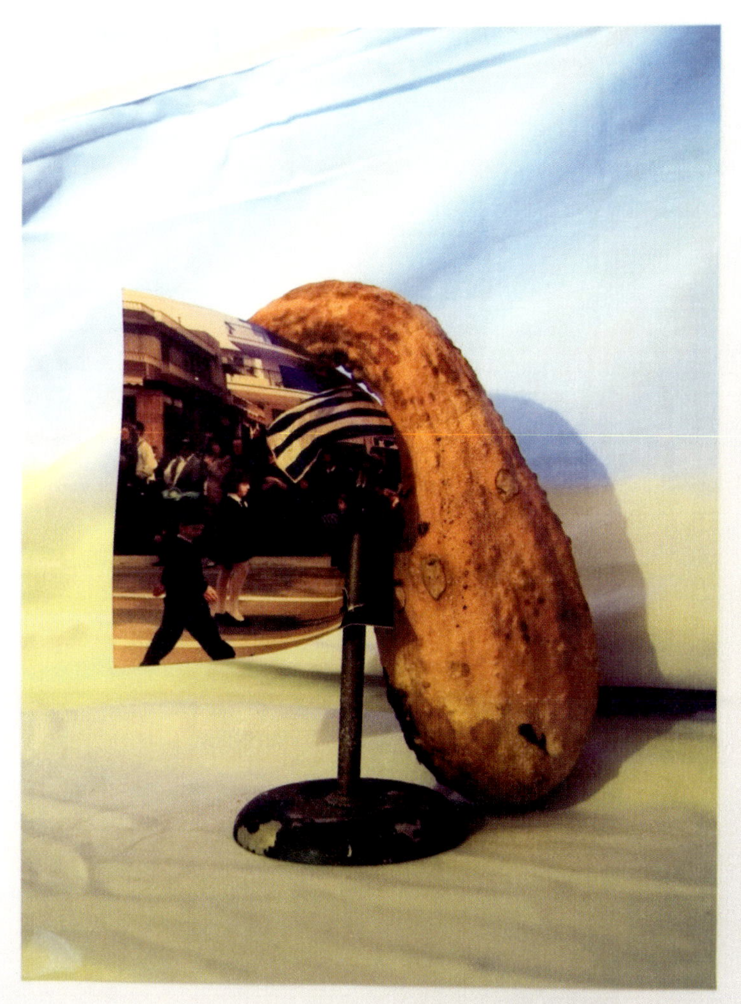

1. *Down with the Abstract. Long Live the Ephemeral!*, 2016 (detail)
Marker on glass, 630 x 320 cm

2.– 3. *God, I Suspect You Are A Leftist Intellectual…*, 2015 (details)
Digital prints on paper, ink on wall, digital prints on textile, and digital prints, drawings, and wood in vitrine, dimensions variable

4. *One Swallow Doesn't Make a Summer*, 2015 (detail)
3,500 calendar pages on wall with transparent tape, dimensions variable

5. *I Love You, You Love Me*, 2013
Digital print on paper, 90 x 60 cm

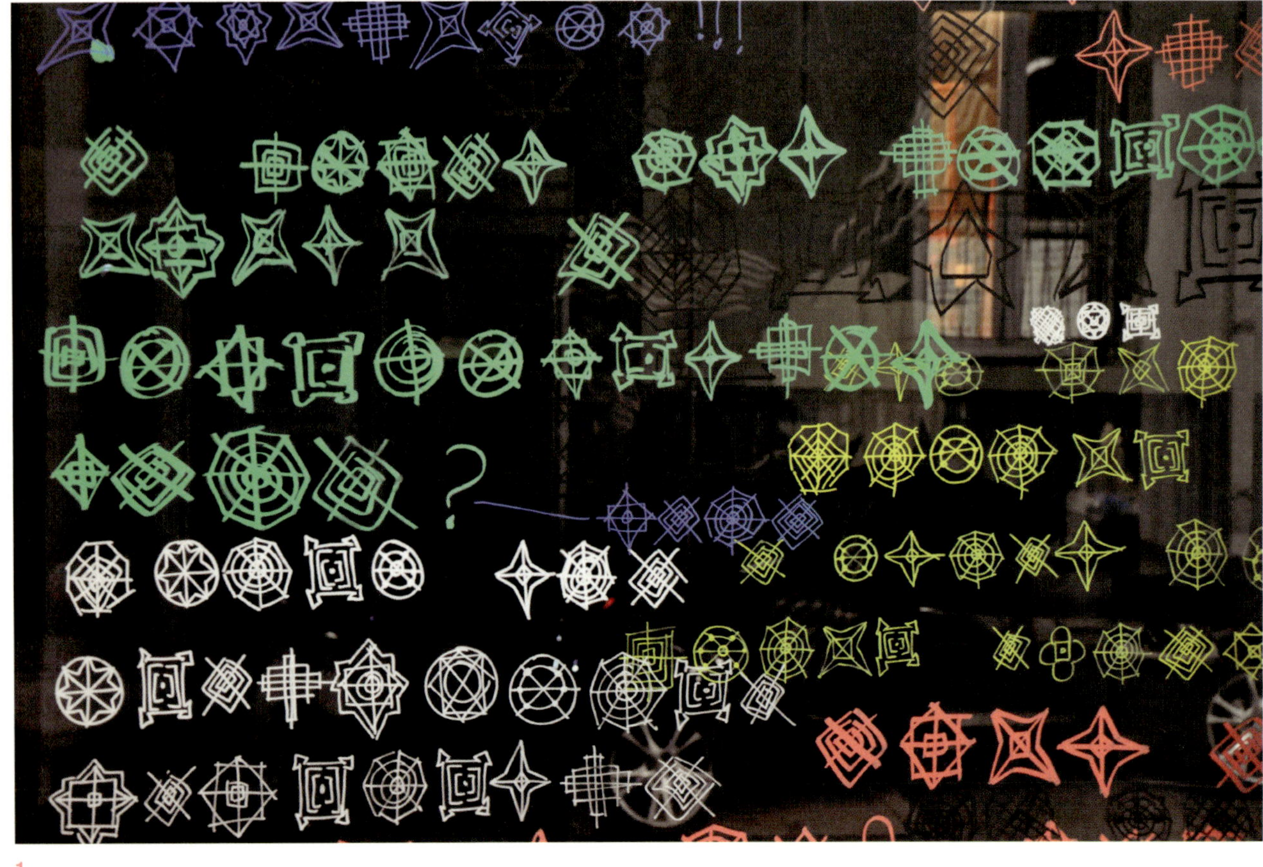

1

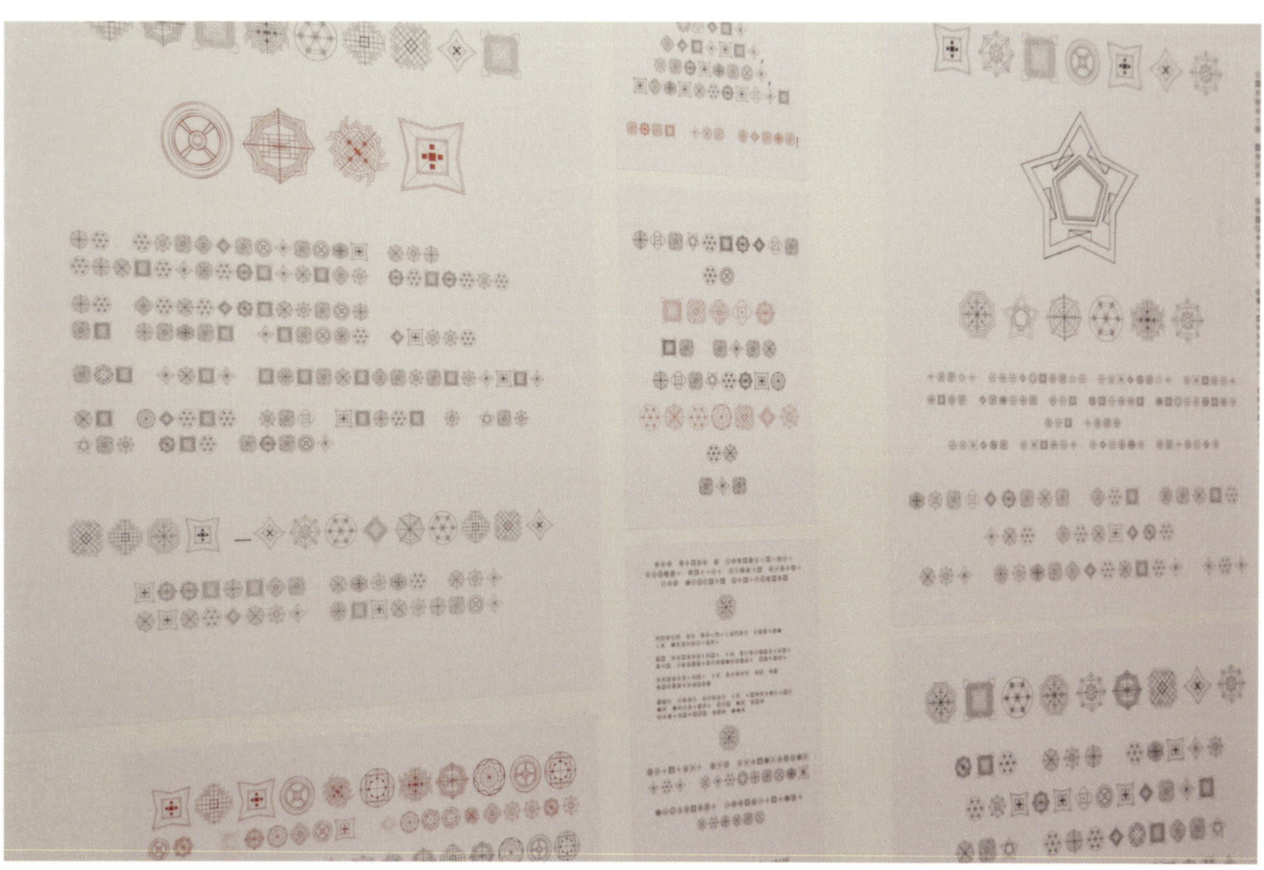

2

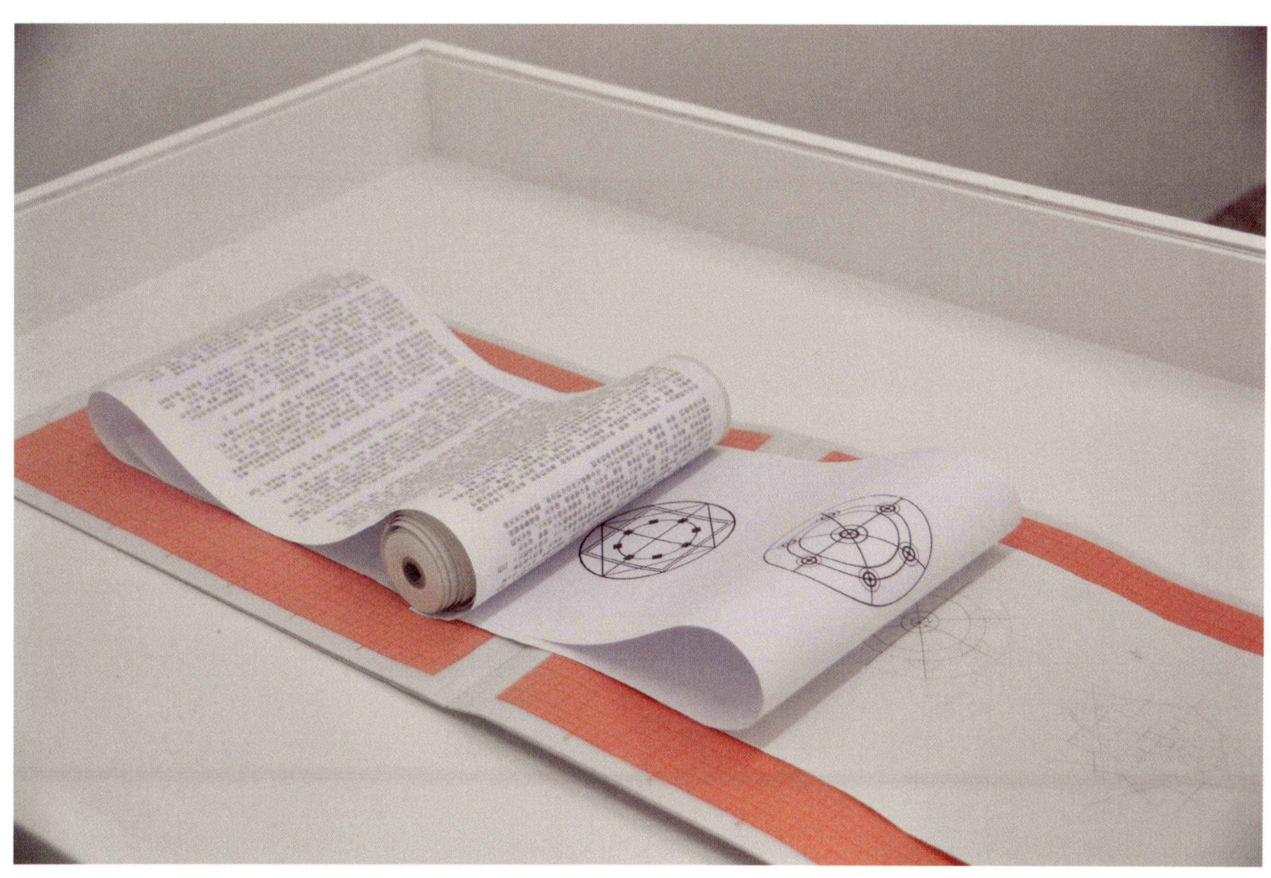

3

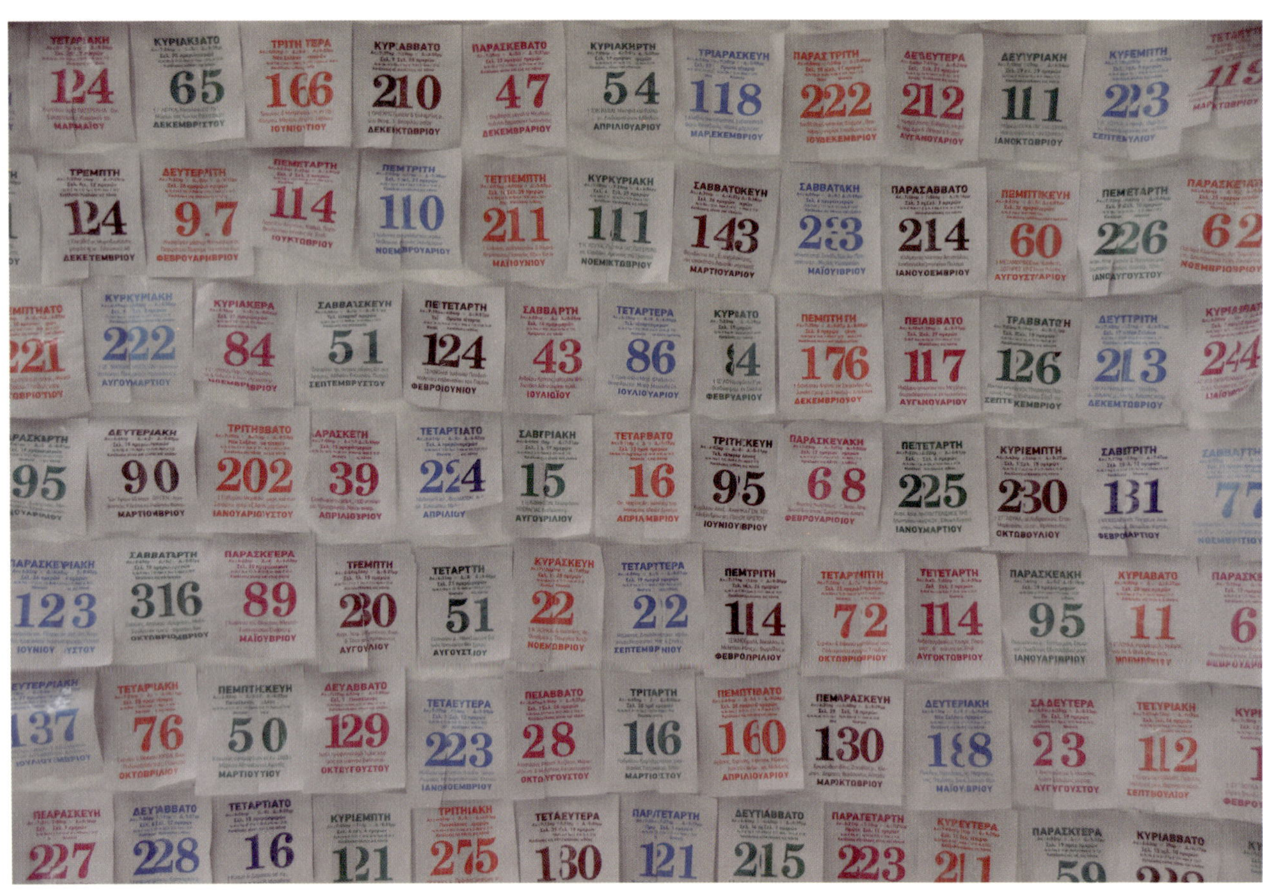

4

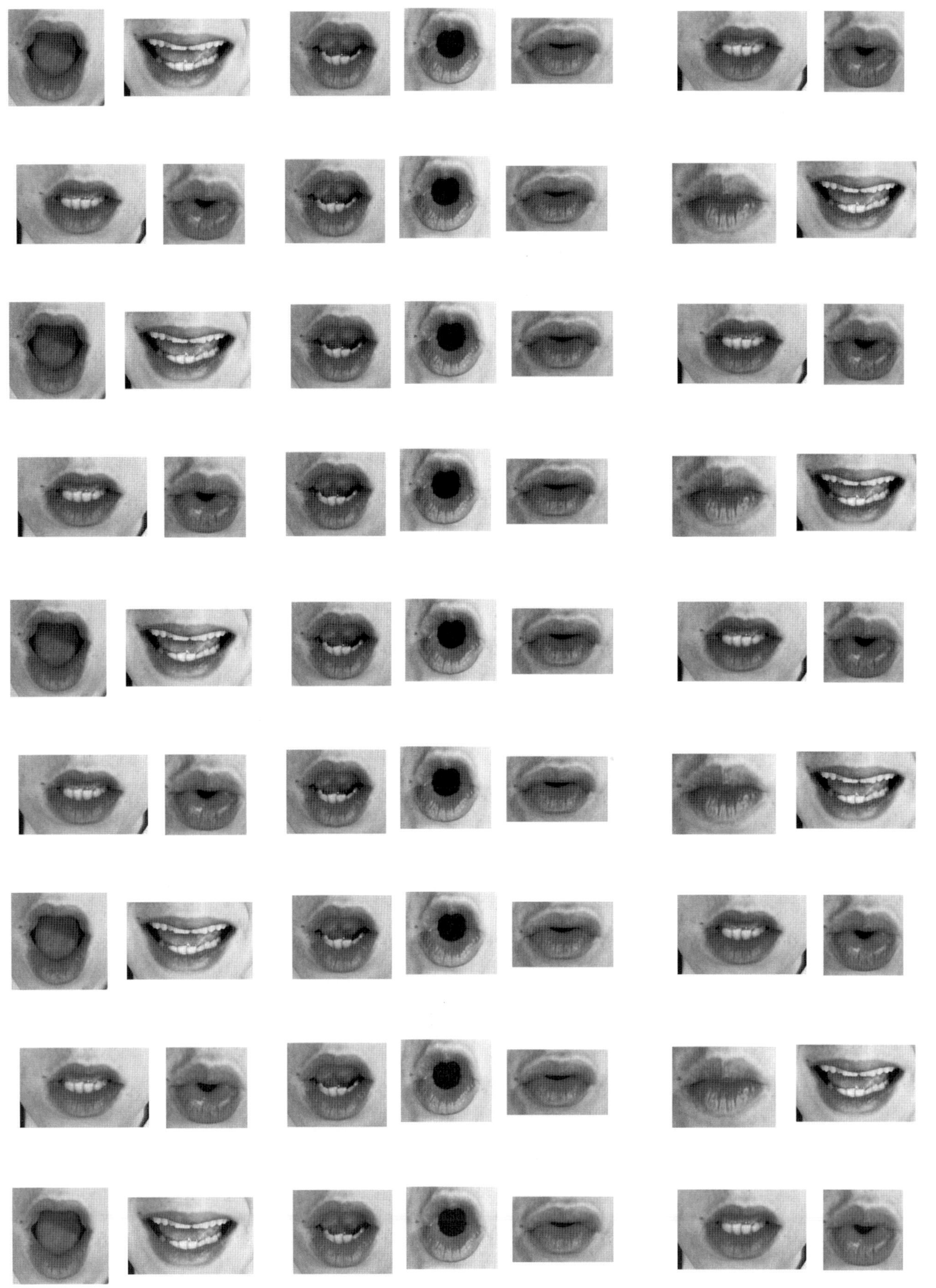

1. *Sunny and Cloudy*, 2013
Blue back paper on billboard, dimensions variable

2. *Attempt to Fly*, 2013 (still)
HD video, color, and sound, 5:00 min

3. – 4. *A Portrait of Her (24/6/2013)*, 2013
Photographic print on cotton paper mounted on Dibond with frame and mandarin orange peel, 17 x 26 cm

5. *Migratory Birds*, 2015
Light box with color transparency, 37 x 55 cm

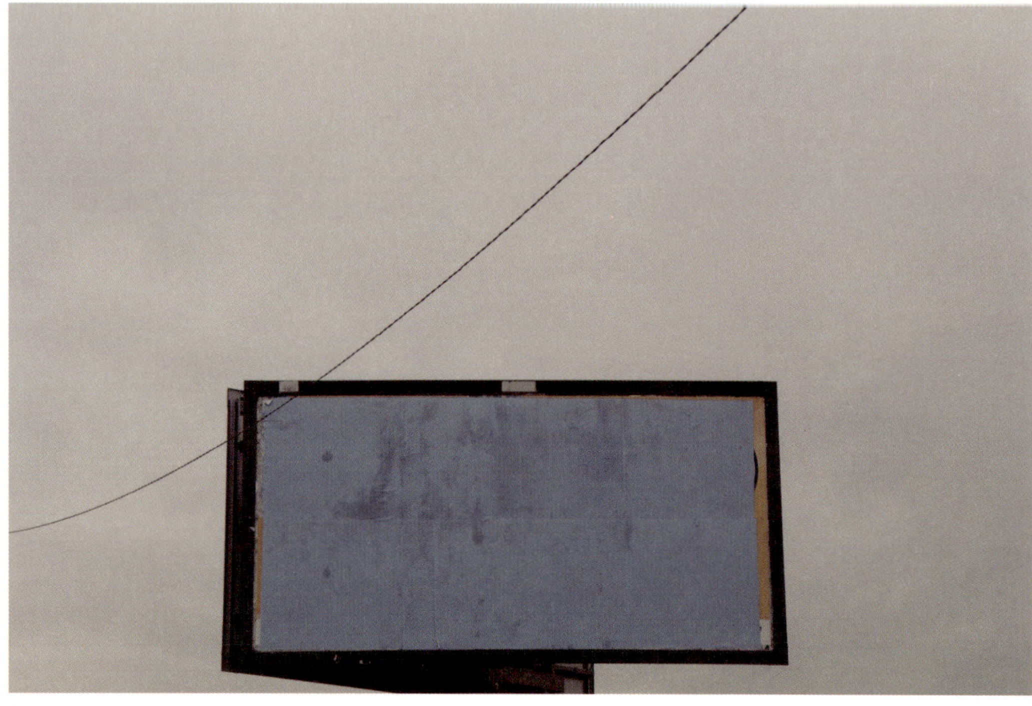
1

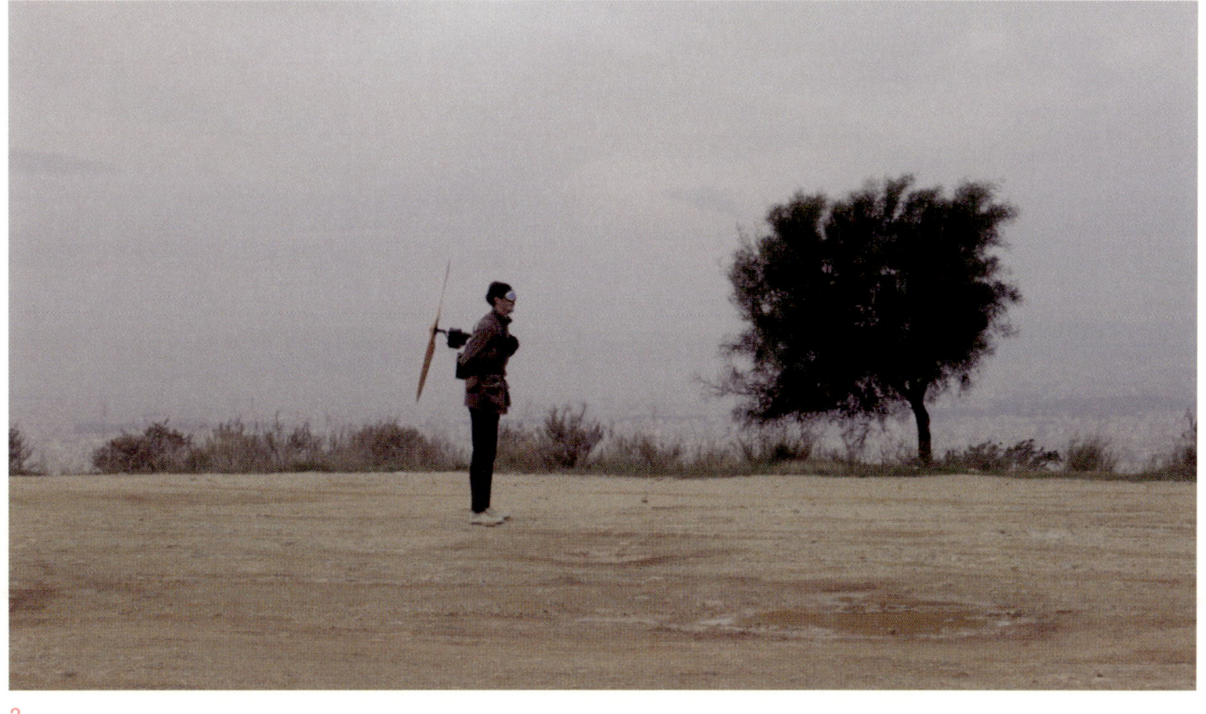

2

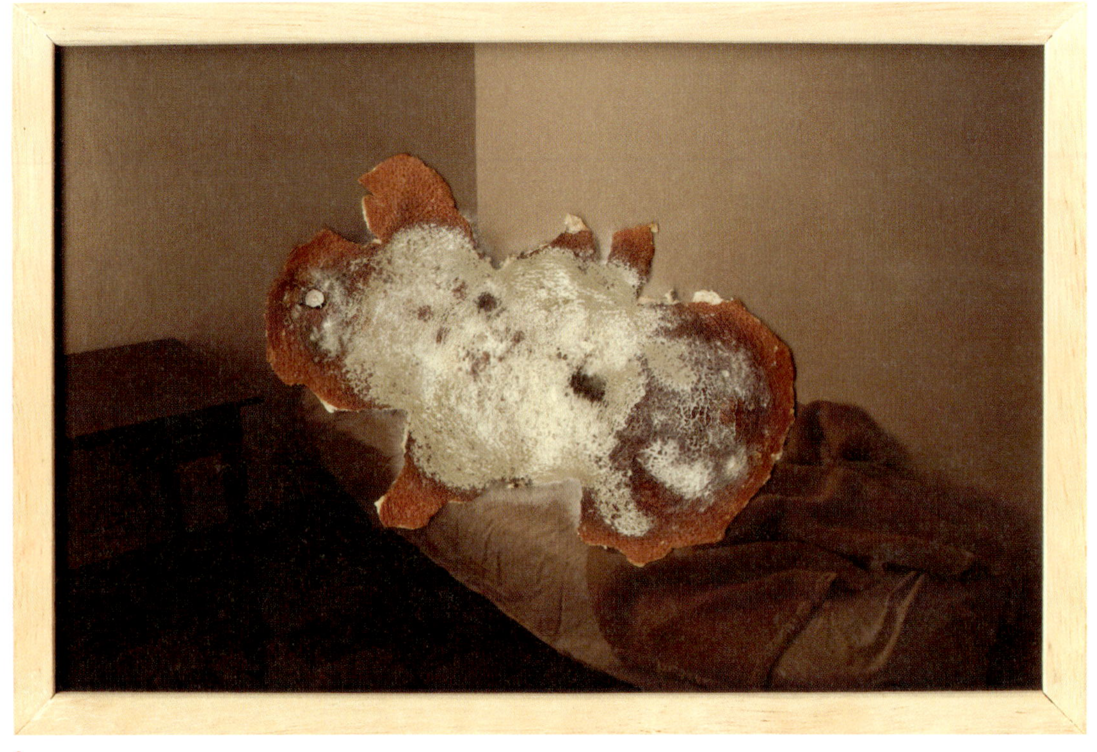

3

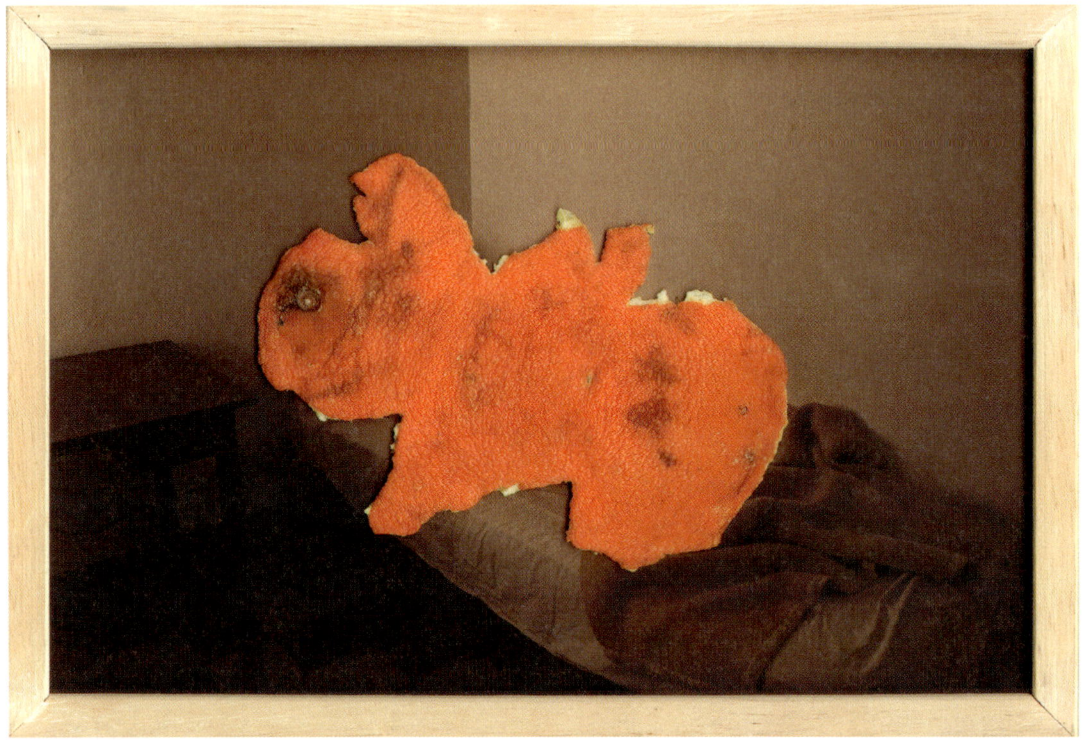

4

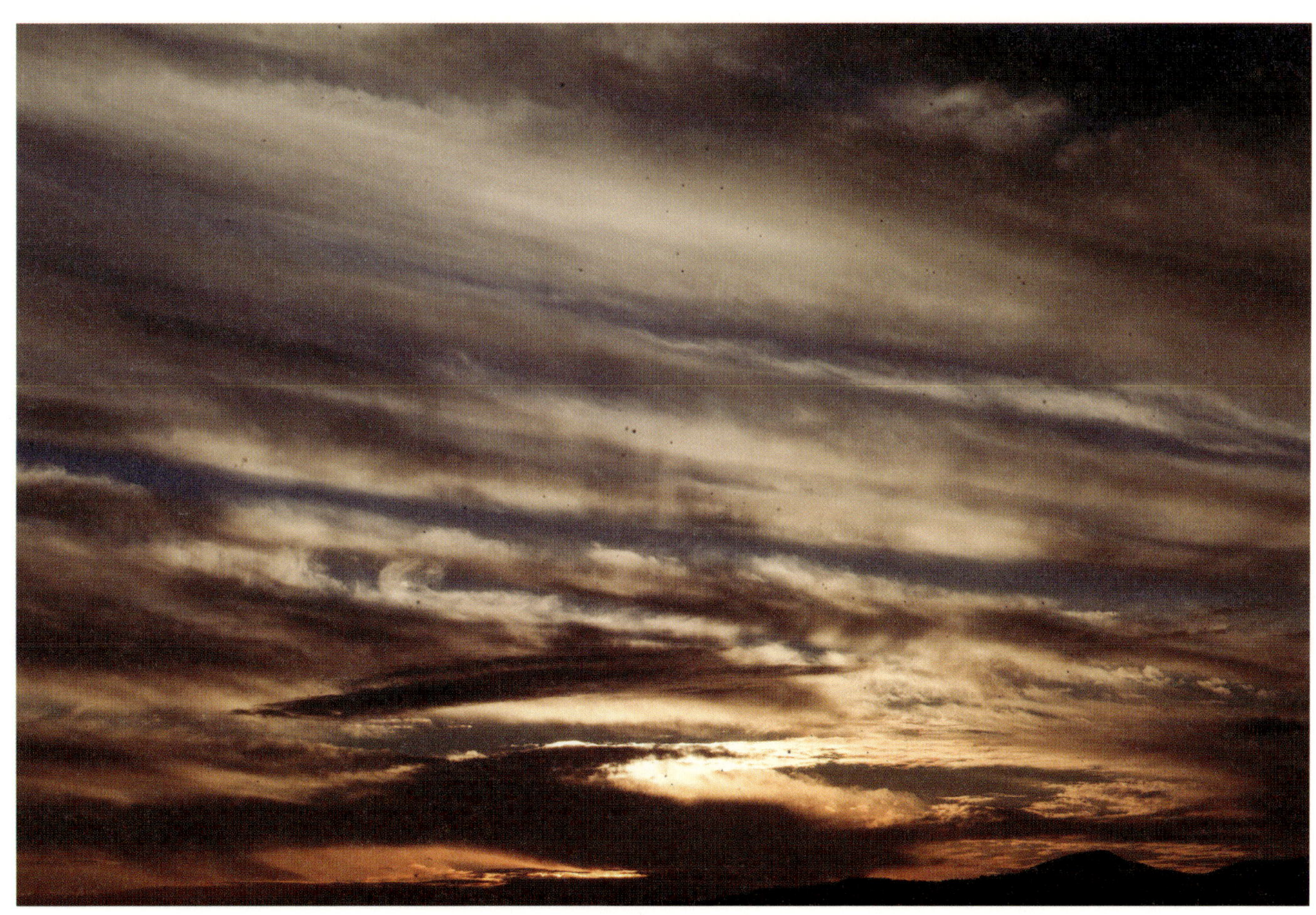

5

1. *One Part Concrete, One Part Ether*, 2014
Wood, ceramic, metal bars, fabric, acrylic paint, india ink, paper, duct tape, drywall, and metal wire, dimensions variable

2. *One Part Concrete, One Part Ether*, 2014 (detail)
Wood, ceramic, metal bars, fabric, acrylic paint, india ink, paper, duct tape, drywall, and metal wire, dimensions variable

3. *When the by the Balcony Likes the by the Kitchen*, 2014 (detail)
Metal, wood, bricks, duct tape, ceramic, felt, acrylic paint, and drywall, 210.8 x 96.5 x 28.6 cm

4. *Before the Warmth of a Fire*, 2014
Wood, acrylic paint, wire, duct tape, and ceramic, 106.7 x 86.4 x 10.2 cm

5. *This Comes When You Lay On a Derivative of a Floor Plan*, 2014
Ceramic, brass, fabric, drywall, cardboard, acrylic paint, marble, cement, kitchen towel, plaster, plastic, and wood, dimensions variable

6. *A Place From a Different Timeline*, 2016 (detail)
White oak, drywall, metal, glazed ceramic, resin, brass, aluminum, shoelace, wire, duct tape, ink, household paint, tools, pencil, print on tissue, print on paper, Band-Aid, wire from broken iPhone, cigarette butt, marble dust, and leftovers of carbon dioxide, water vapor, oxygen, and nitrogen, dimensions variable

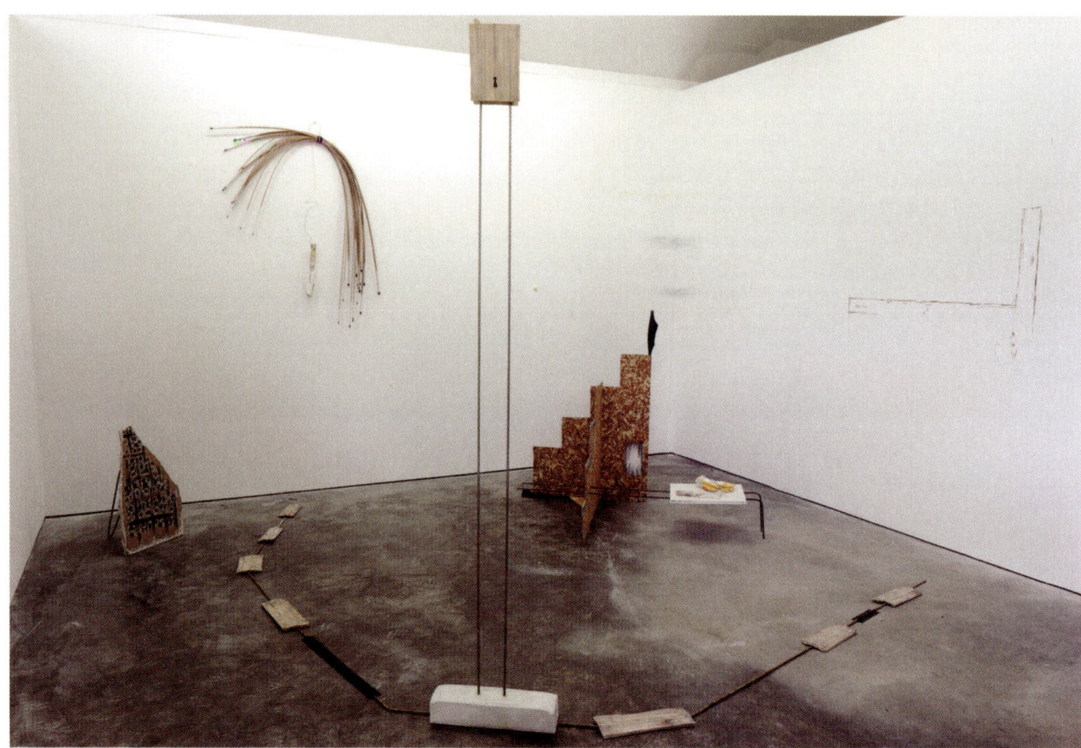

1

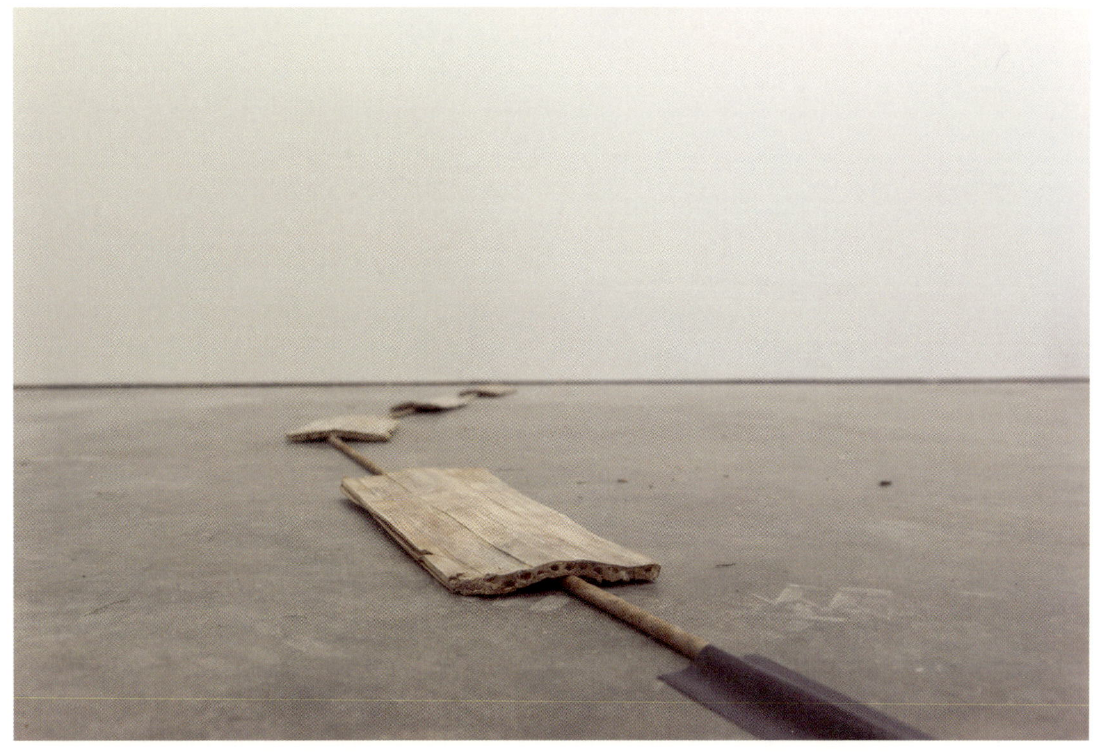

2

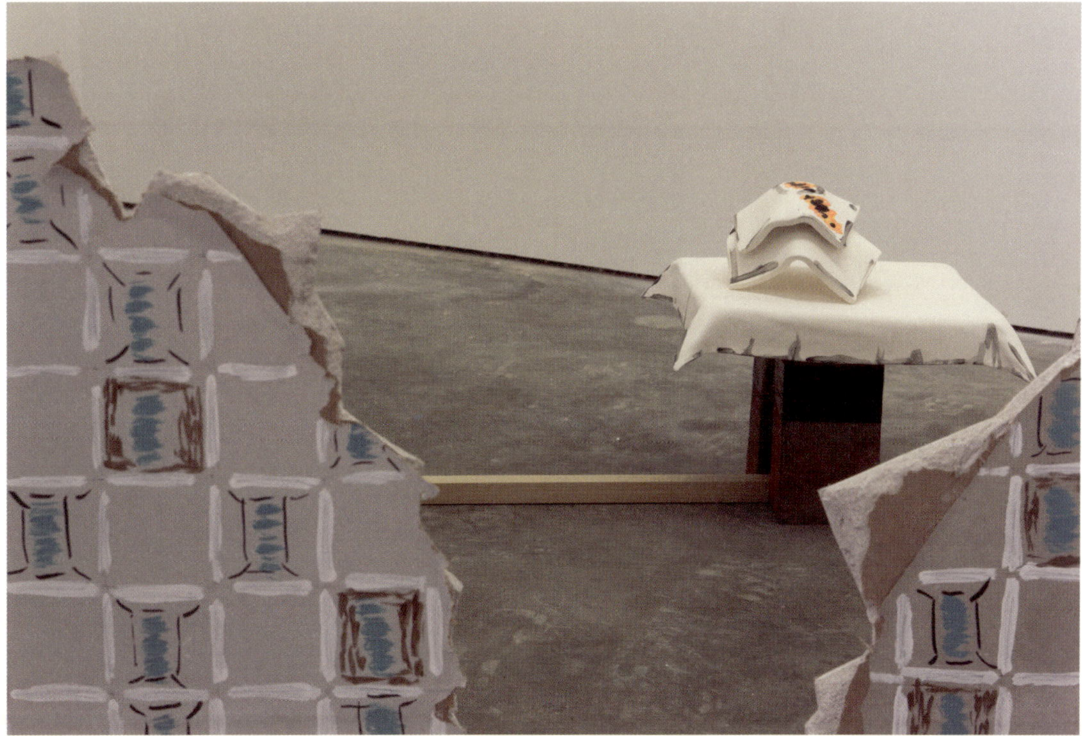

3

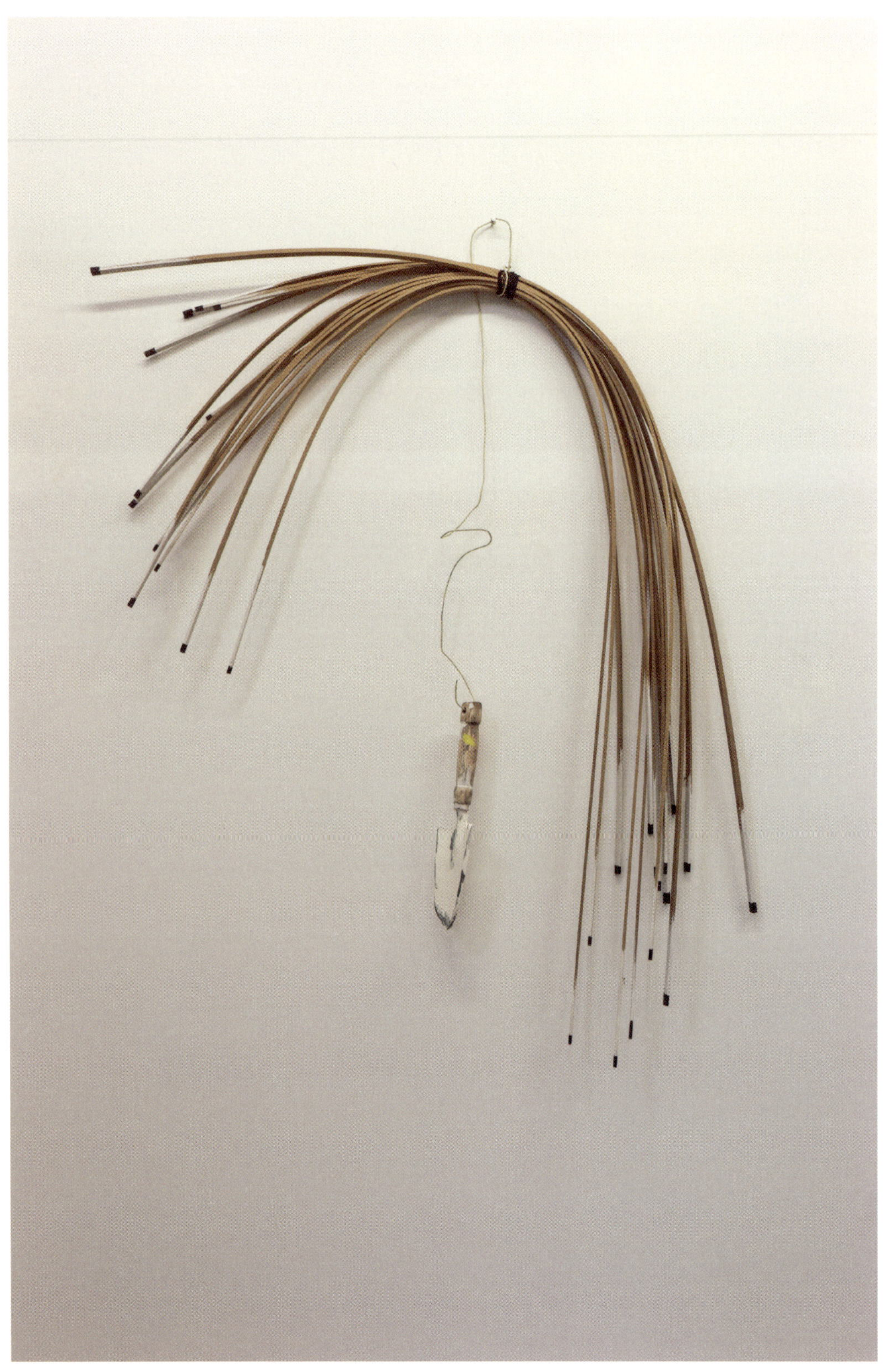

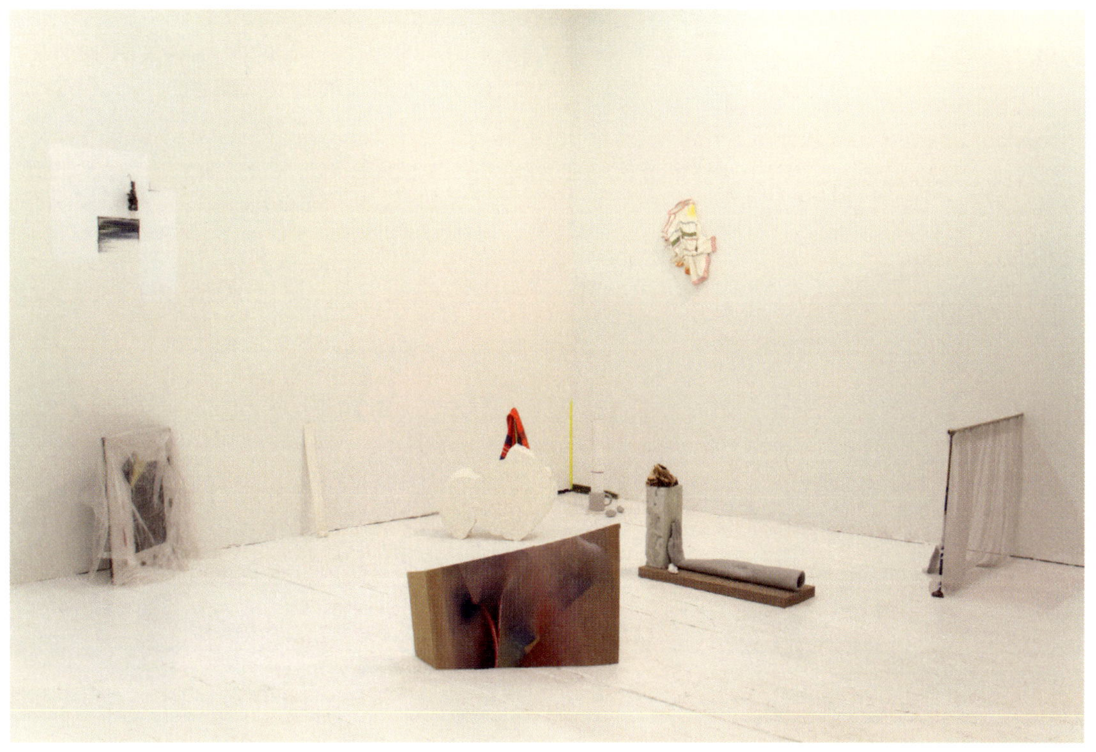

5

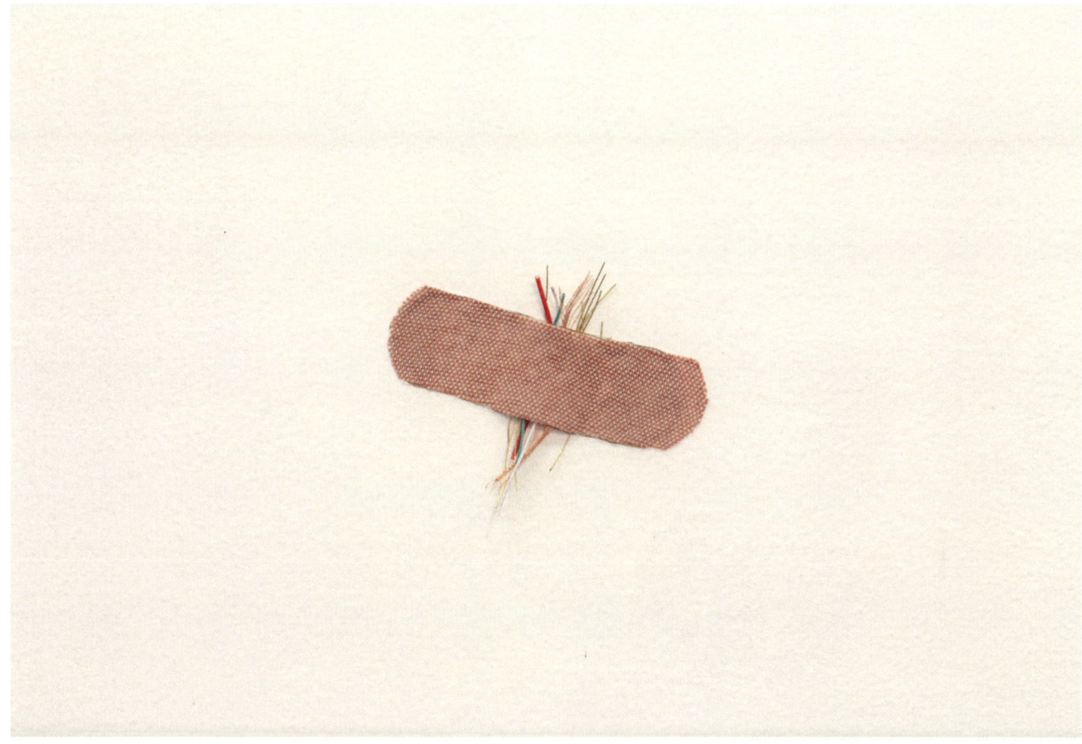

6

1. *All the Guys She's Fucked, Part I*, 2014
Ink and digital print on fabric, 220 x 140 cm

2. *All the Guys She's Fucked, Part II*, 2014
Ink and digital print on fabric, 220 x 140 cm

3. *Koleti Street*, 2015
Ink and digital print on canvas, 140 x 100 cm

4. *Nudists*, 2015
Ink and digital print on canvas, 145 x 240 cm

5. *Olay Oldu*, 2014
Ink and digital print on canvas, 180 x 140 cm

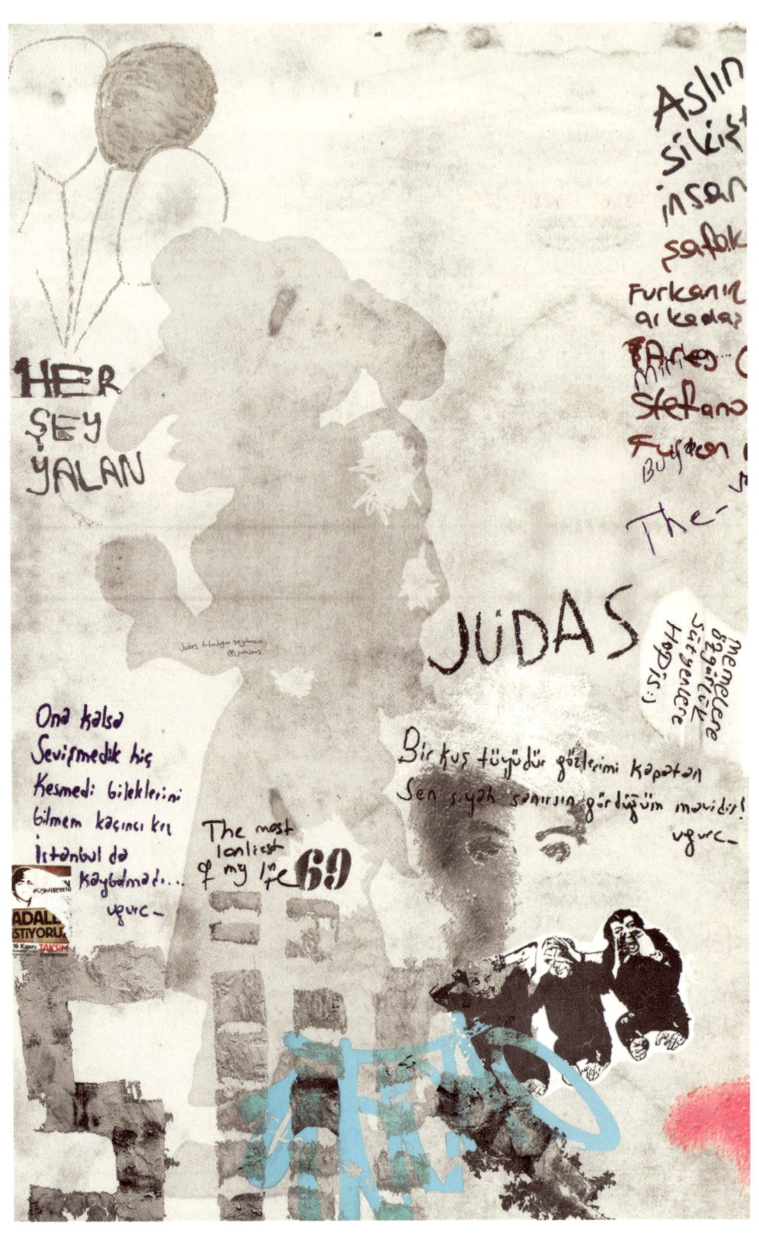

1

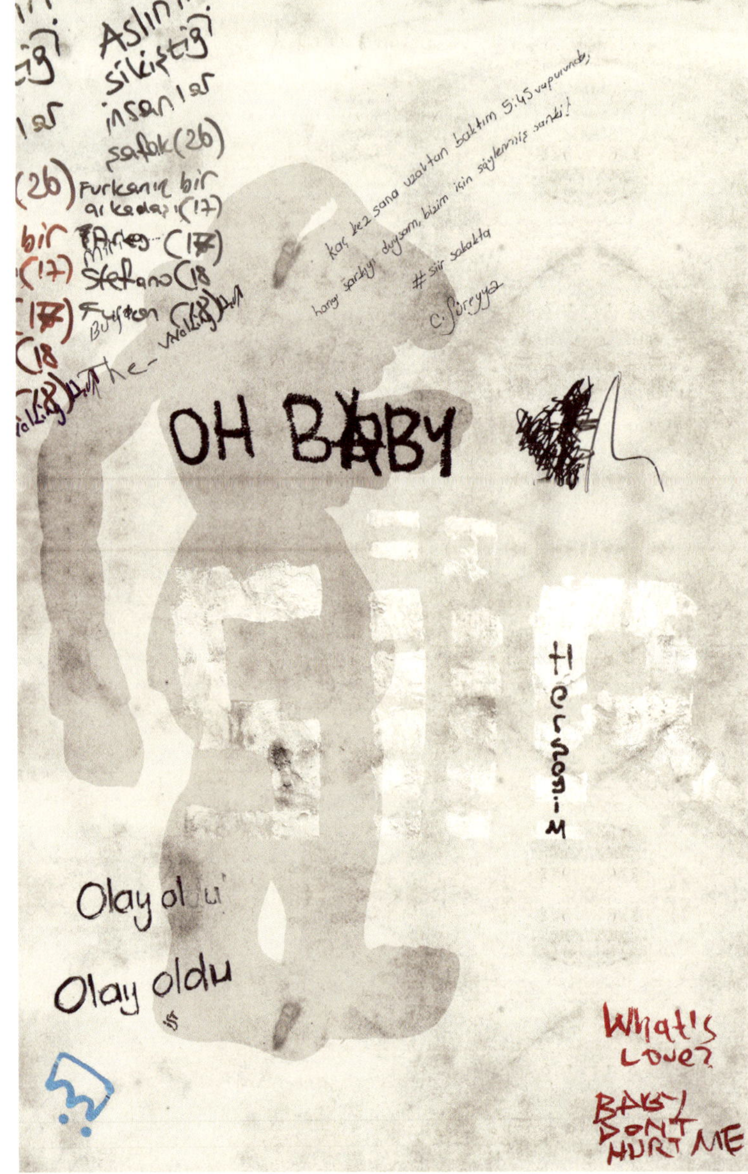

2

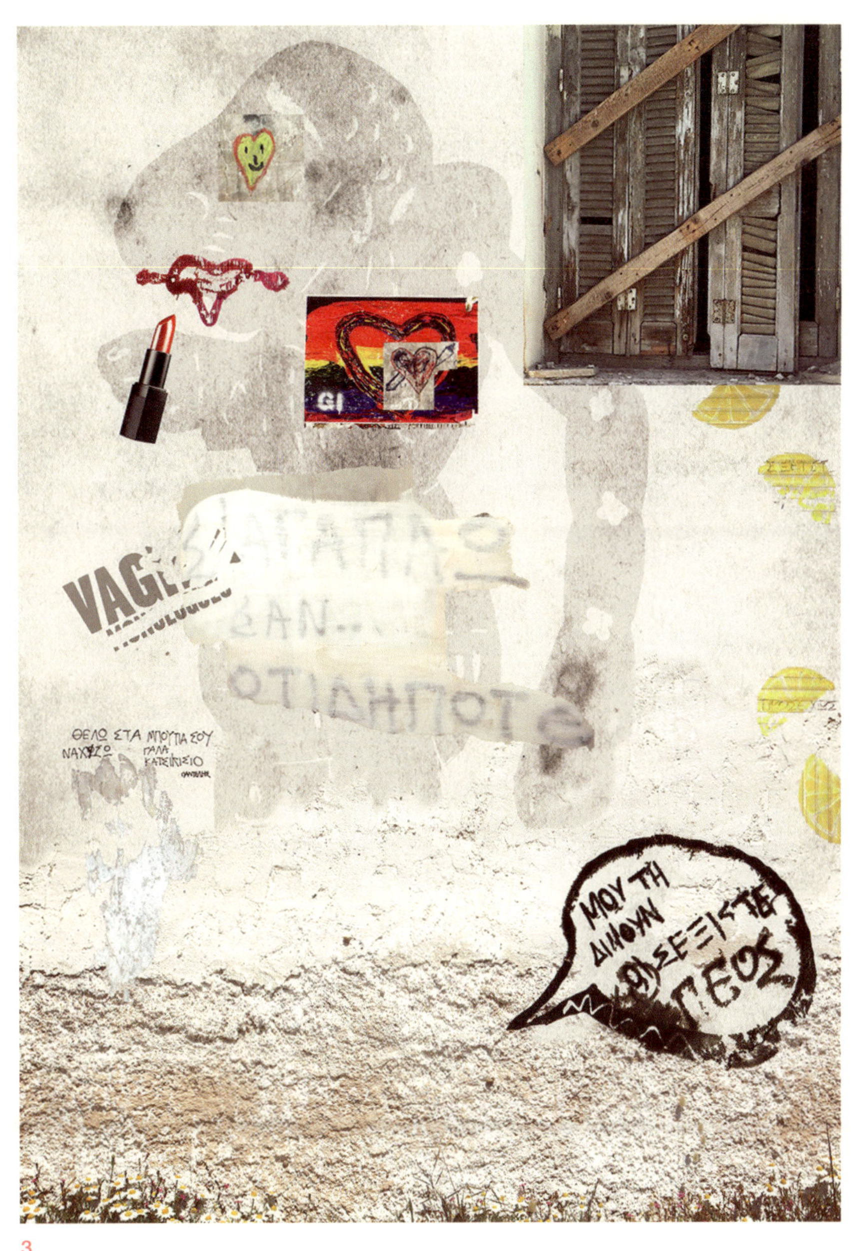
VAGI
ΘΕΛΩ ΣΤΑ ΜΠΟΥΤΙΑ ΣΟΥ
ΝΑΧΥΖΟ ΓΑΛΑ ΚΑΤΕΥΘΕΙΟ

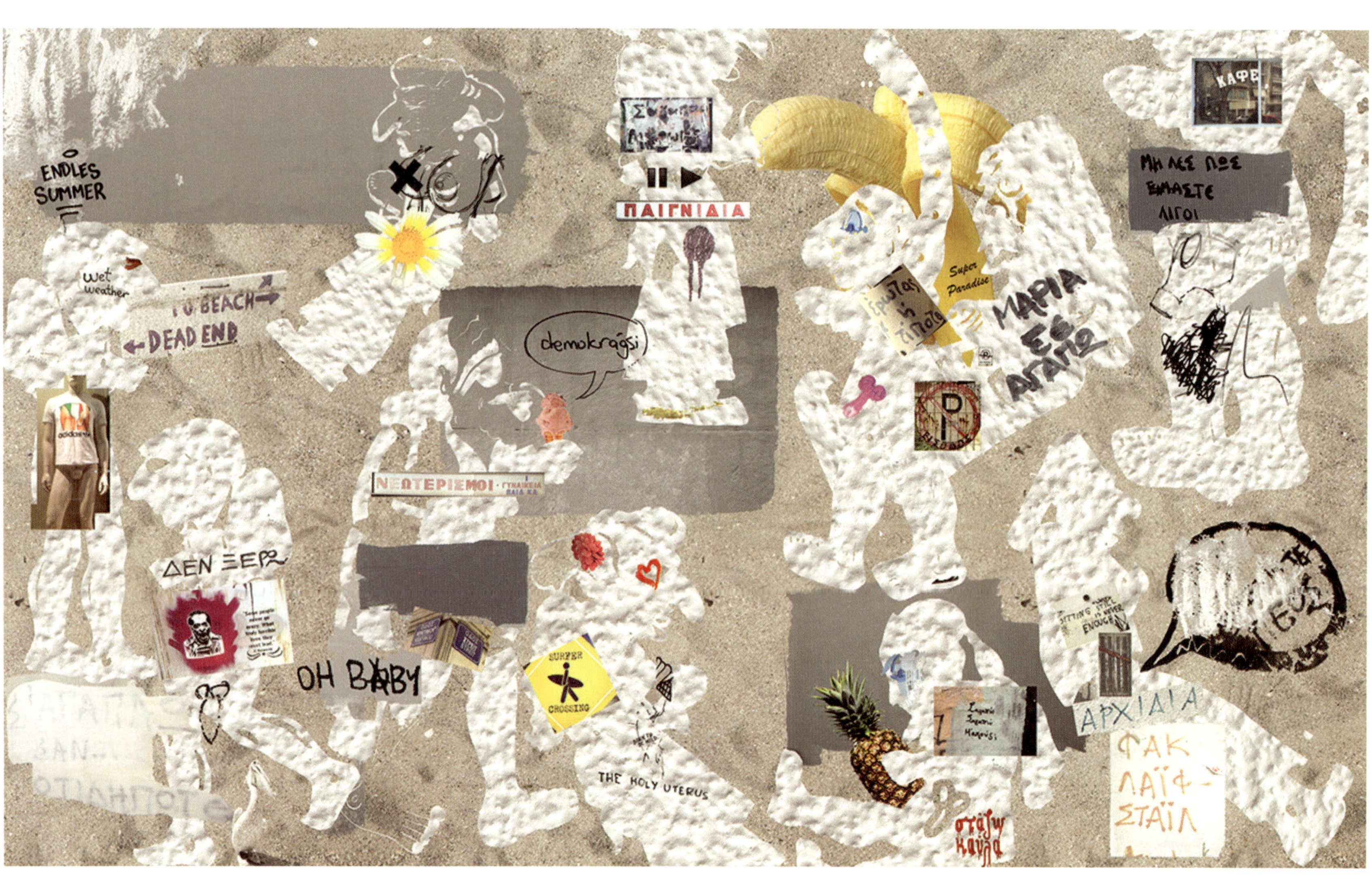

ENDLES SUMMER
Wet weather
TO BEACH →
← DEAD END
ΠΑΙΓΝΙΔΙΑ
demokraqsi
ΝΕΩΤΕΡΙΣΜΟΙ
ΔΕΝ ΞΕΡΩ
OH BABY
SURFER CROSSING
THE HOLY UTERUS
Super Paradise
ΜΑΡΙΑ ΣΕ ΑΓΑΠΩ
ΚΑΦΕ
ΜΗ ΛΕΣ ΠΩΣ ΕΙΜΑΣΤΕ ΛΙΓΟΙ
P
ΑΡΧΙΔΙΑ
ΦΑΚ ΛΑΪΦ ΣΤΑΪΛ

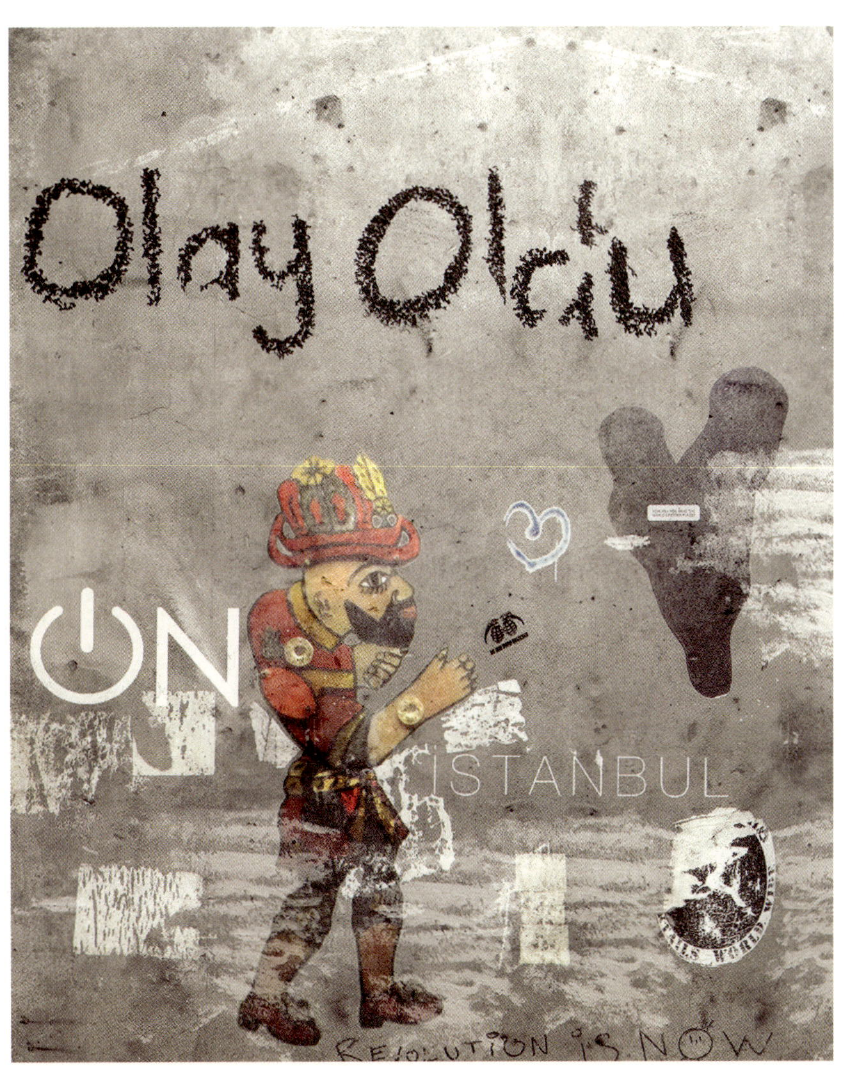

5

1. *Leda, Daphne, Daphne, Medusa, Leda*, 2015
Plaster and traces of extruded polystyrene, dimensions variable

2. *Columns (Time, Brain, Transformation, Skeleton)*, 2015 (detail)
Steel, plaster, and traces of extruded polystyrene, dimensions variable

3. *Alone (Chara)*, 2015
Photograph, dimensions variable

4. *Hunt (Patras)*, 2015
Steel and digital print on elastic insulation sheet, 215 x 240 cm

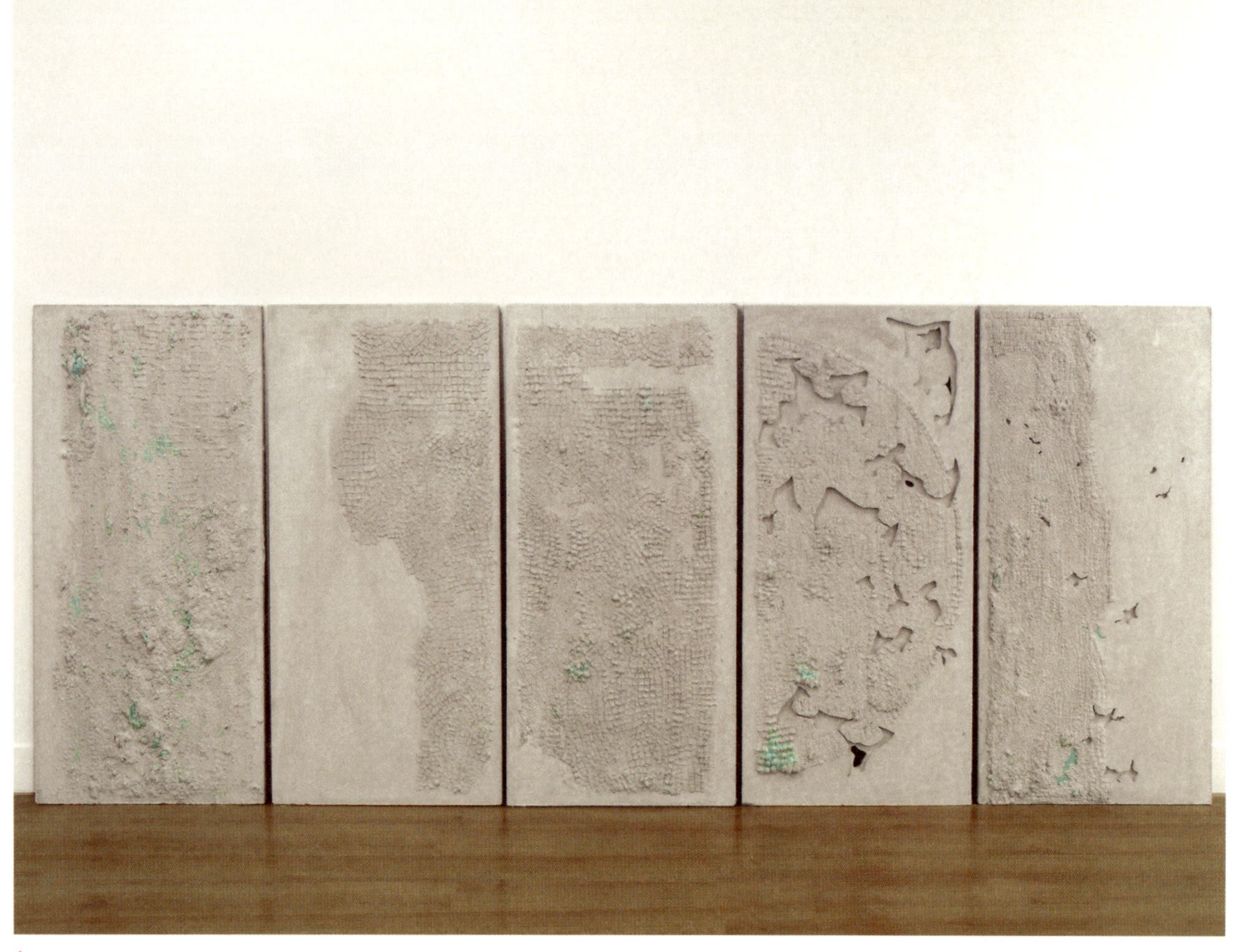

1

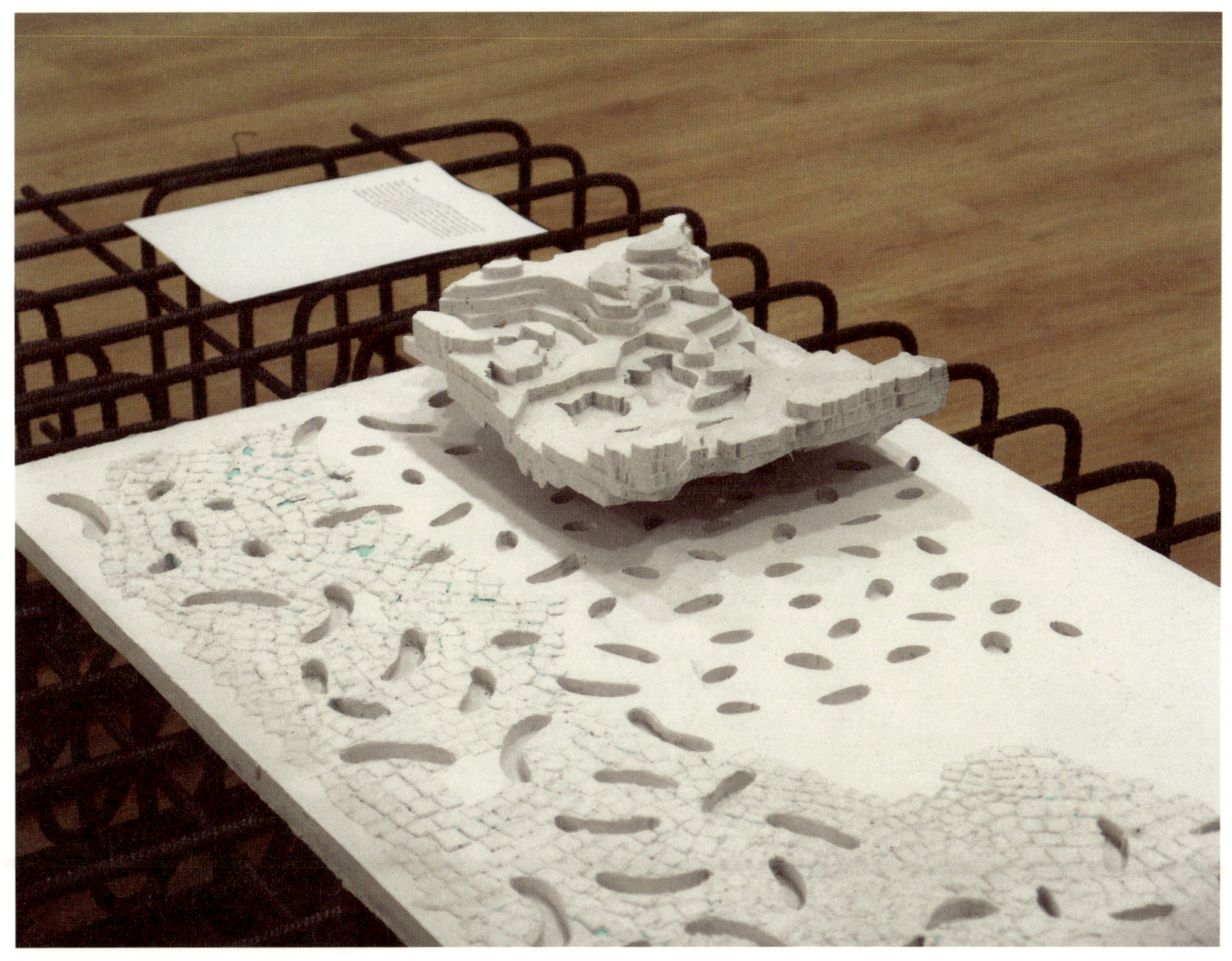

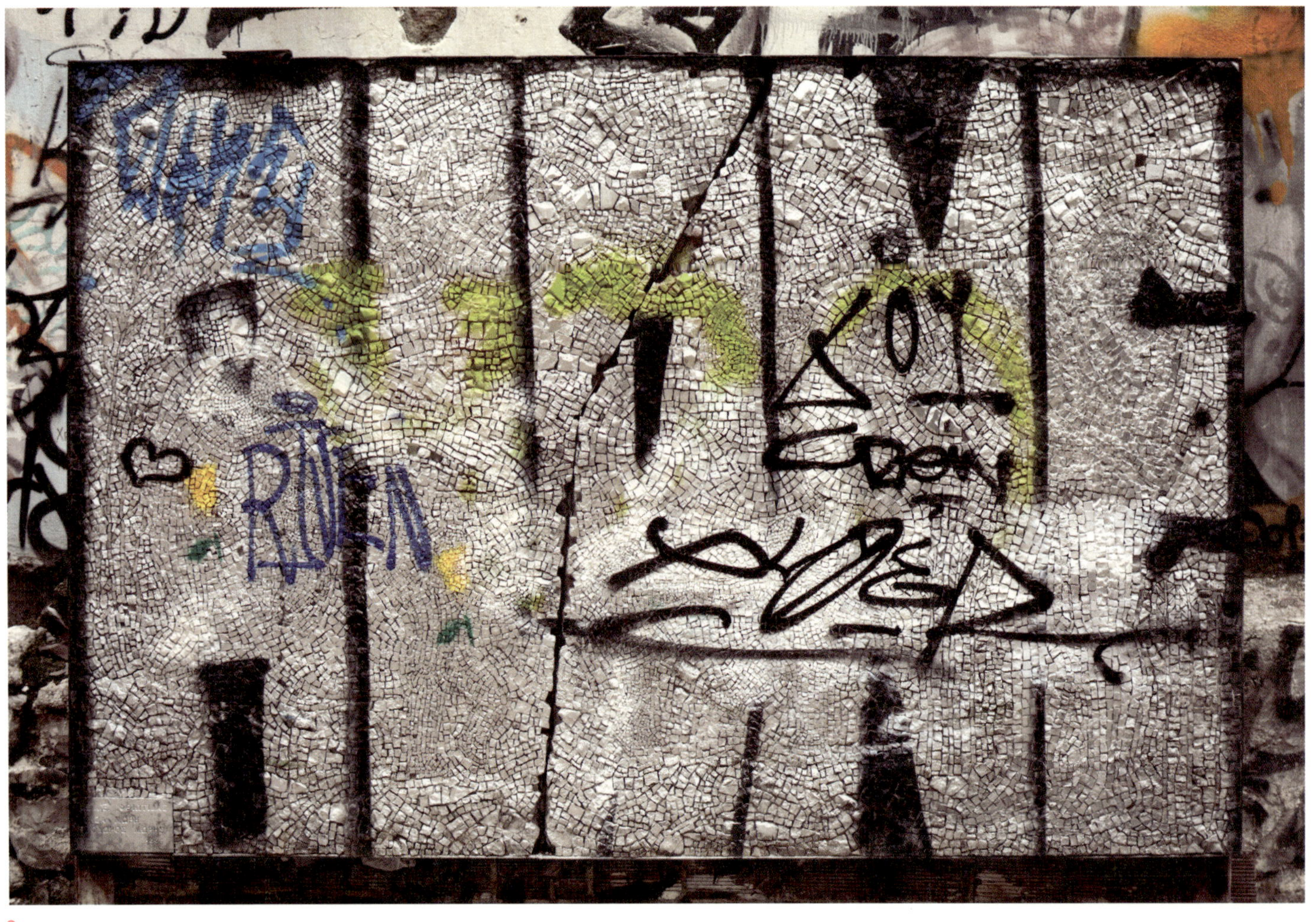

3

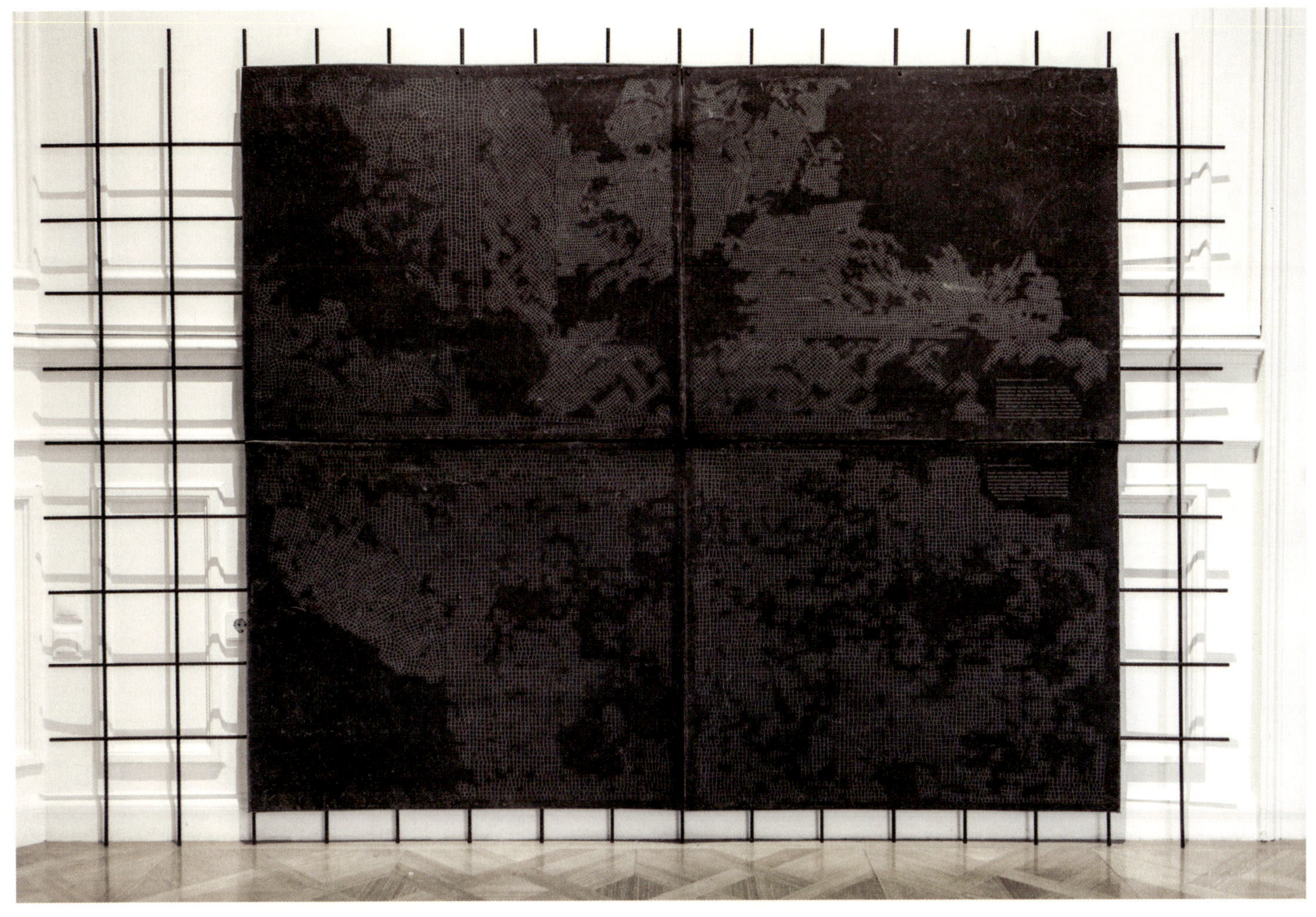

4

1. – 3. *Maltepe Gelinler / Maltepe Brides*, 2015–ongoing
Video, 13:44 min

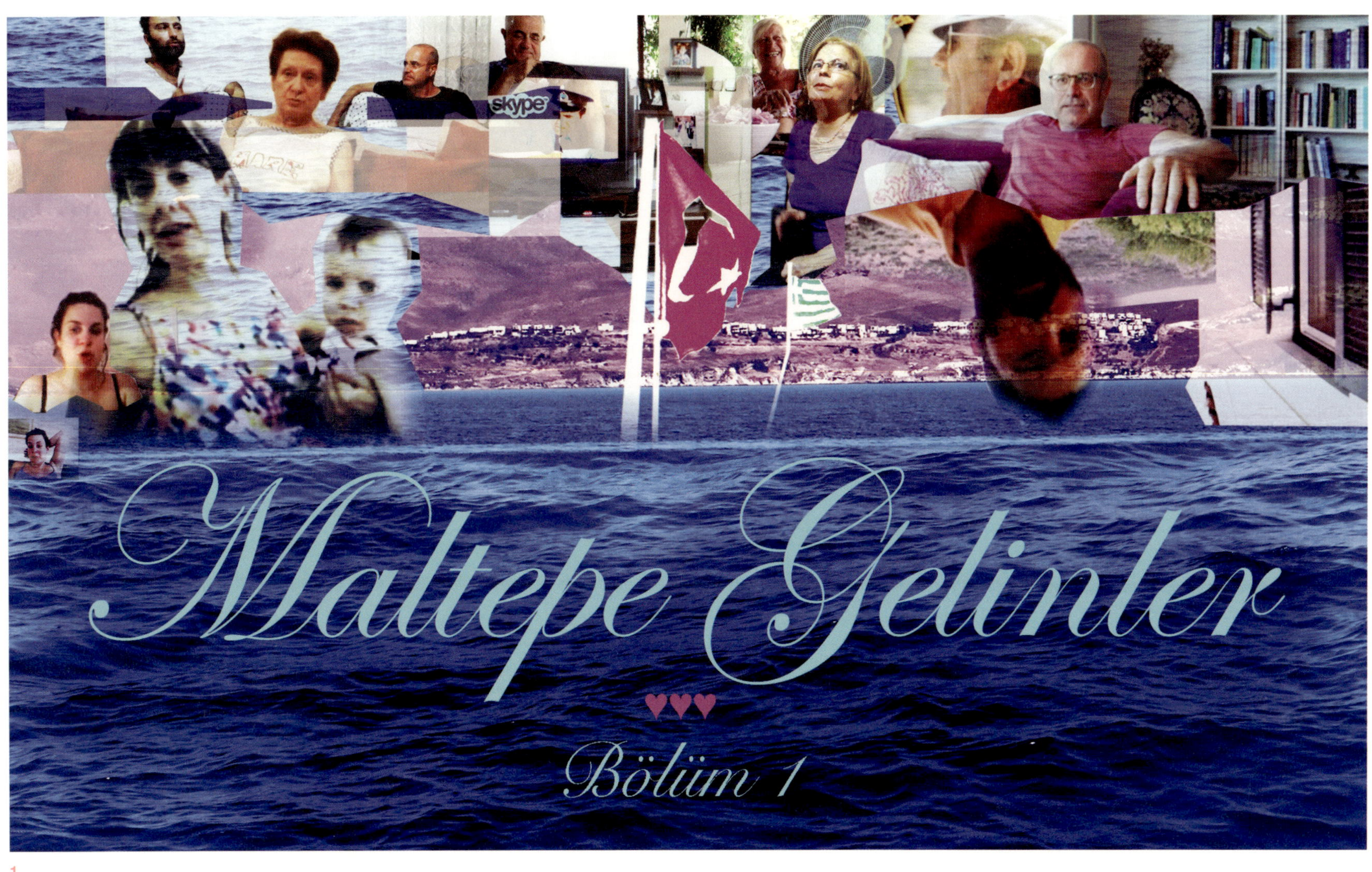
skype
Maltepe Gelinler
Bölüm 1

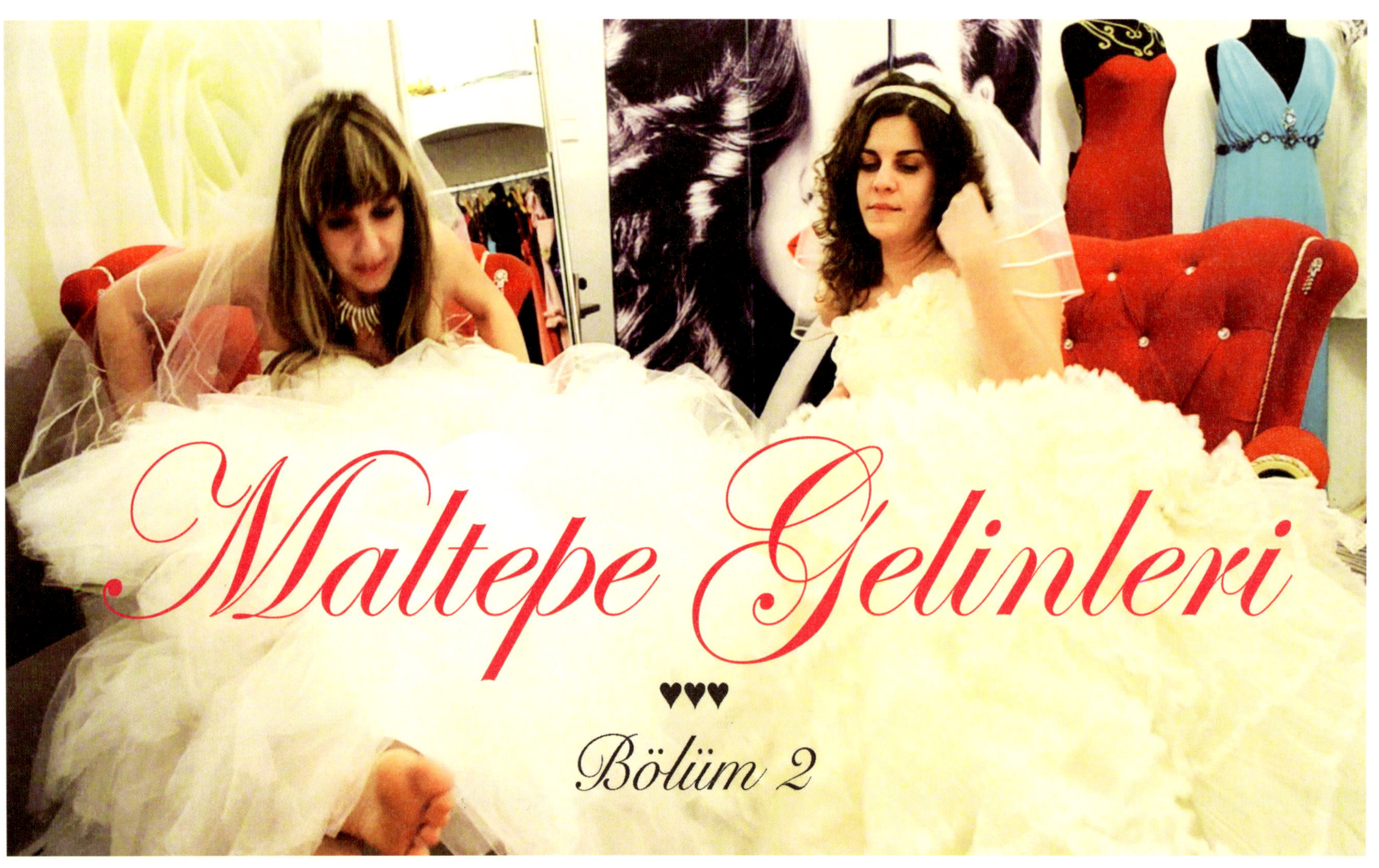

Maltepe Gelinleri
Bölüm 2

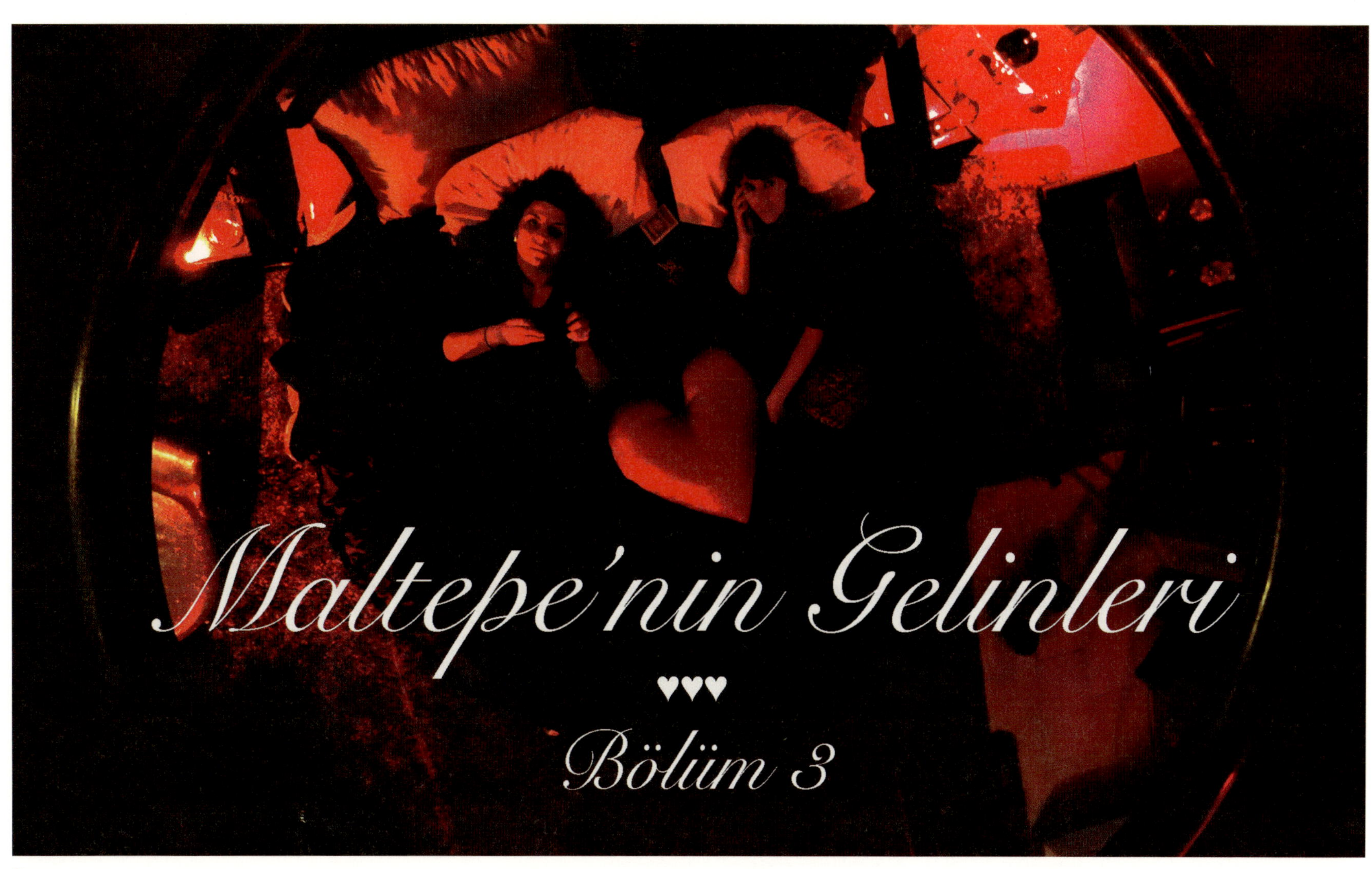
Maltepe'nin Gelinleri
♥♥♥
Bölüm 3

1. *Ghost Relief I (The Mansion of the Kontou Family)*, 2015
Paraffin wax, pigment, wick, and wood, 157 x 60 x 35 cm

2. *Ghost Relief IV (Villa Kazouli)*, 2015
Paraffin wax, pigment, wick, and wood, 176 x 51 x 35 cm

3. *Ghost Relief II (The House on Smolensky Street)*, 2015
Paraffin wax, pigment, wick, and wood, 147 x 45 x 35 cm

4. *Ghost Relief I–IV*, 2015
Paraffin wax, pigment, wick, and wood, dimensions variable

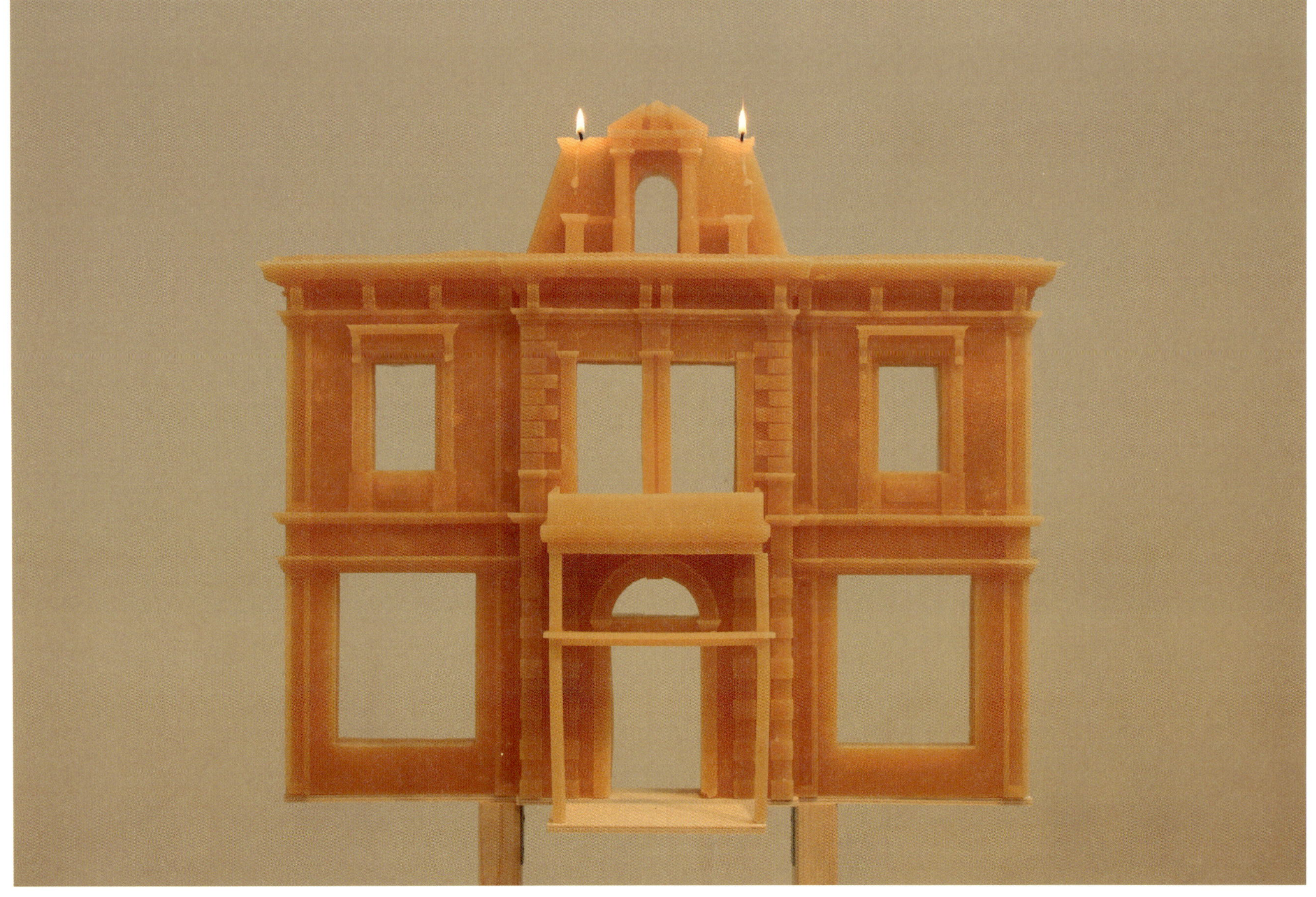

1

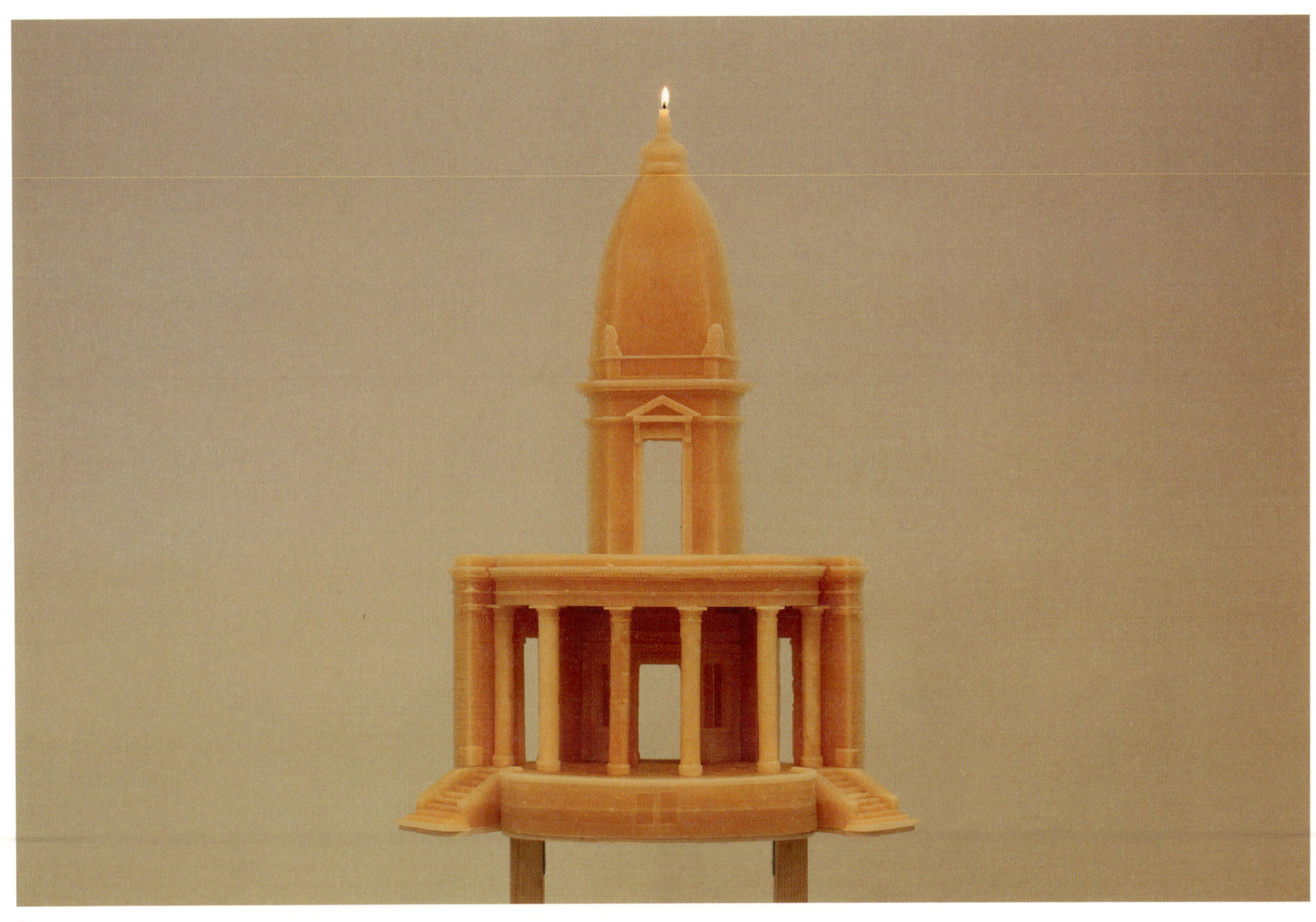

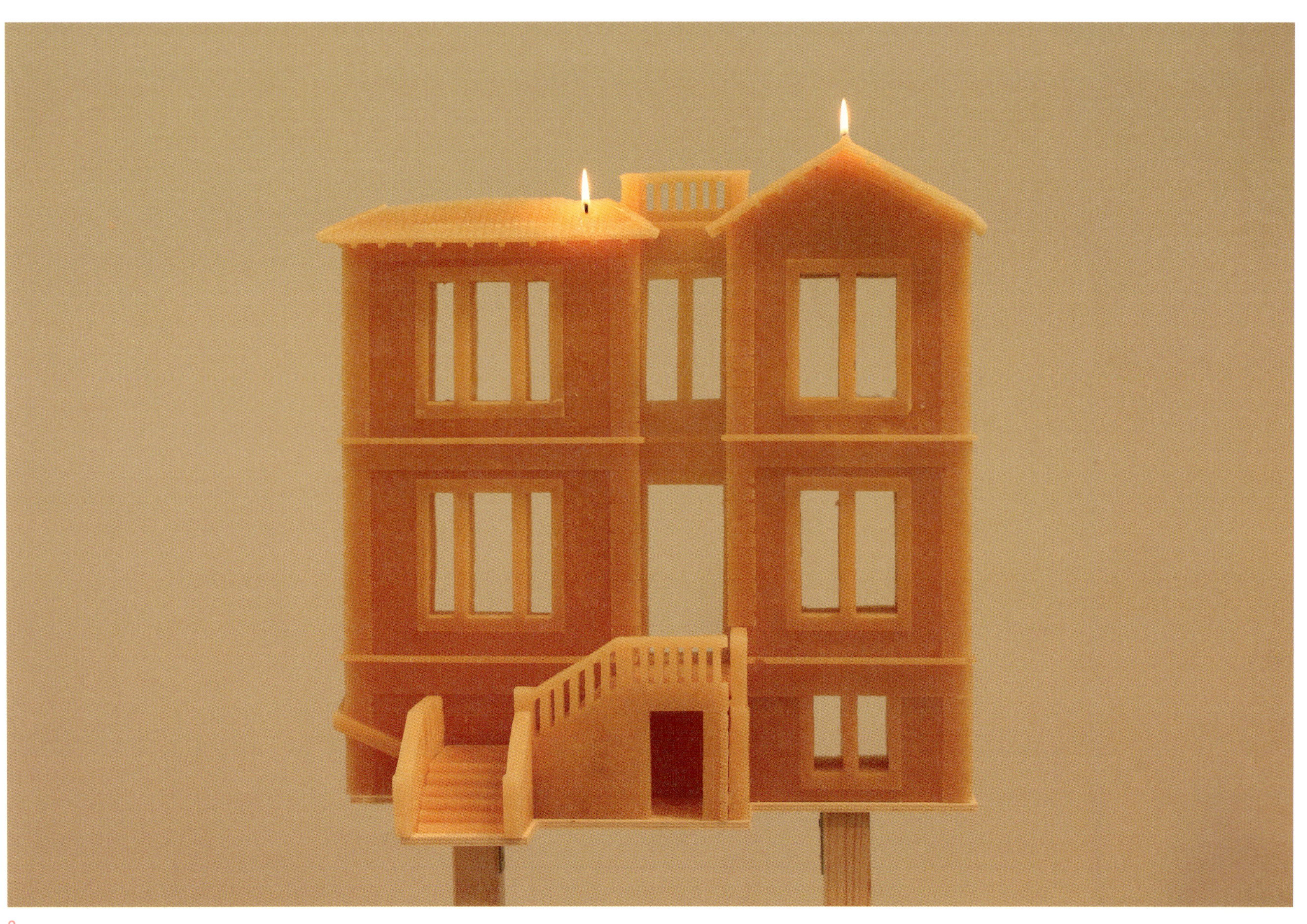

3

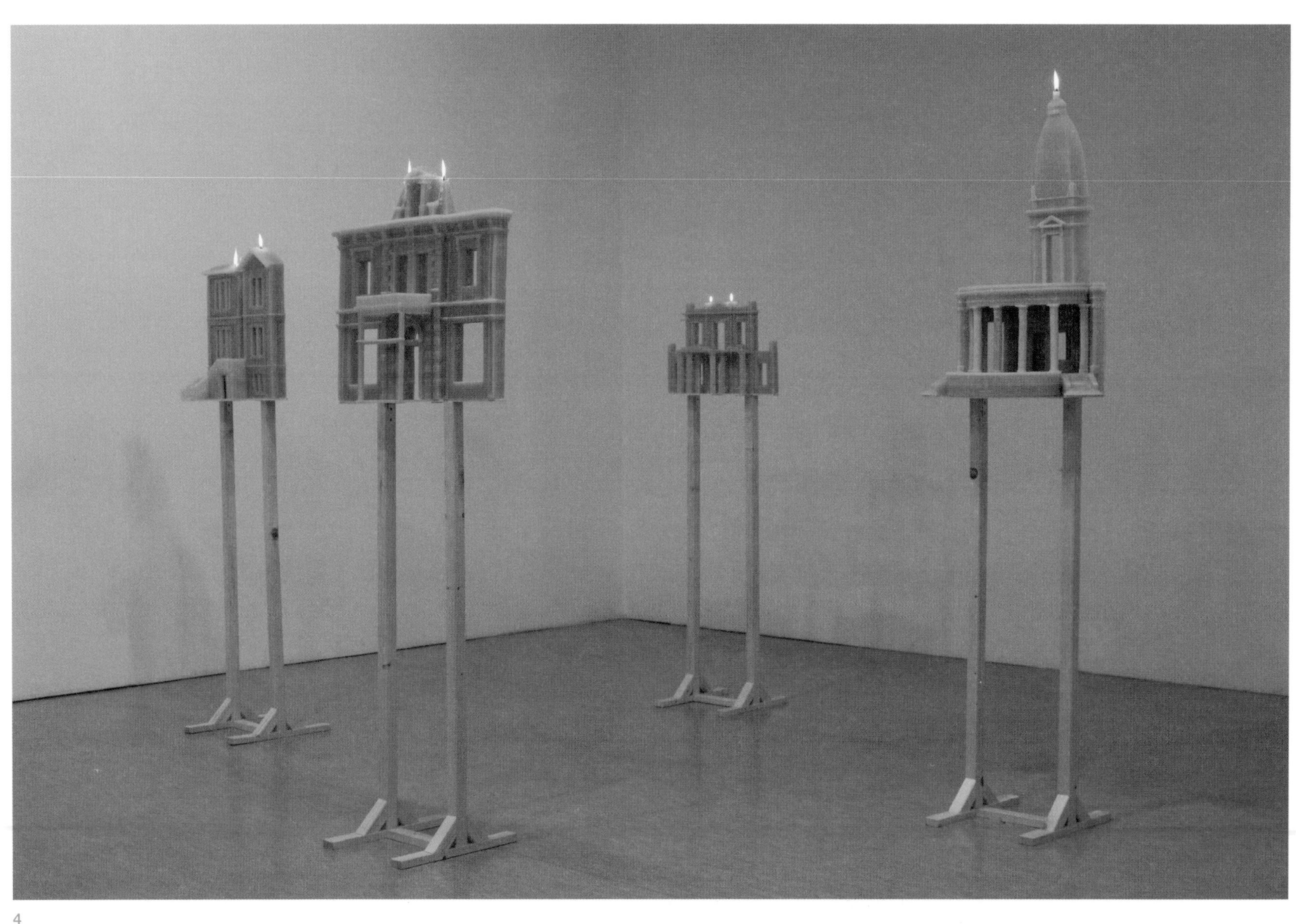

4

1. *Glove and permanent blue page test*, 2016
2. *Altitude*, 2016 (detail)

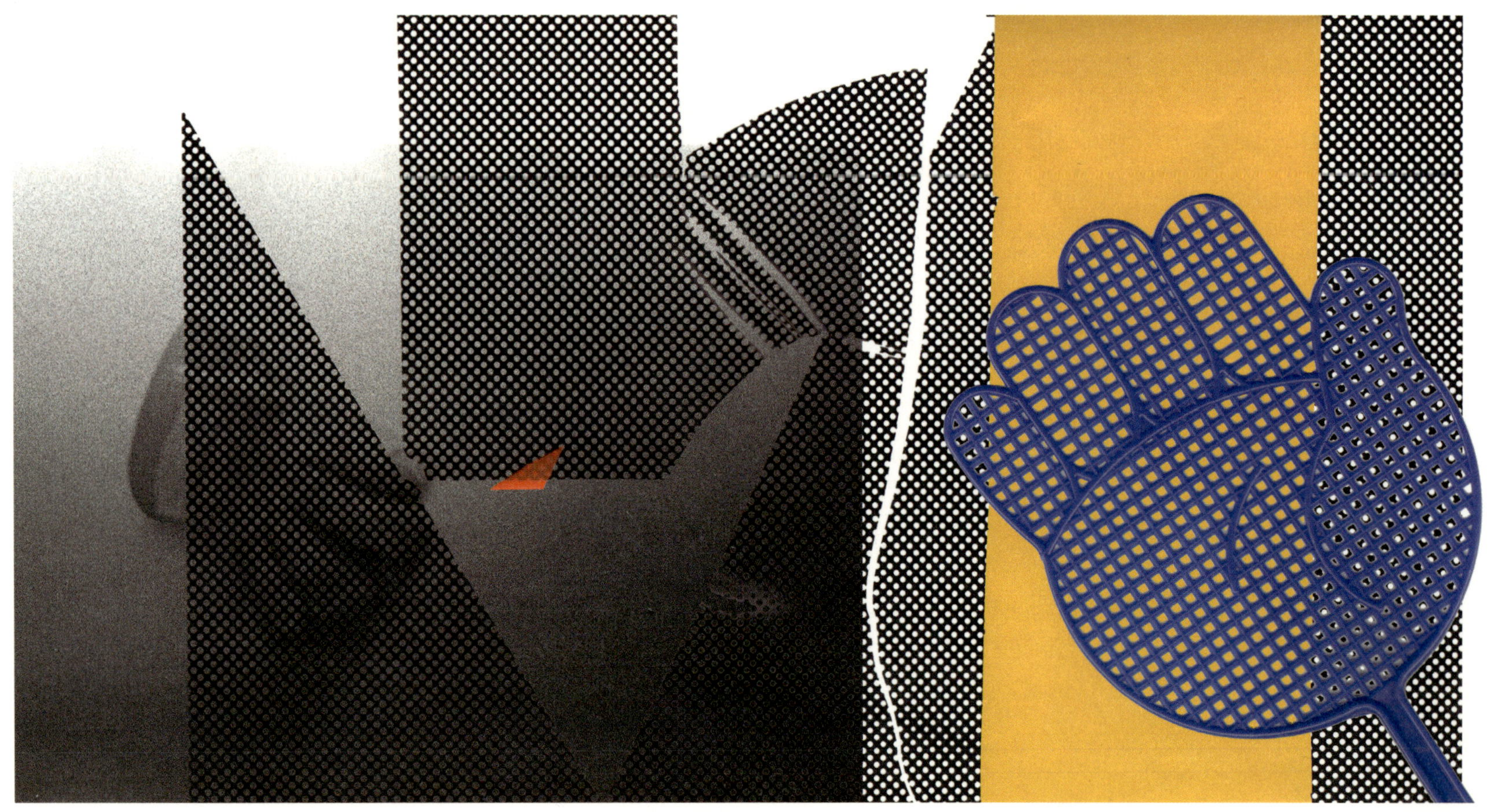

1

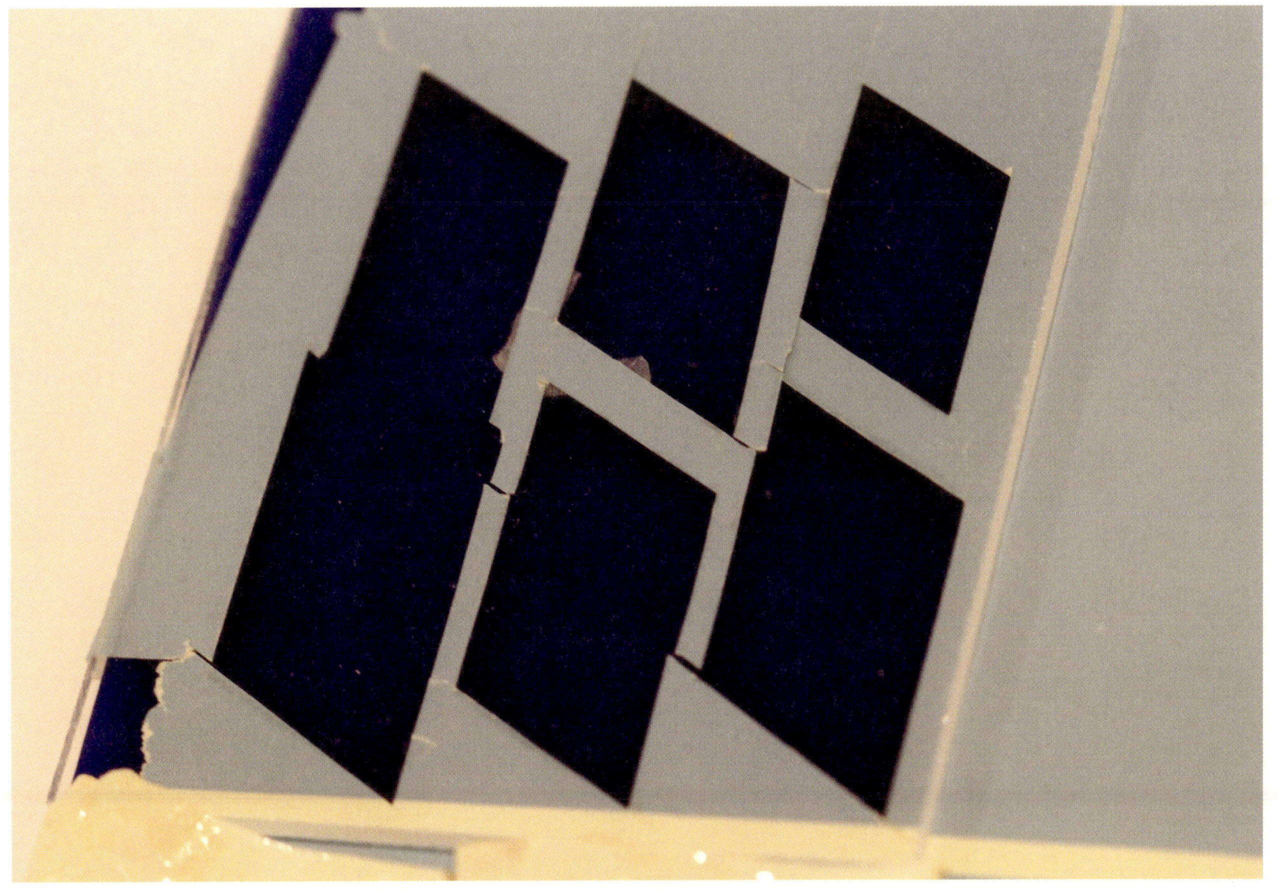

1. – 3. *Factitious Imprints*, 2016 (details)
Single-channel video, sound, and color, 9:30 min, and seven prints on polar fleece, Lycra sheen, suede, and voile fabric with scroll, dimensions variable

2. *Flagas Fragment*, 2015
Print on polyester, 300 x 100 cm

3. *Someday I Will Buy an Ikea Chair with Bitcoins*, 2015
Digital print on towel and HD video with color and sound, 3:35 min

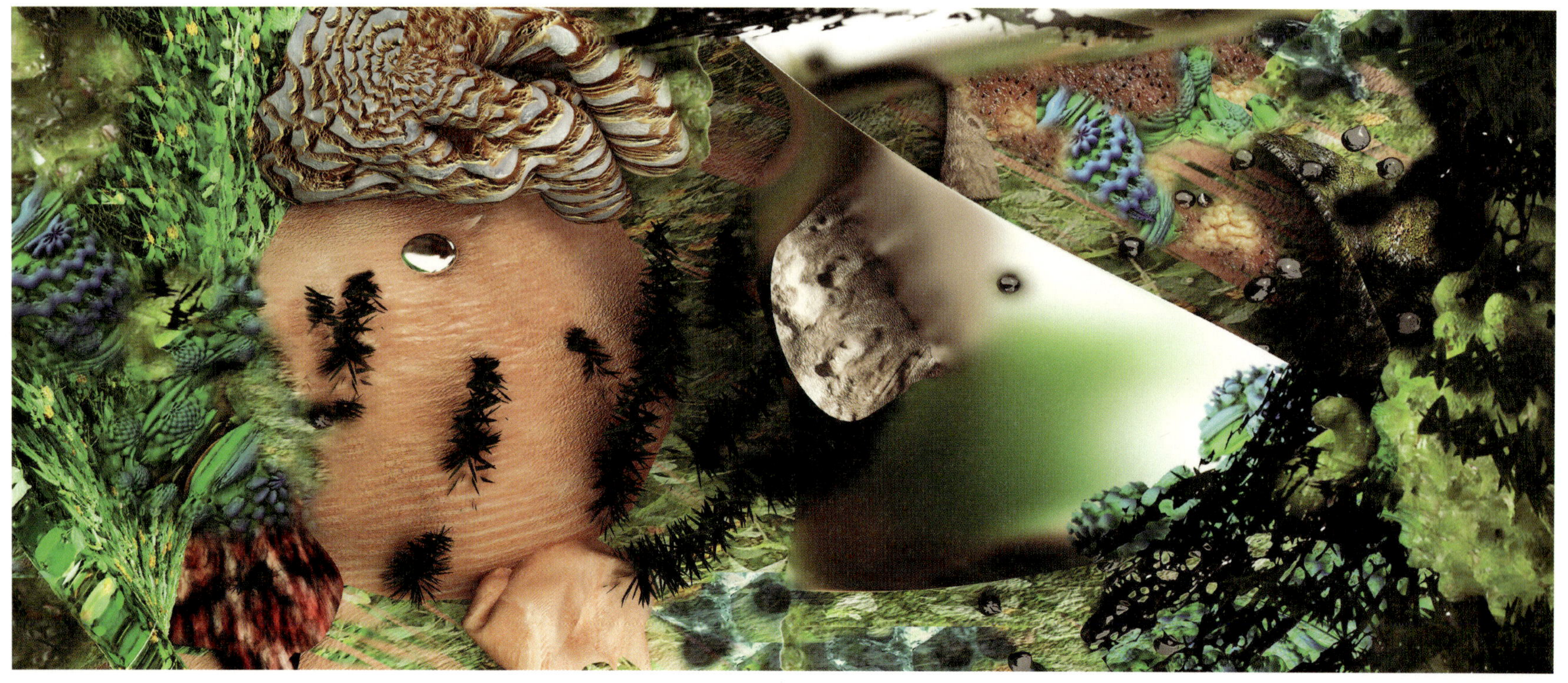

1

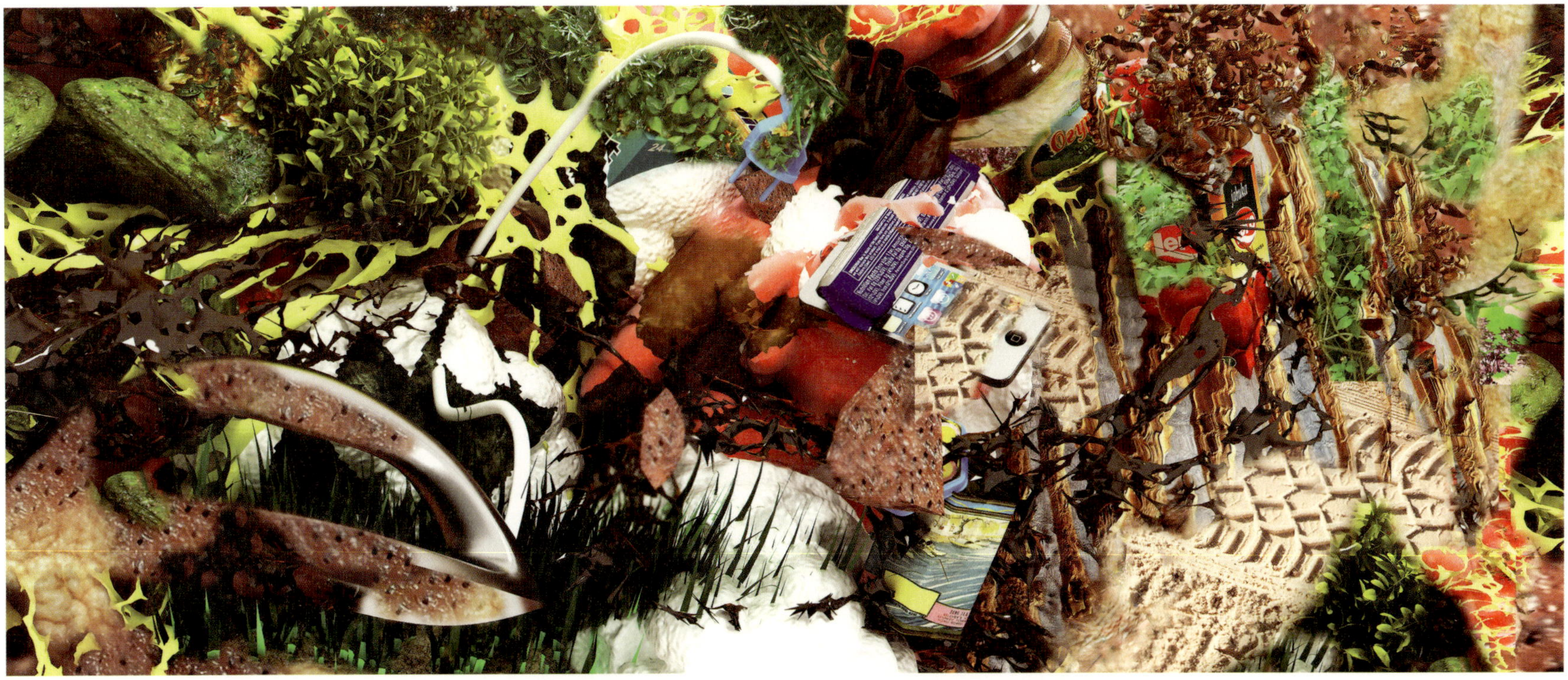

2

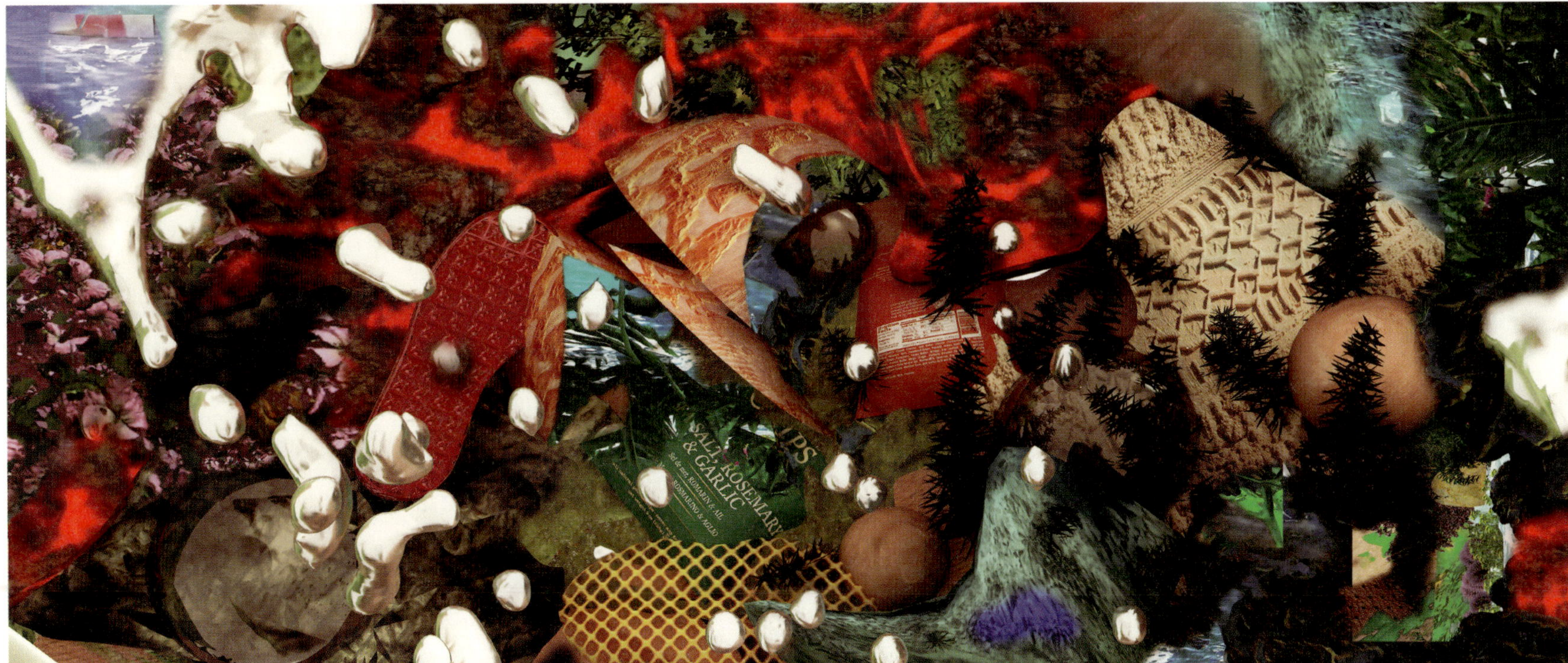

3

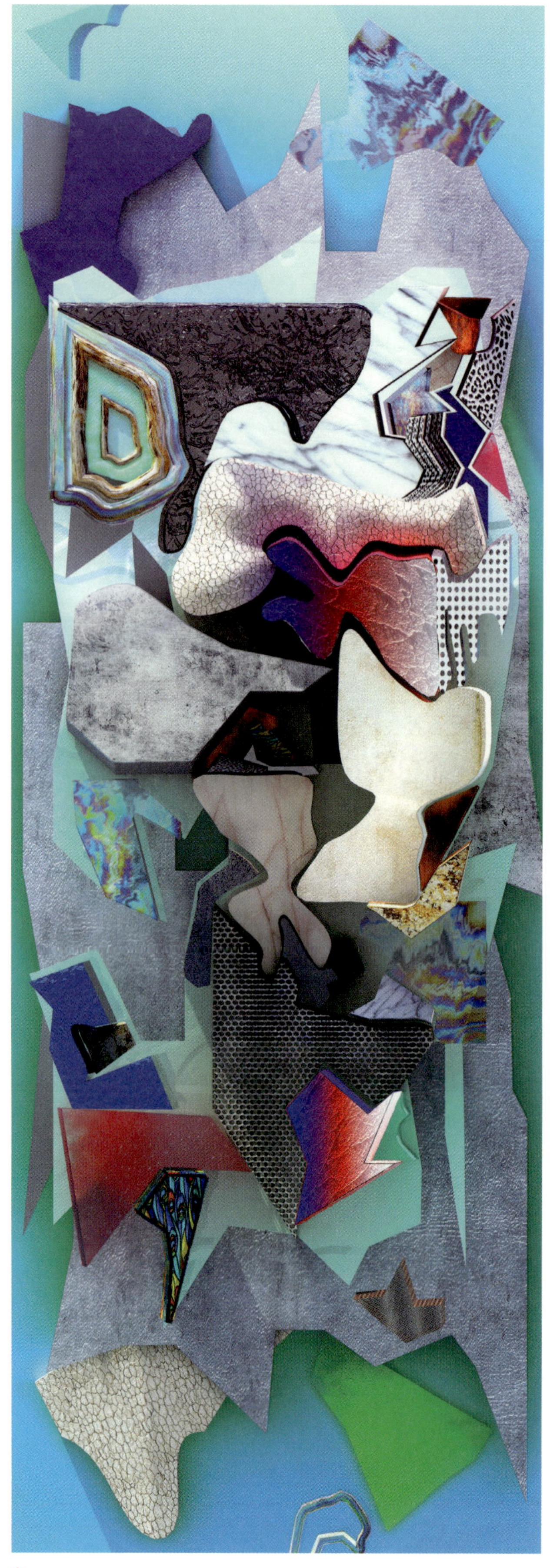

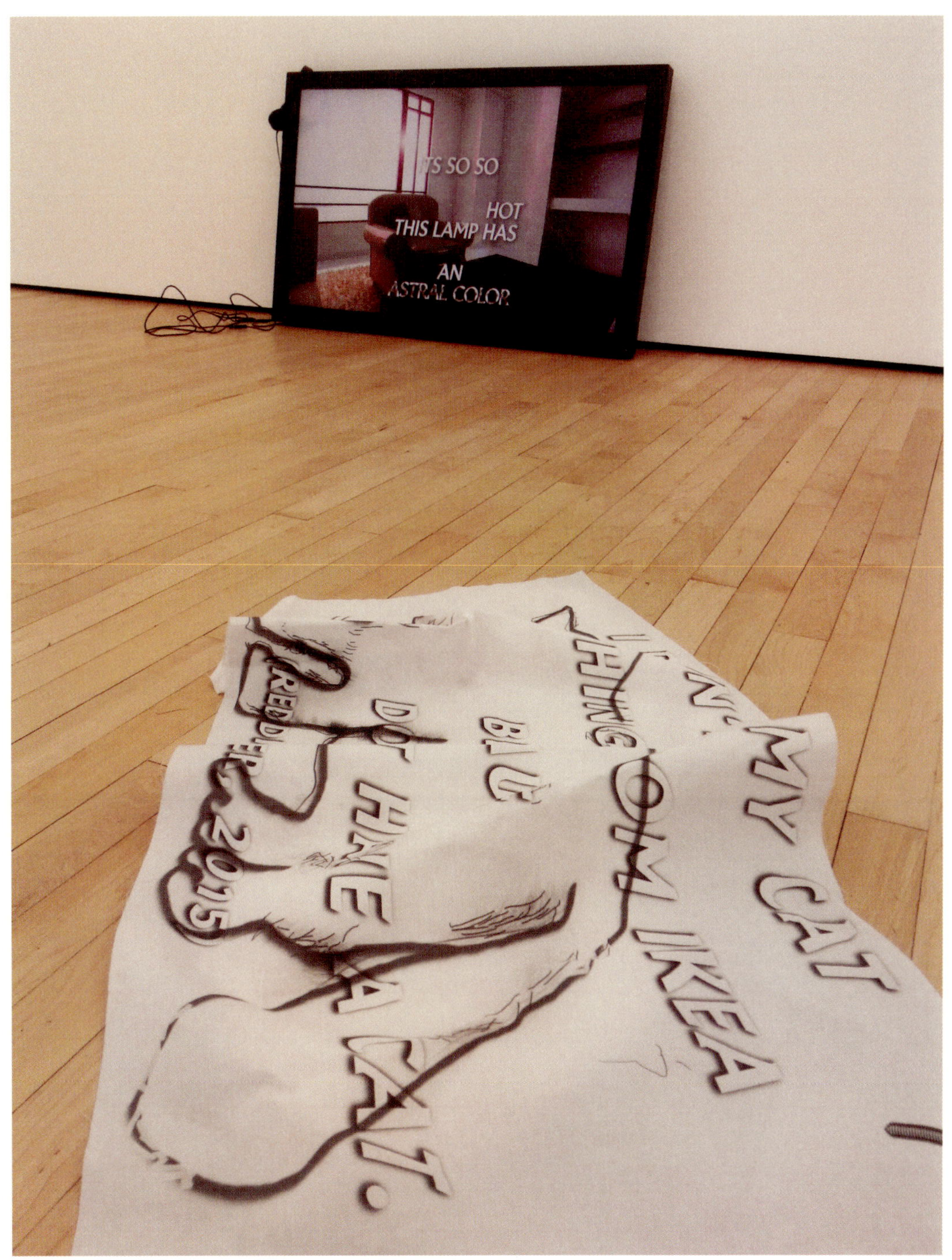
TS SO SO
HOT
THIS LAMP HAS
AN
ASTRAL COLOR.

1. *The Taste of a Cosmopolitan Shepherd with an Excellent Long Term Memory,* 2014
Semi-fired ceramic beads and metal, 200 x 120 cm

2. *Front Line Accomplice,* 2014
Carved wooden chair with wool fabric, dimensions variable

3. – 4. Exhibition view: Zoë Paul, "A Goat Named Hermés," NAM Project, Milan, Italy, 2014

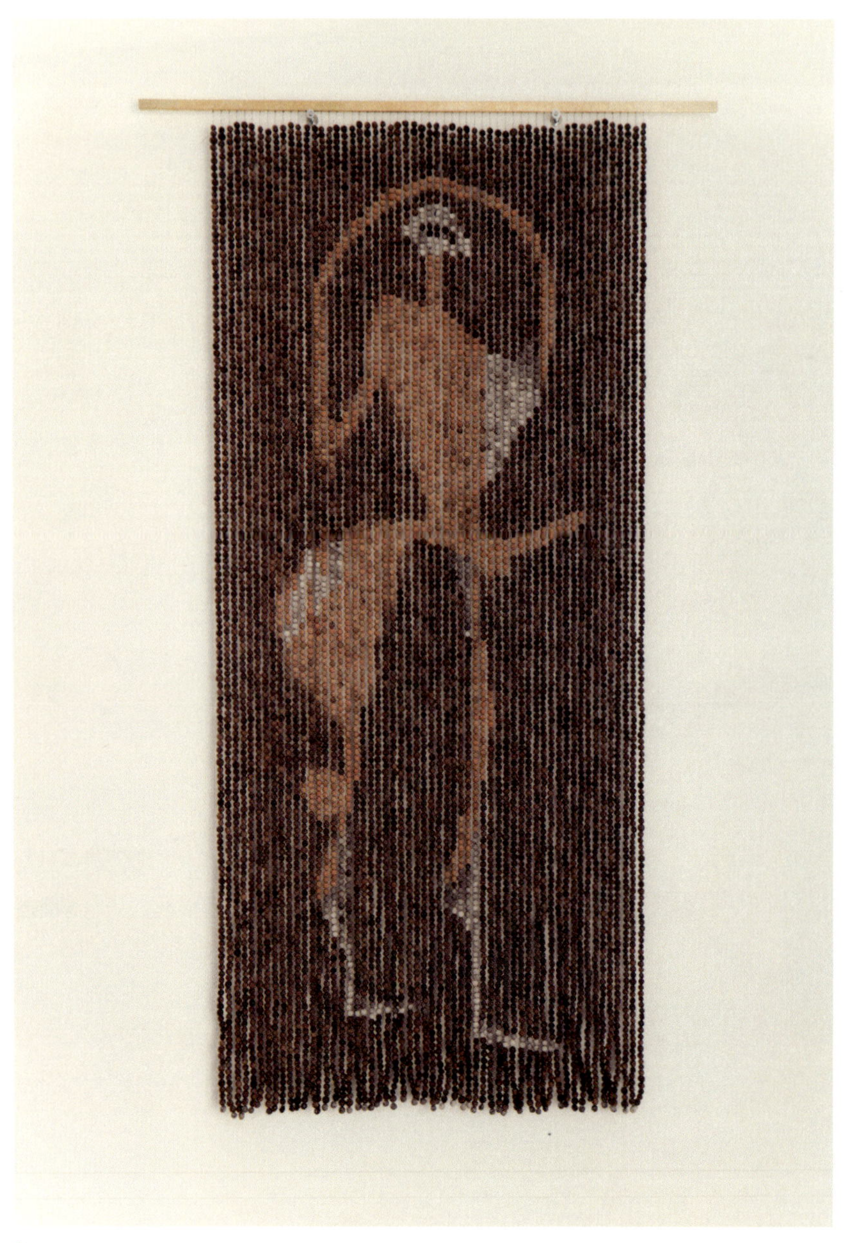

1

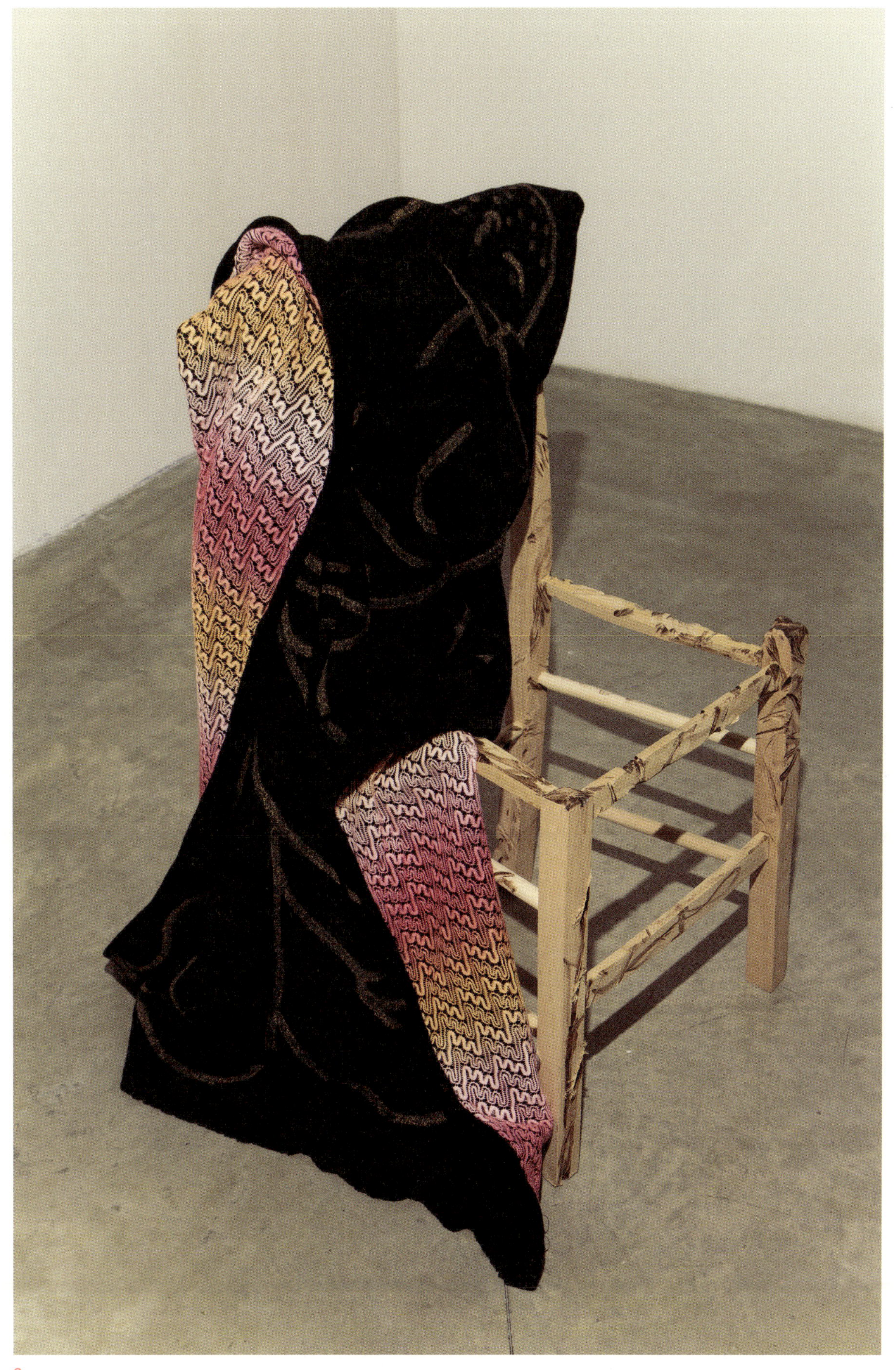

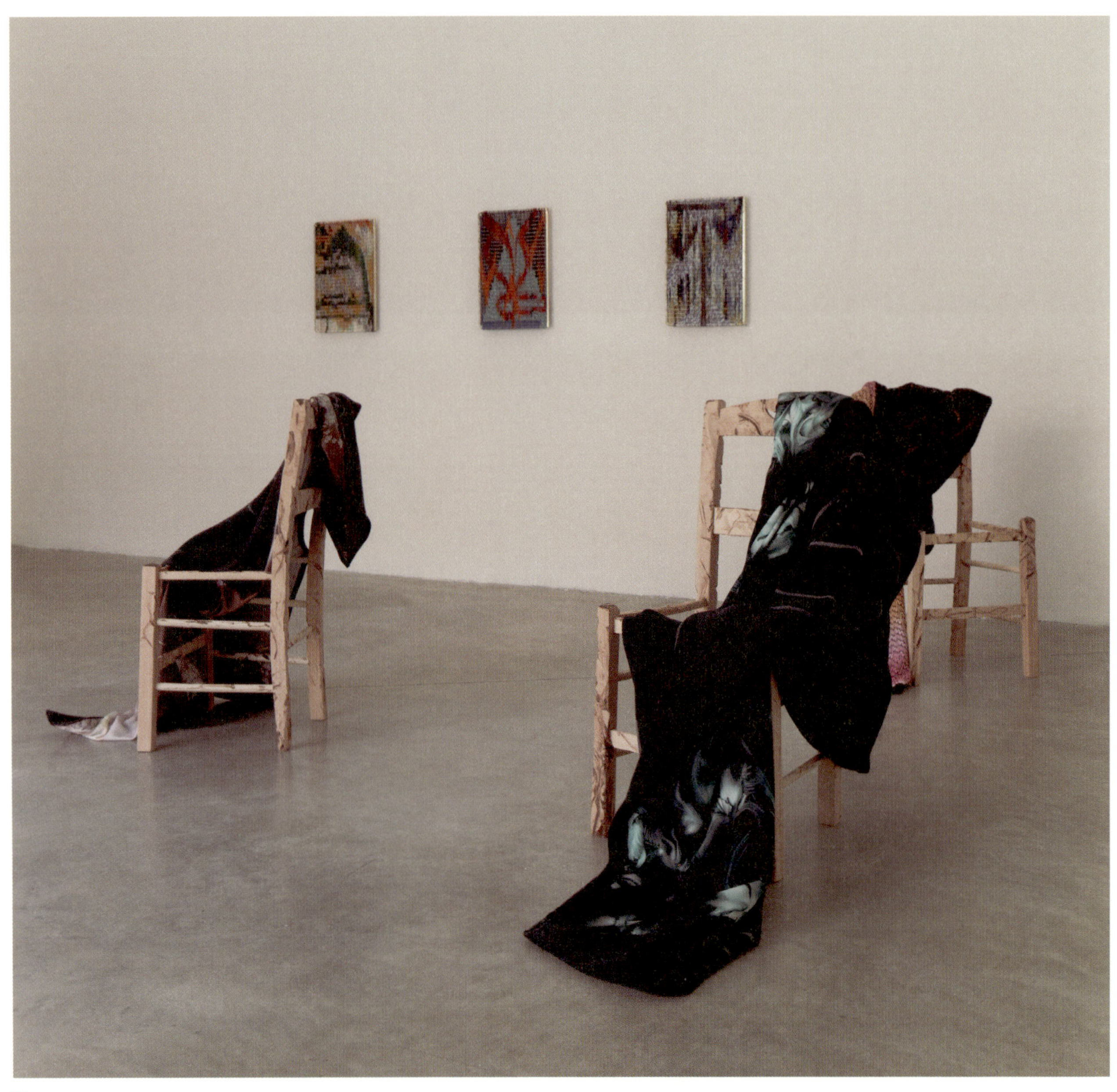

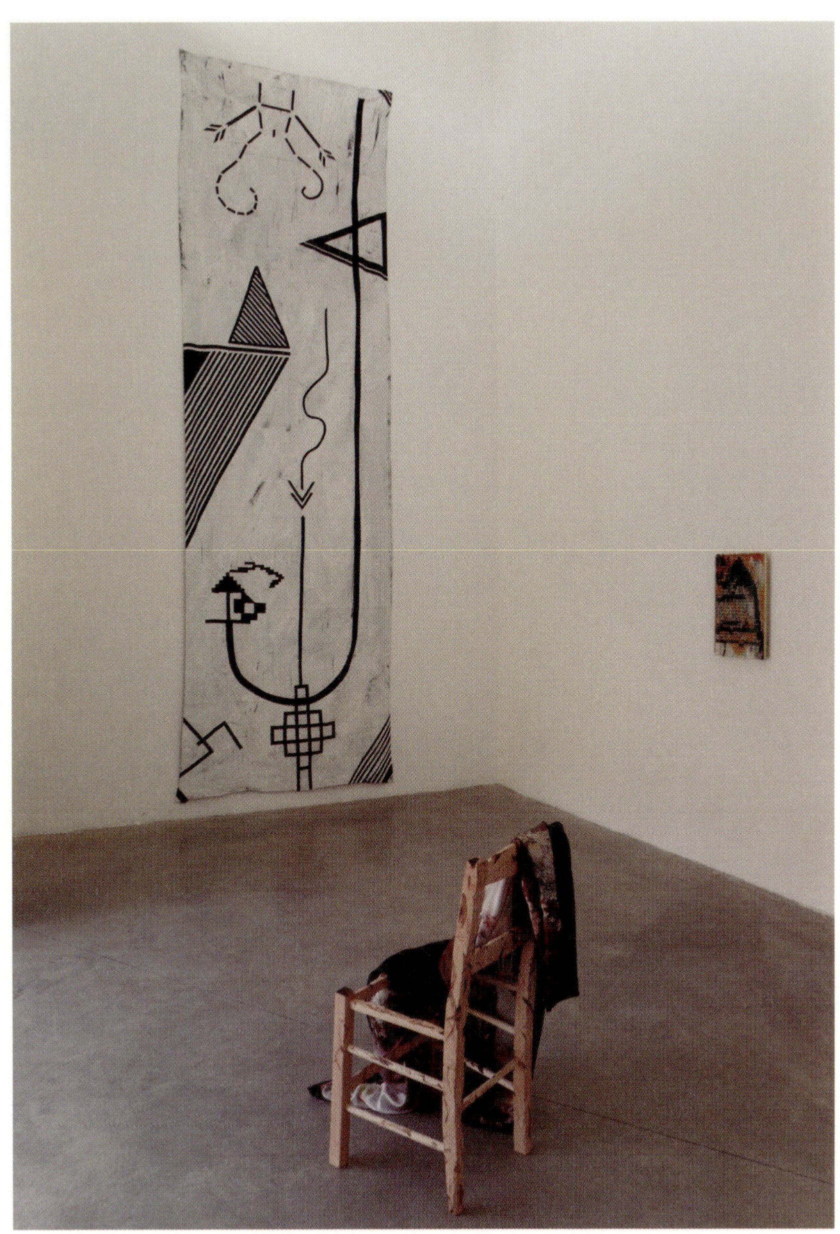

4

1. *Processing Love*, 2015
Sumi ink, acrylic, and gouache on cotton, 150 x 100 cm

2. *How To Eat Things That Don't Exist*, 2016
Sumi ink and gouache on cotton, 75.5 x 72 cm

3. *Fingers Follow*, 2016
Sumi ink and acrylic on cotton, 150 x 100 cm

4. *Monoliths*, 2015
Acrylic, pastel, and ink on cotton, 150 x 100 cm

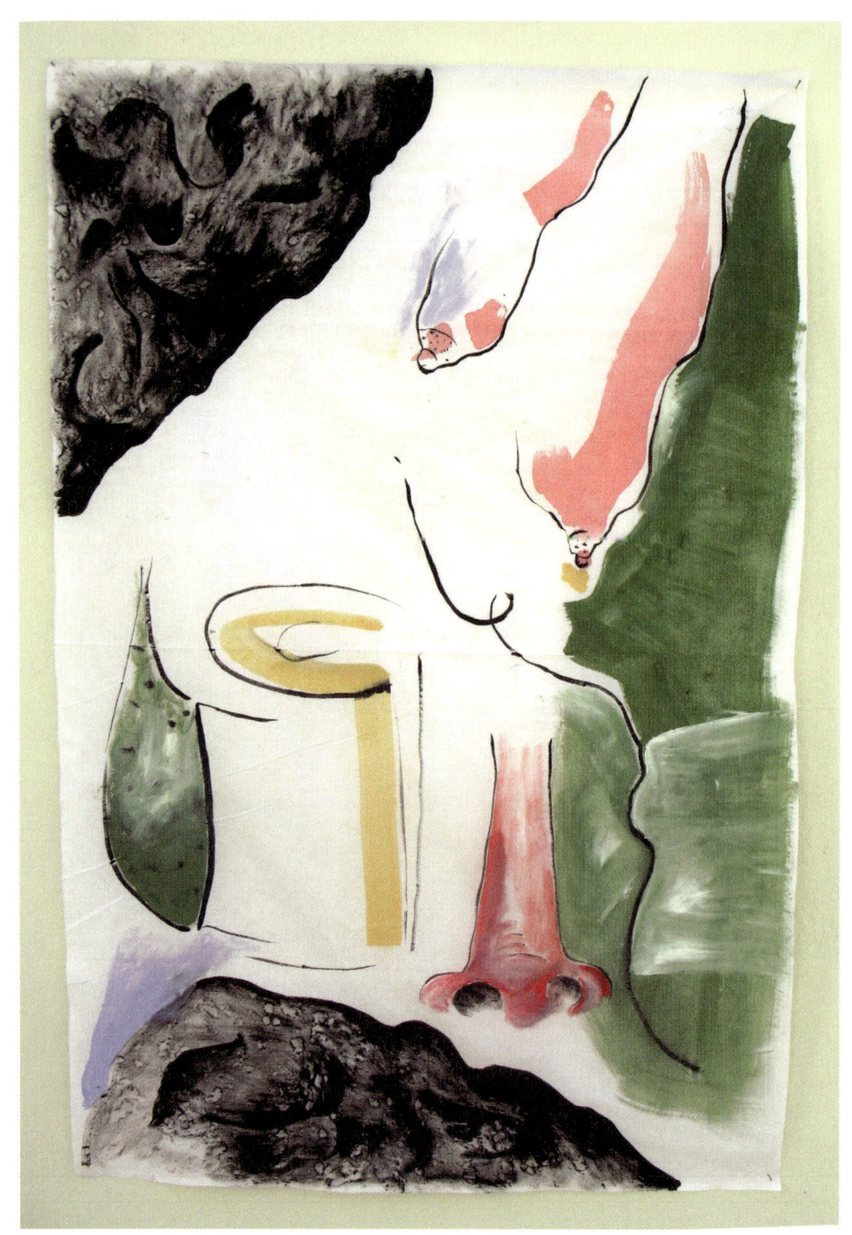

1

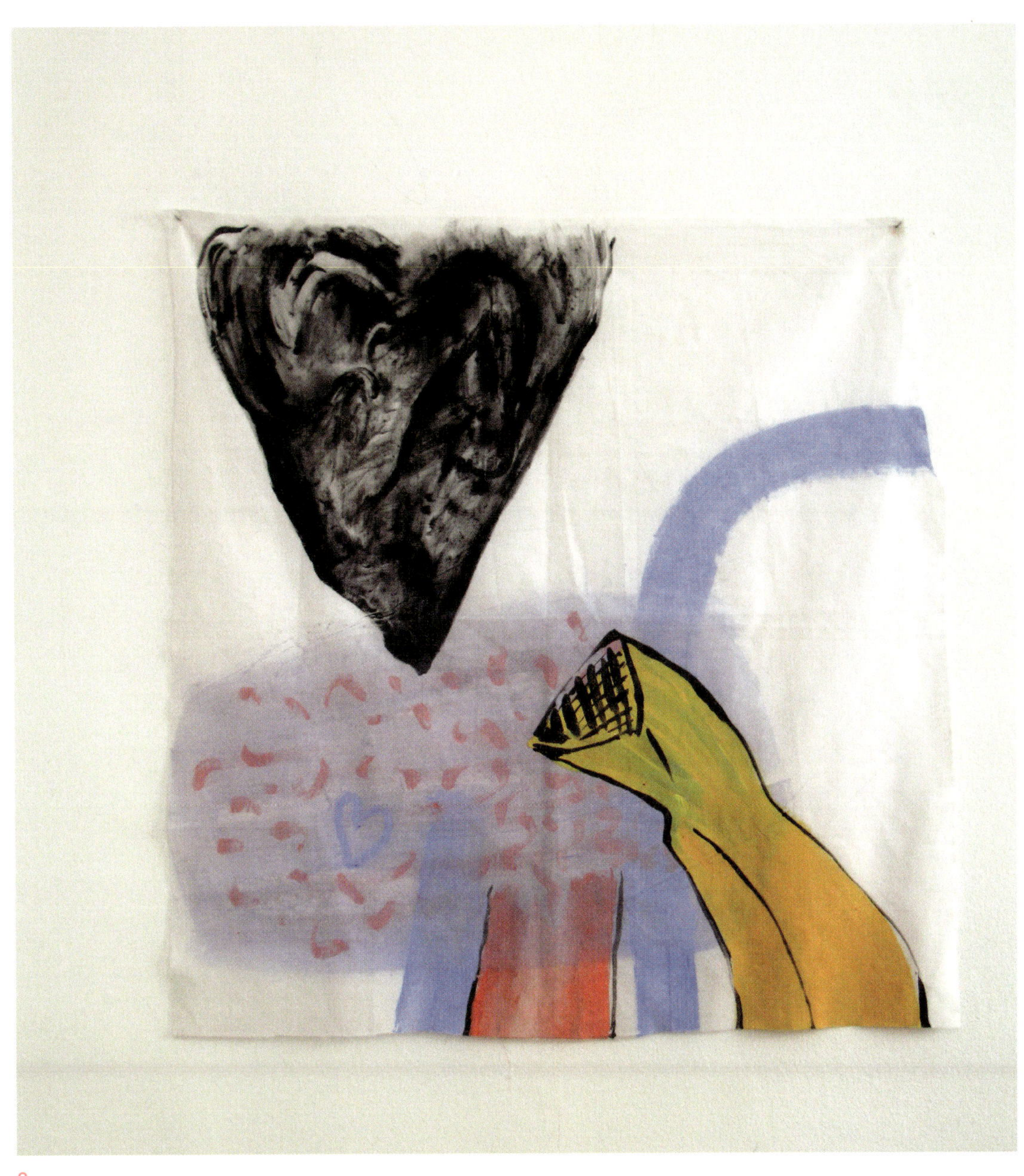

2

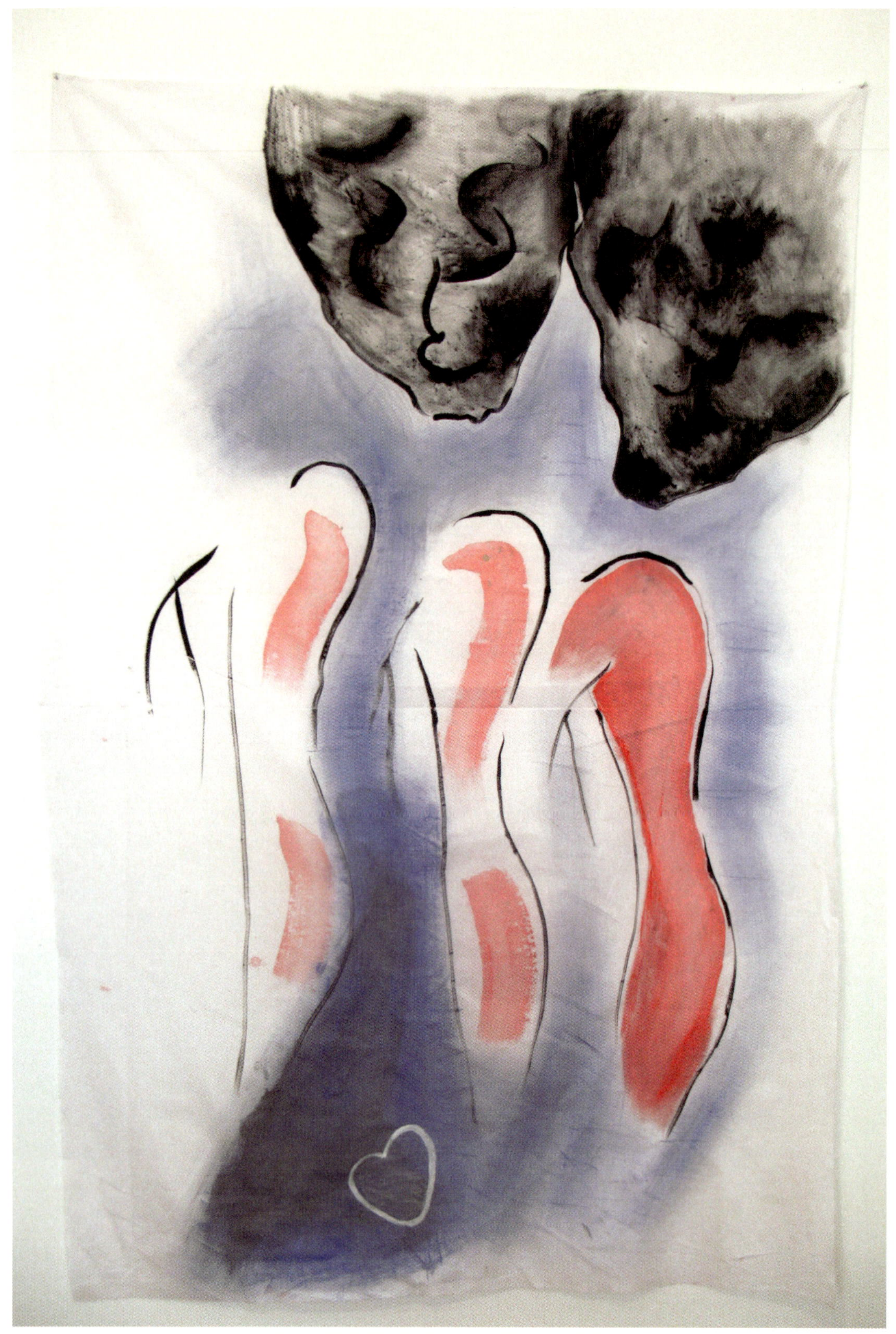

3

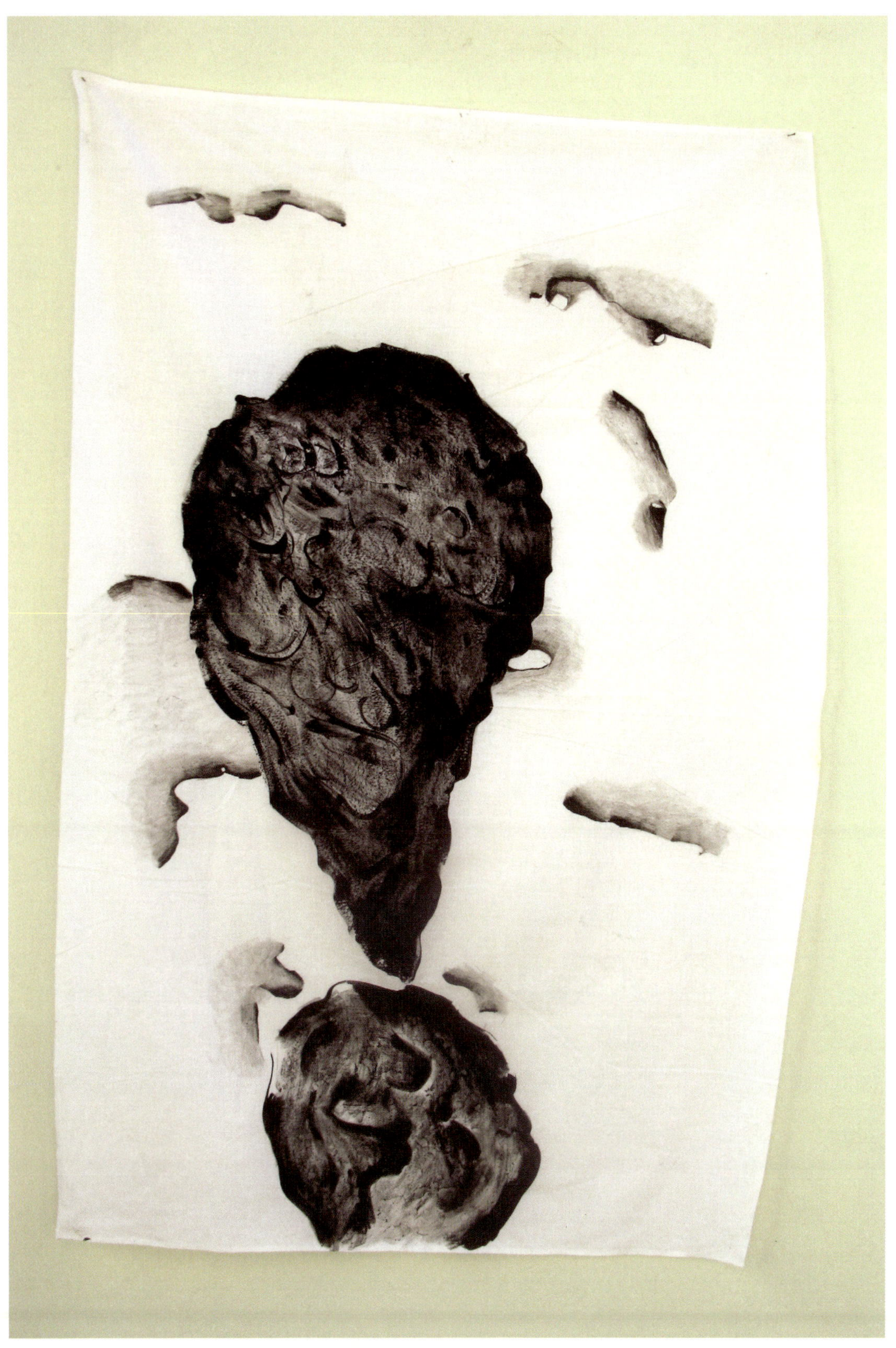

4

1. *Untitled (Simulacra #6)*, 2012
Eighteen graphite on paper drawings, 40 x 30 cm each

2. *Viniani, 10 April 1944 (ver. 1–3)*, 2013
Digital print, charcoal, and graphite on fine art paper, 37.5 x 85 cm

3. *Adamantios Korais from the series Ubi nunc*, 2013–14
Pencil on paper, 4 x 3 cm

4. *A Photograph of a White Paper and an Unprinted White Paper*, 2012
Inkjet print and inkjet photographic paper mounted on aluminum, 55.5 x 80 cm each

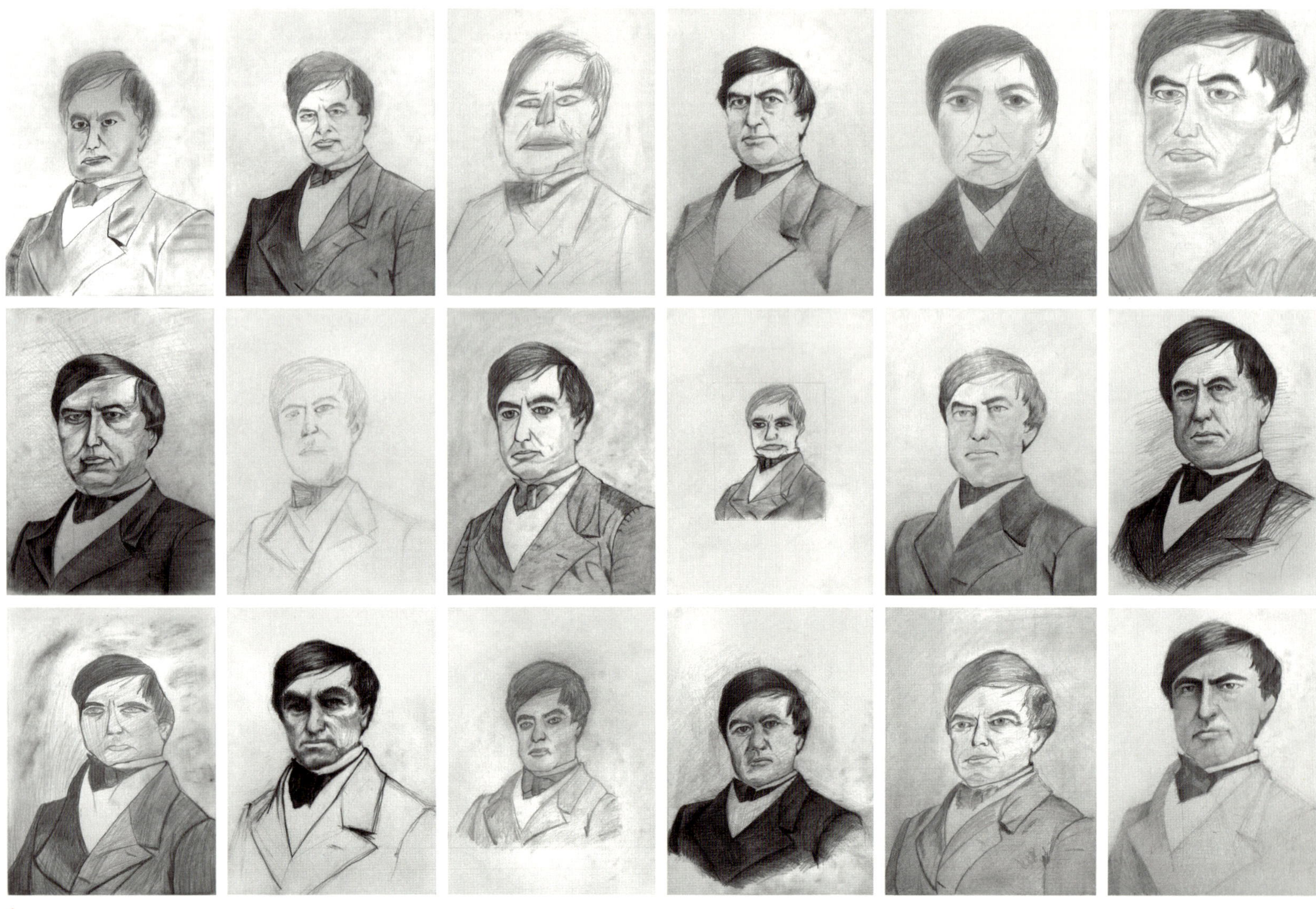

1

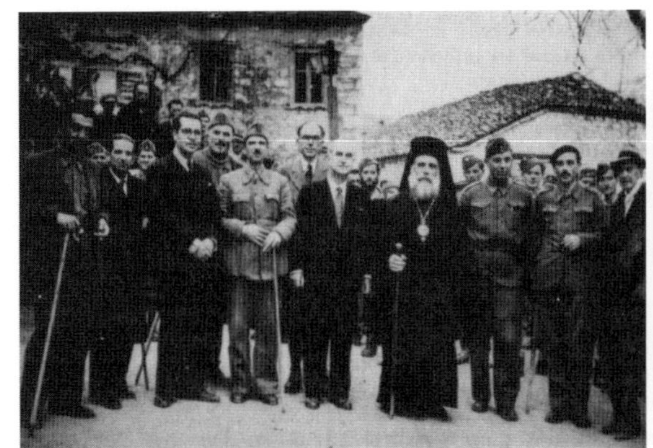
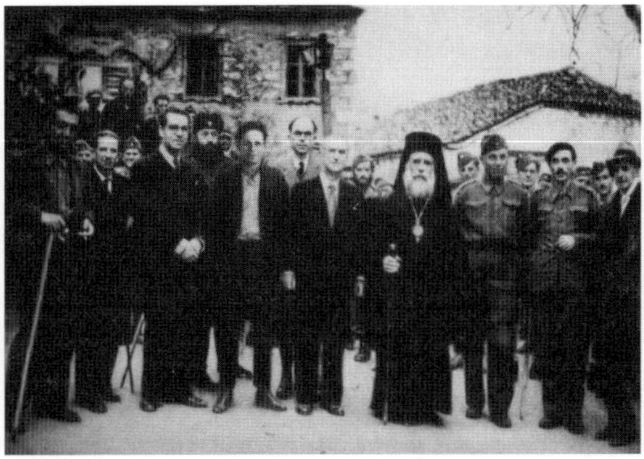
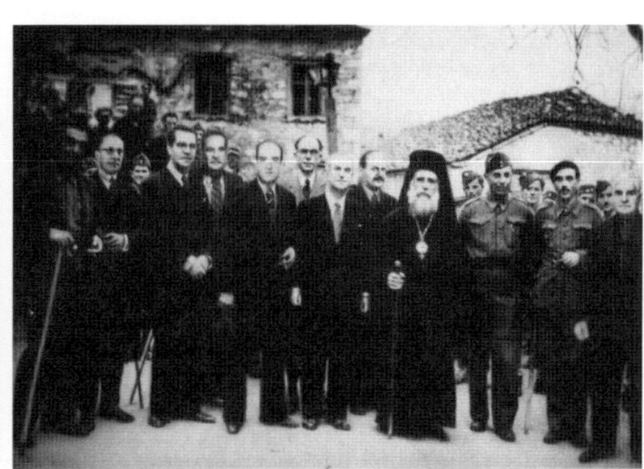

2

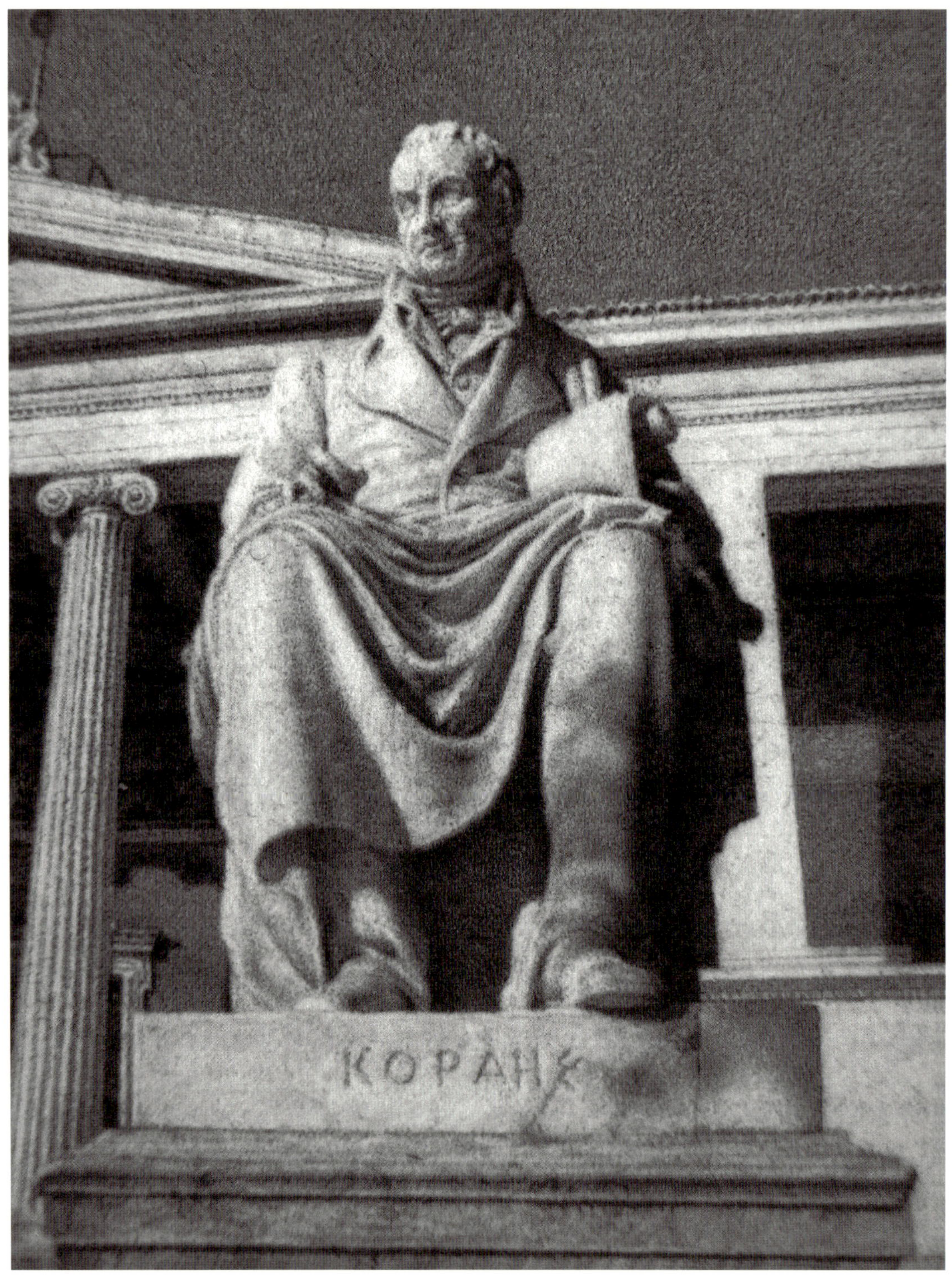

3

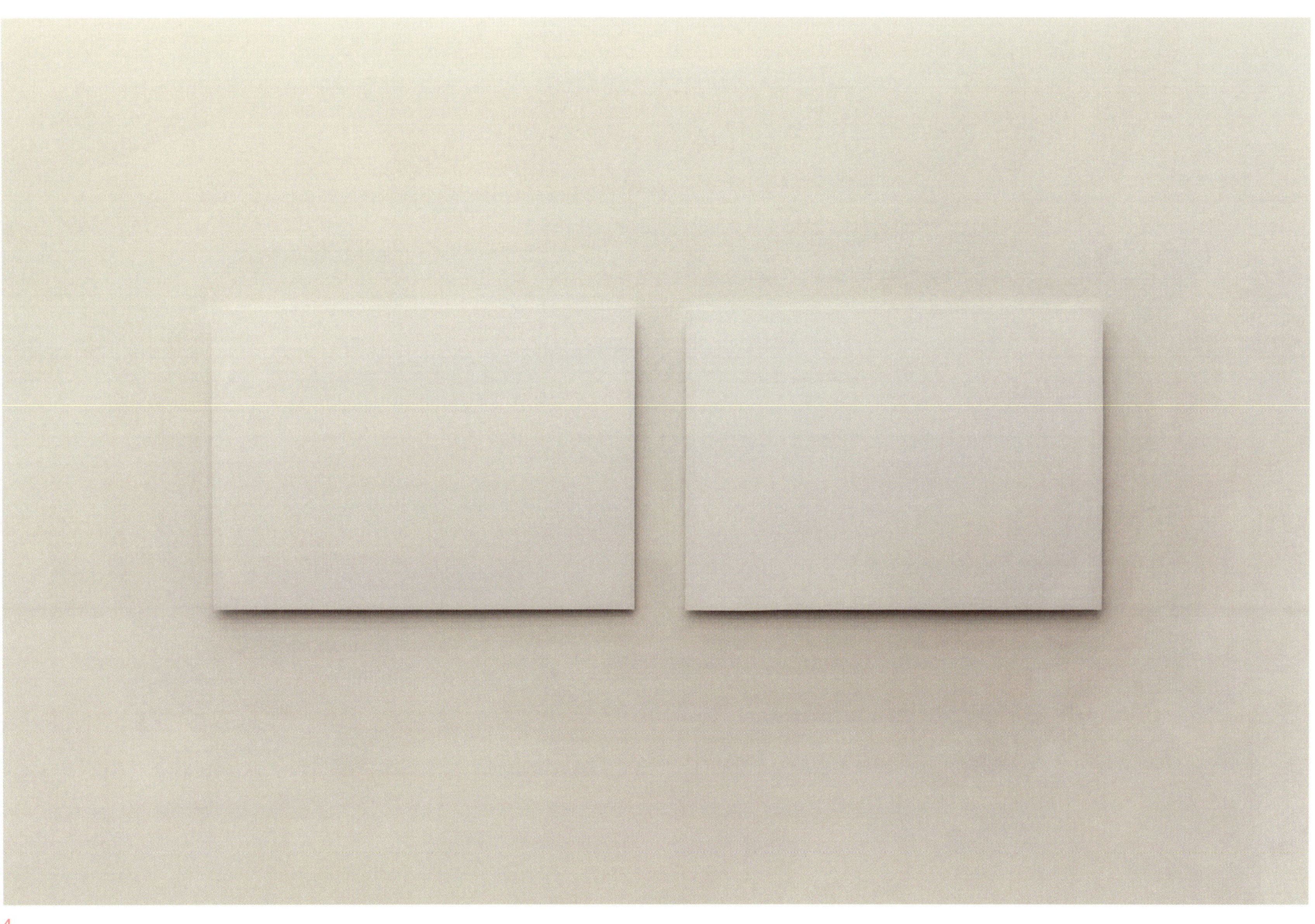

4

1. – 2. *The Gravestone Doji*, 2015 (stills)
Video triptych and webpage, dimensions variable

3. – 4. *Bones_ΔΔΔY*, 2015
Asphalt, jesmonite, steel frames, LED strip sculptures, and HD video triptych, dimensions variable

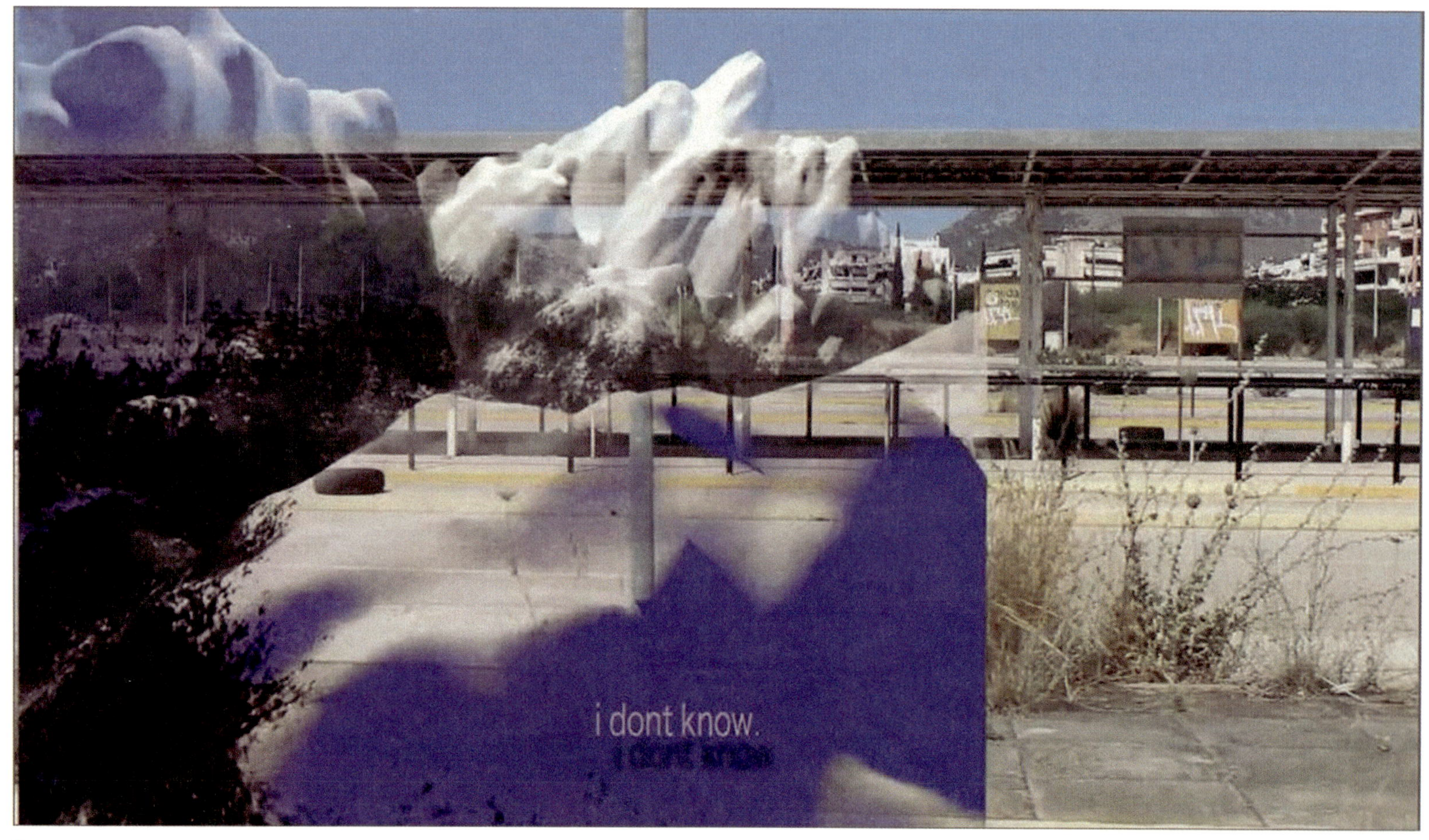

1

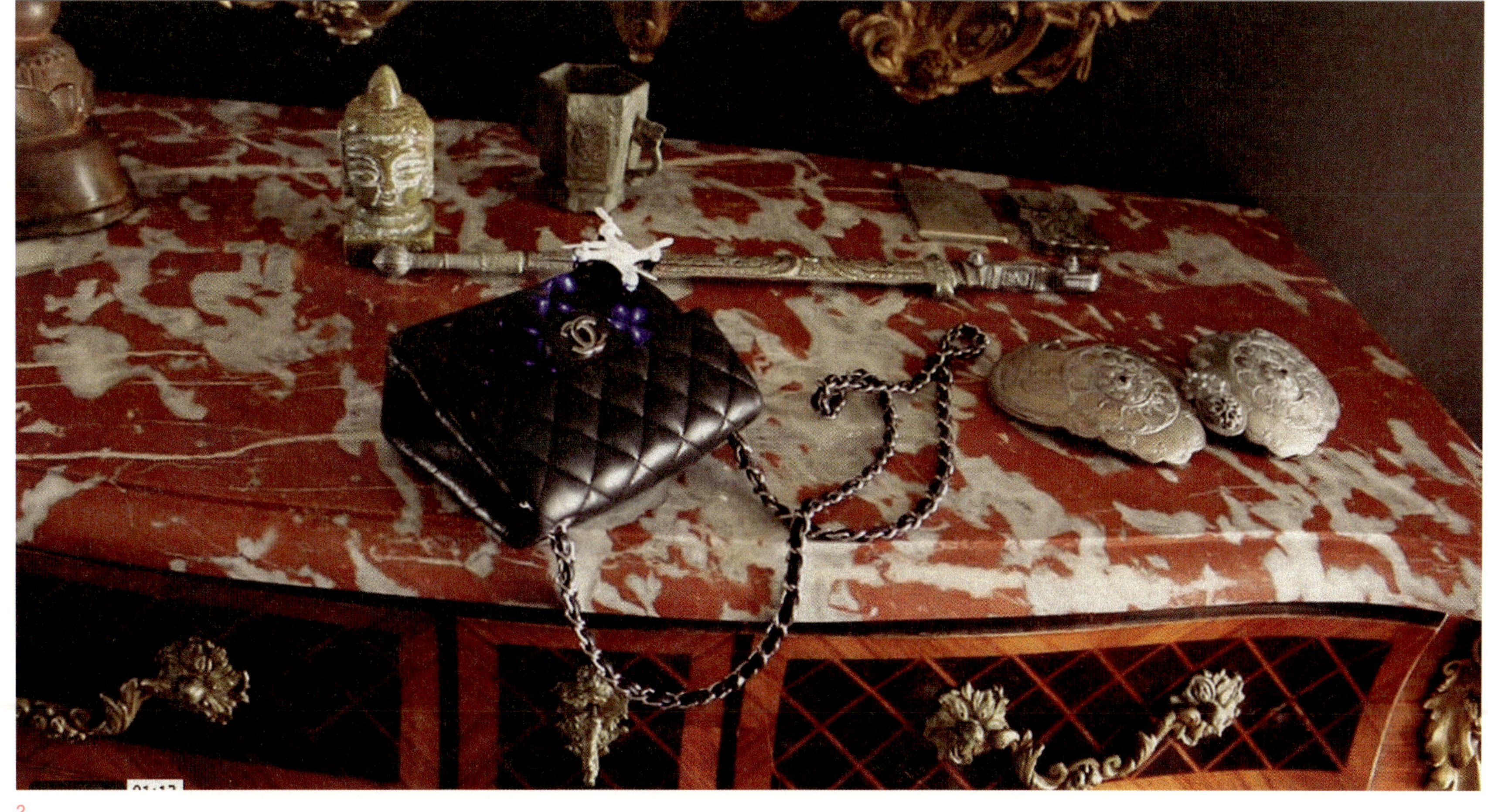

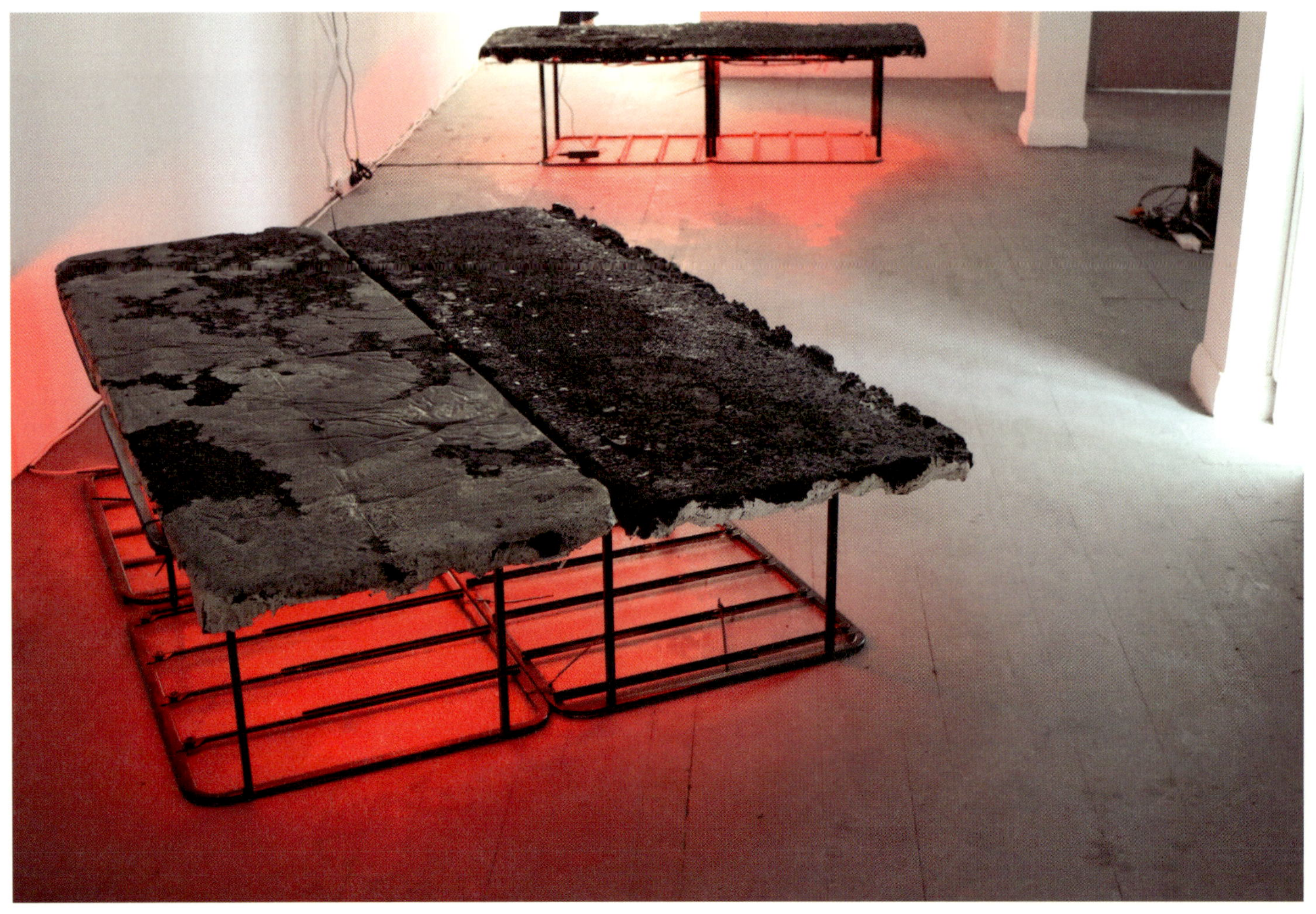

3

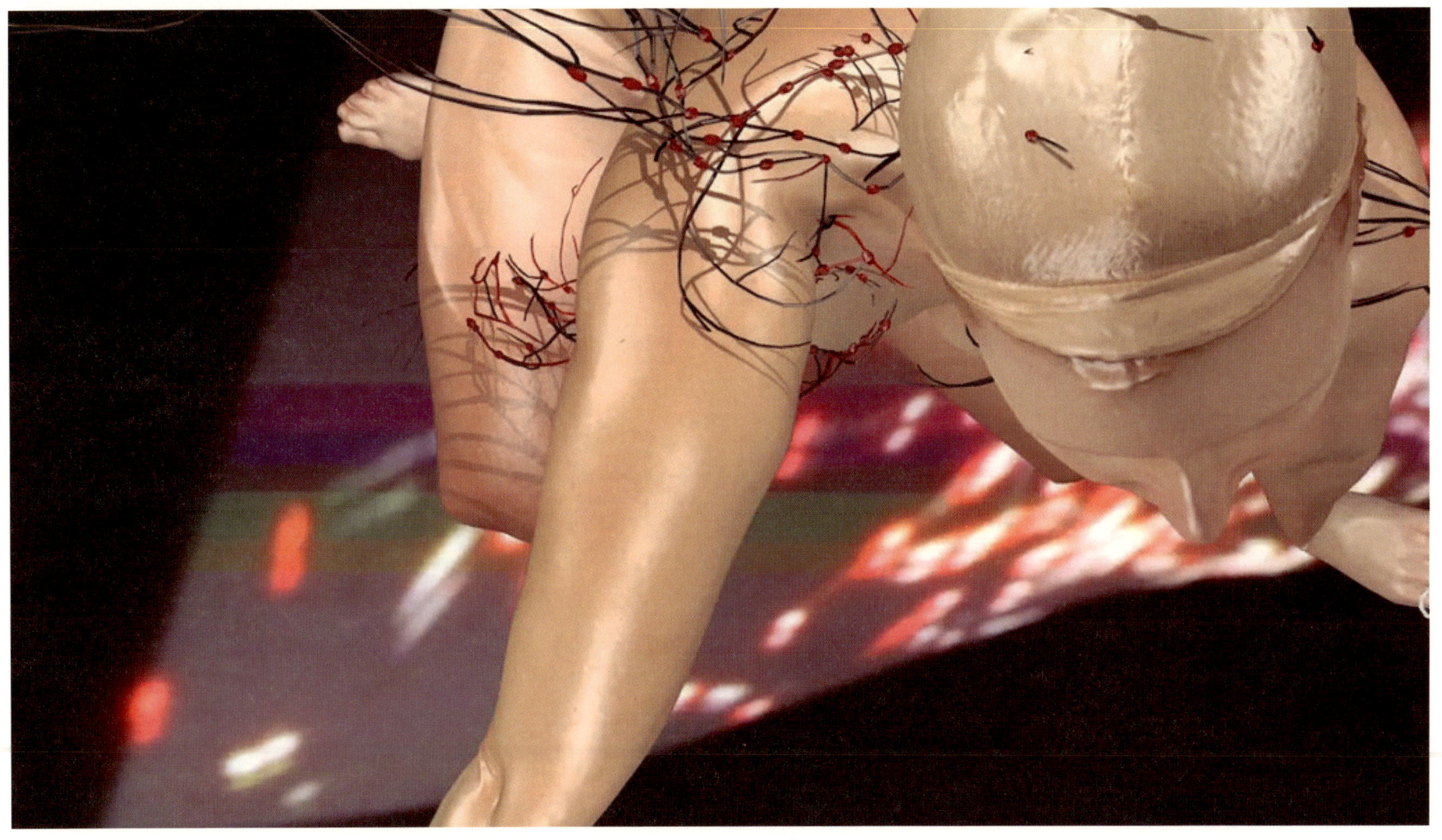

1. *Aquaggaswack*, 2015
Steel, camping lanterns, and twine, 220 x 210 x 45 cm

2. *33,478*, 2014
Book spines, wood and marble offcuts, and plexiglas, 85 x 530 x 70 cm

3. *It Is Everything White*, 2014
Book spines, wood and marble offcuts, plexiglas, white clay, industrial shelves, found images, tape, and correction fluid, dimensions variable

4. *AEK, CULTURA, SEPULTURA (Hagia Sophia)*, 2015
Plastic, archival material, tape, clay, and plastic, 100 x 70 x 21 cm

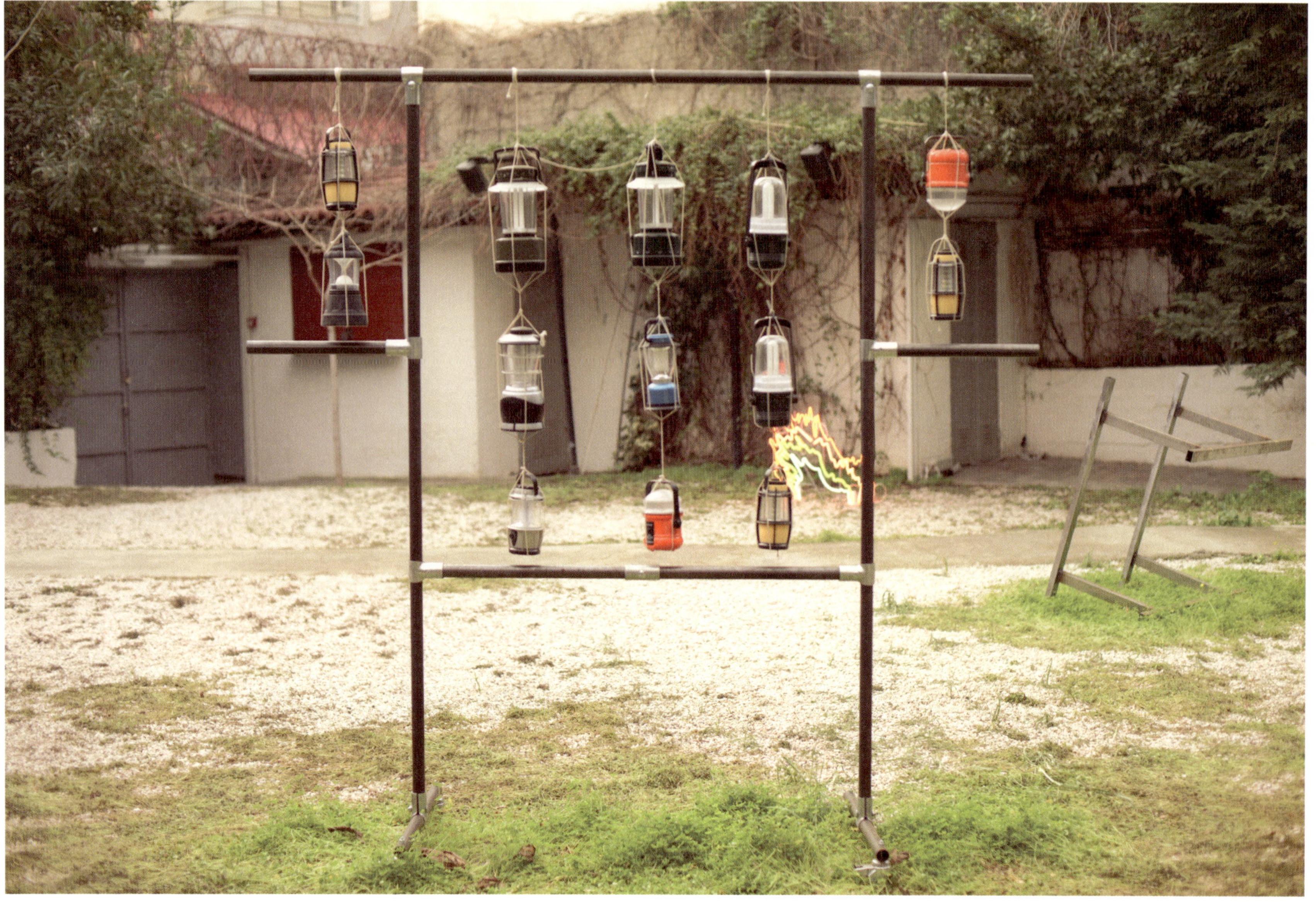

1

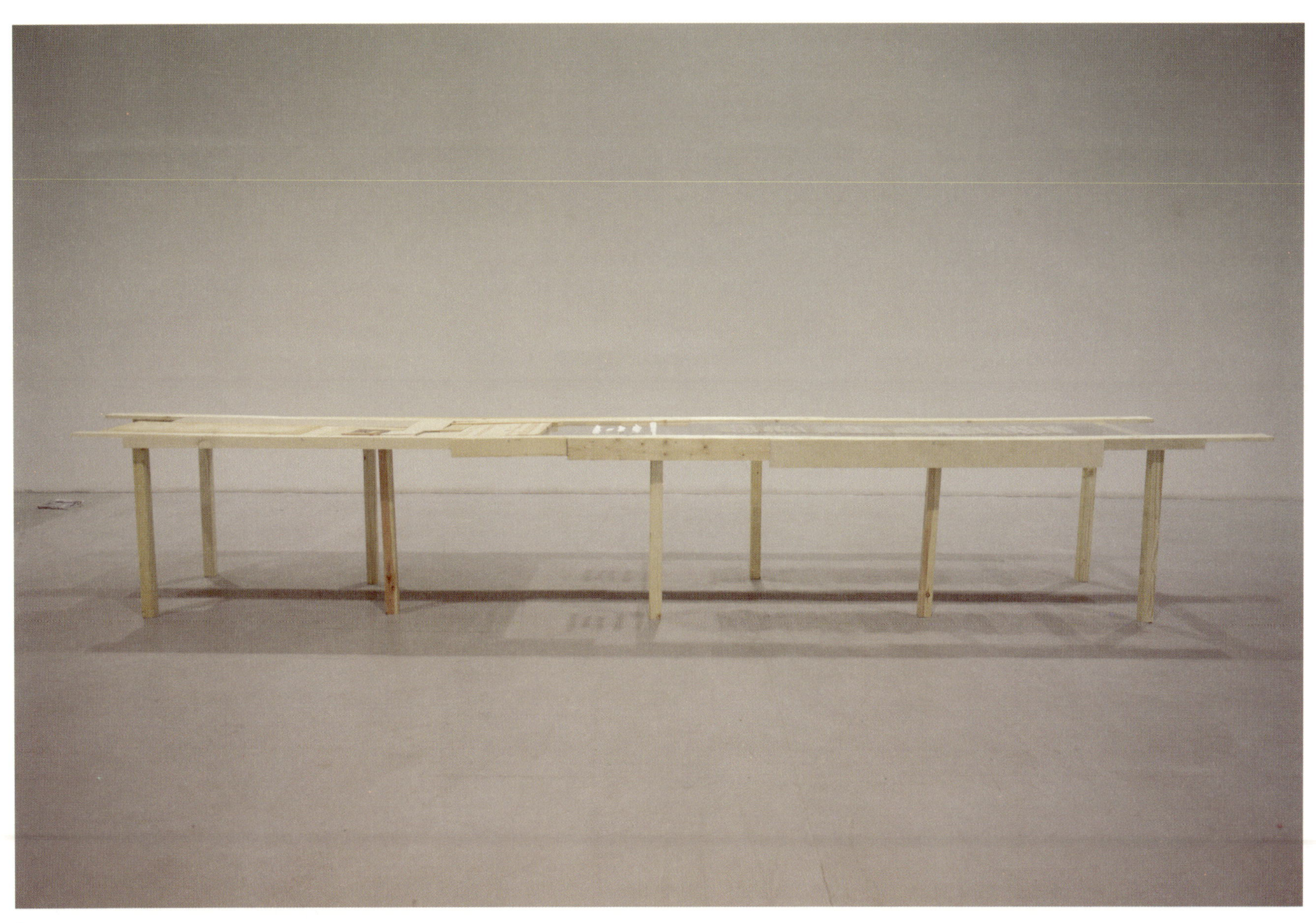

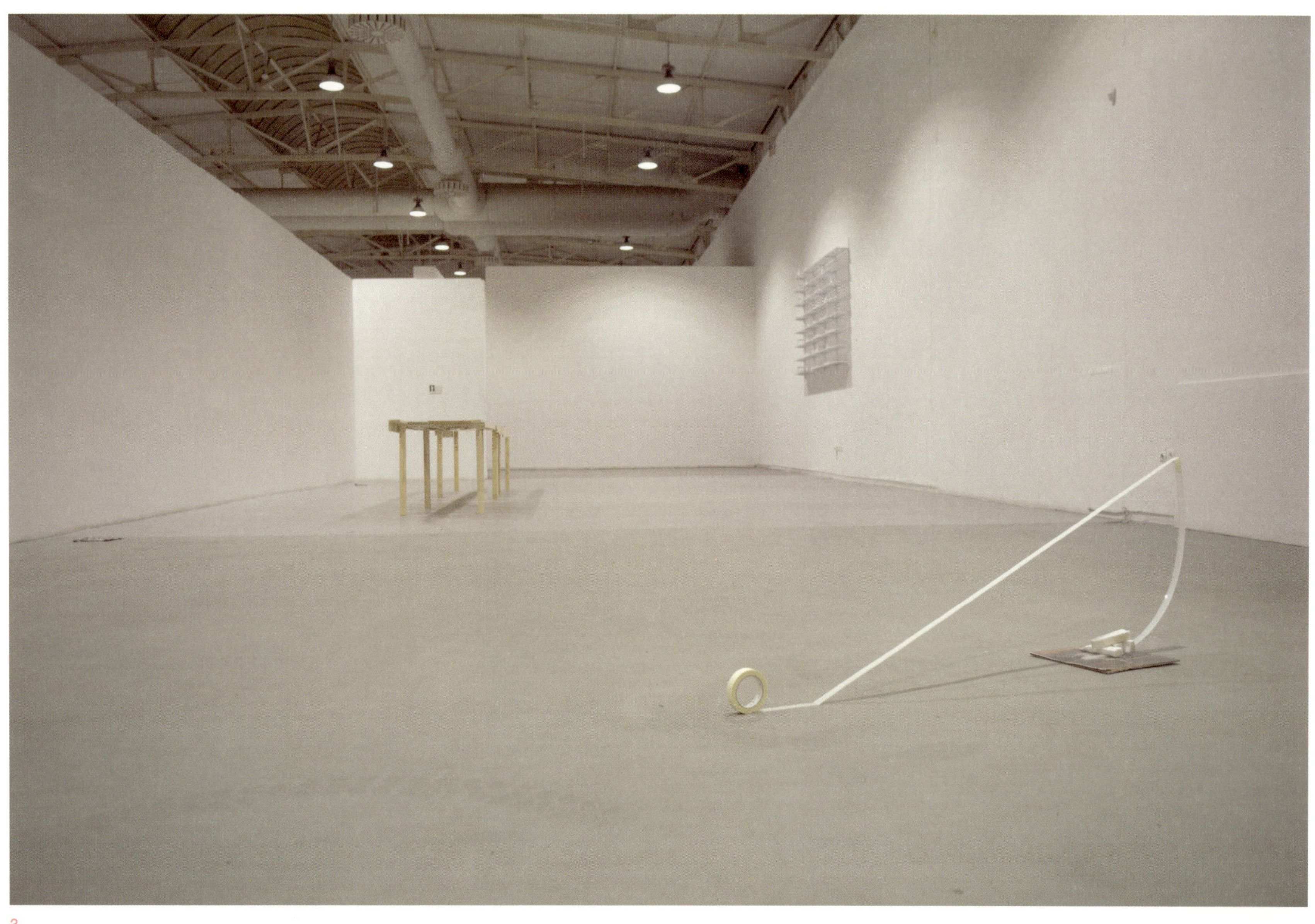

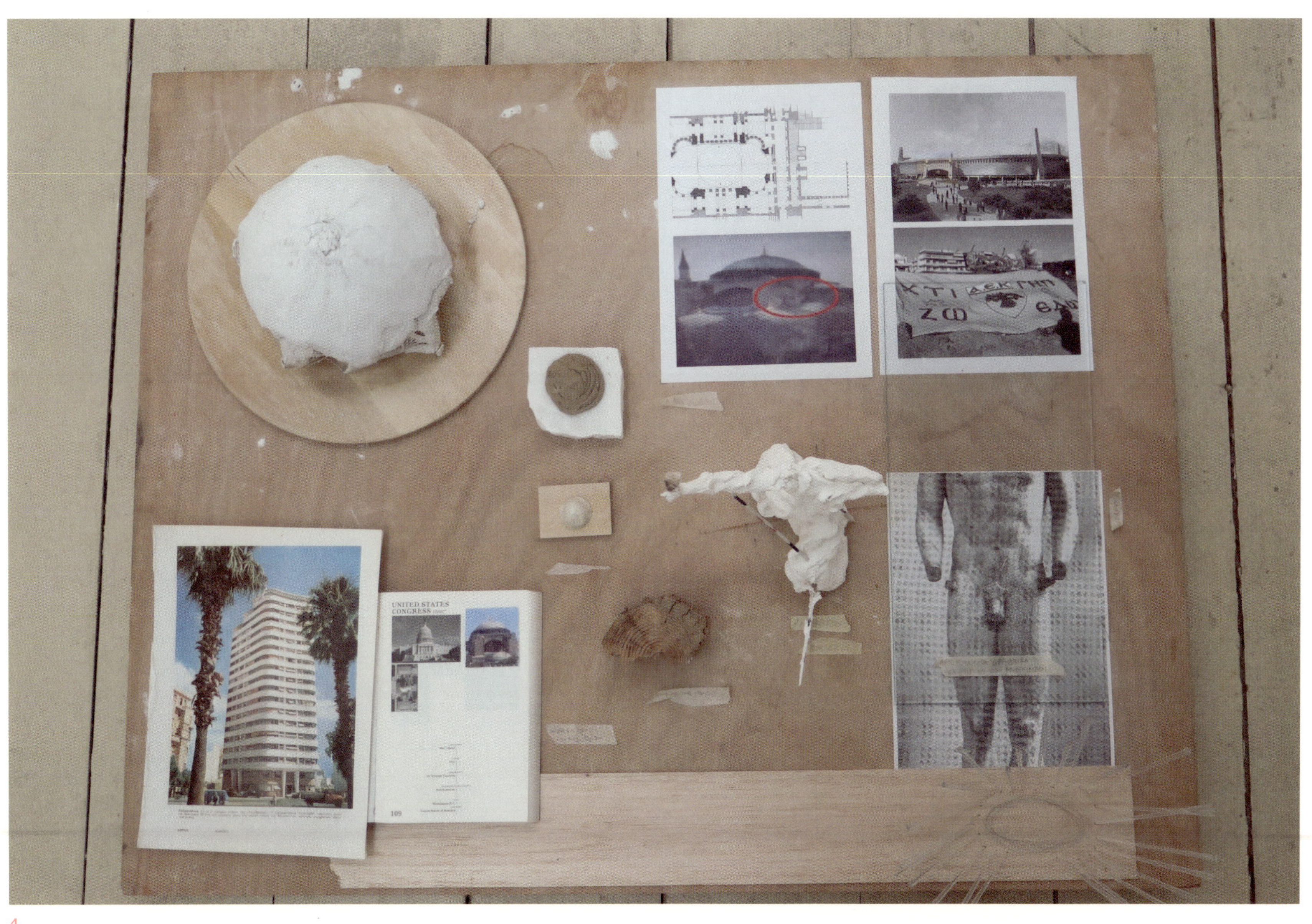

1. *The Afternoon*, 2015
Paper and sanding paper, 56 x 42 cm

2. *Beers, Tangerines and Ruins 2/2*, 2014 (detail)
Pen on plastic, 200 x 90 cm

3. *The Cicadas*, 2015 (detail)
Four monotype prints, 56 x 42 cm each

4. *Fossils*, 2015 (detail)
White carbon paper, clear acrylic paint, and fluorescent lamp, 58 x 50 cm

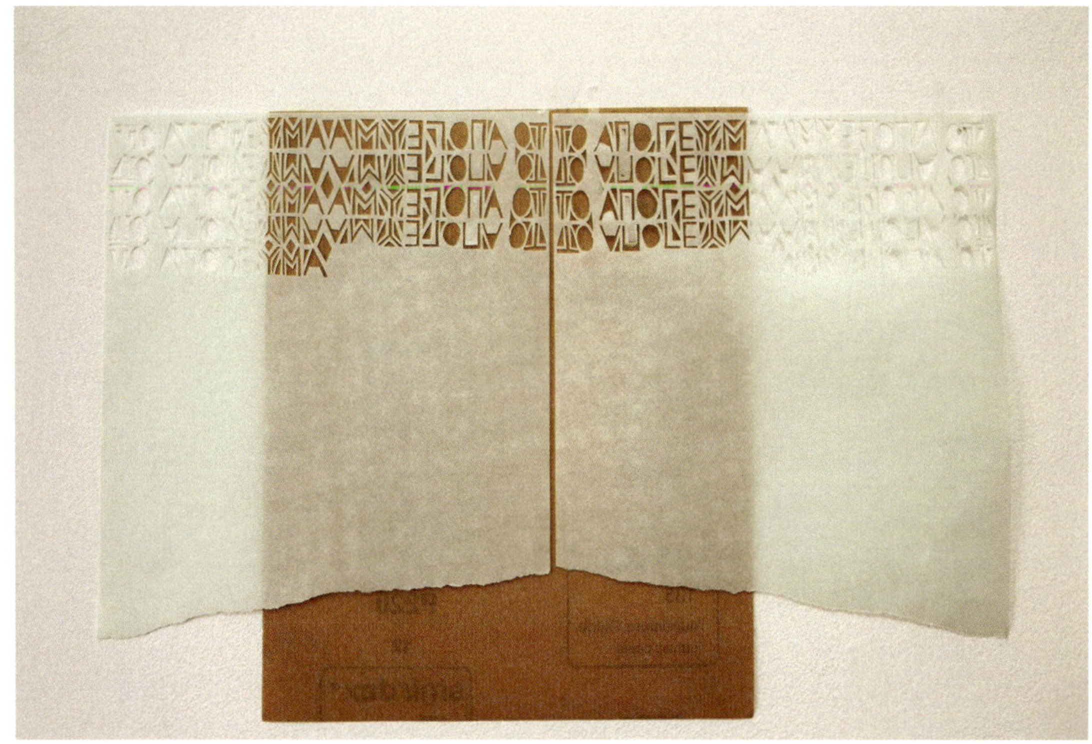

1

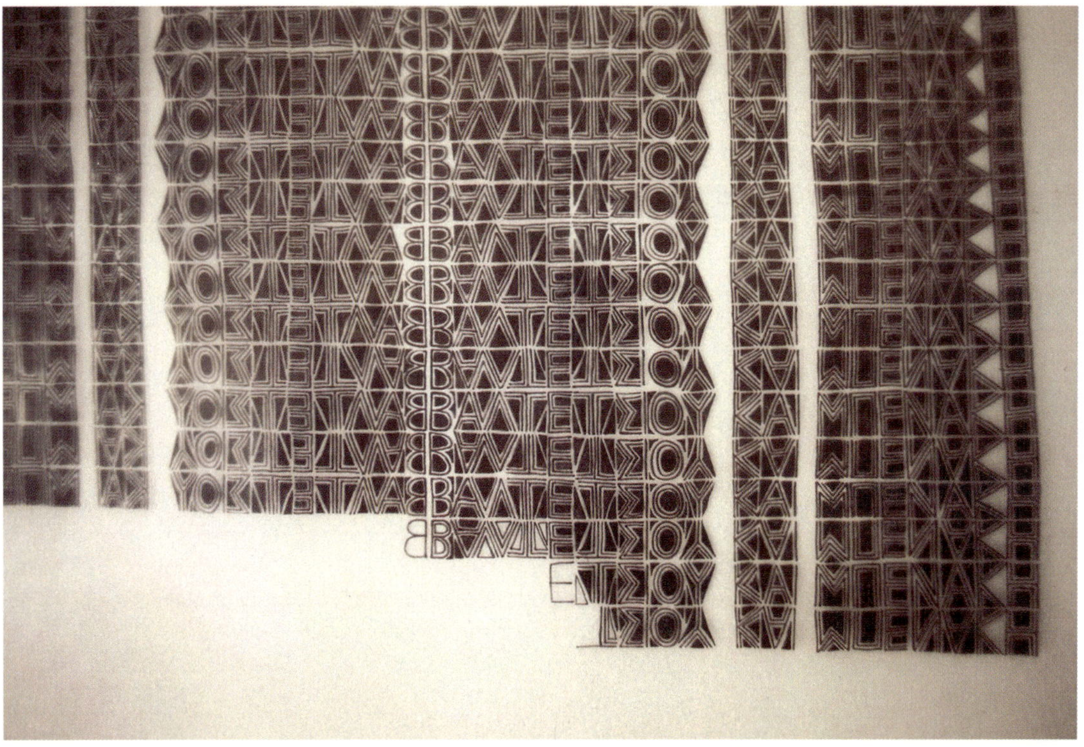

2

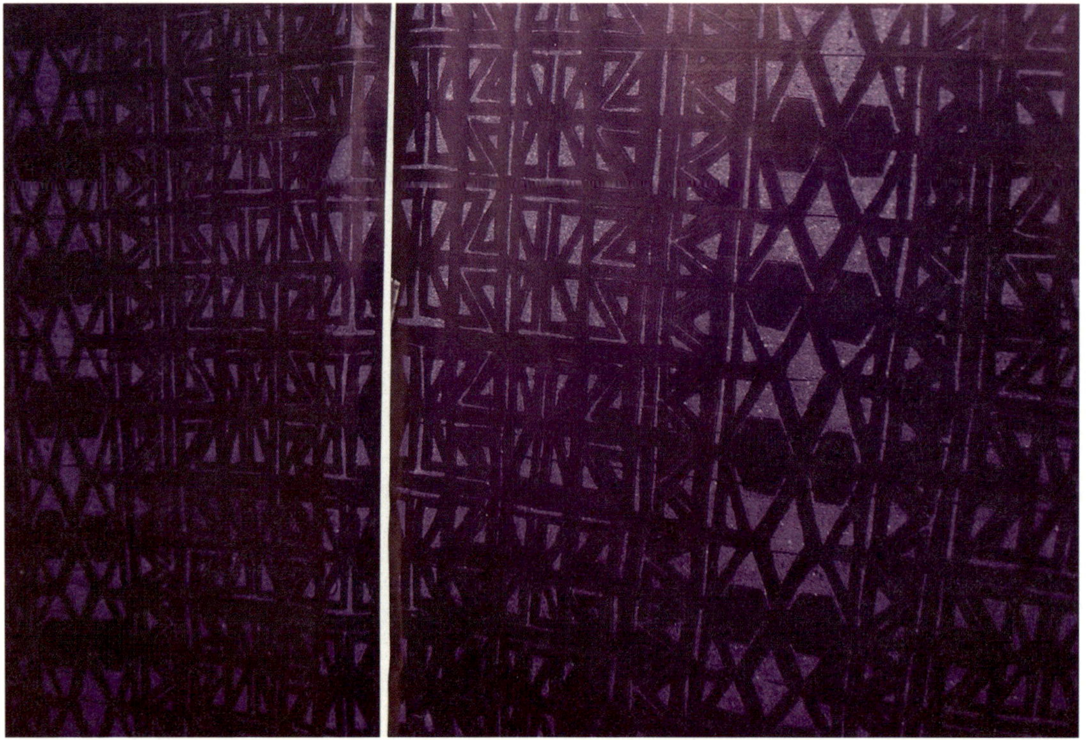

3

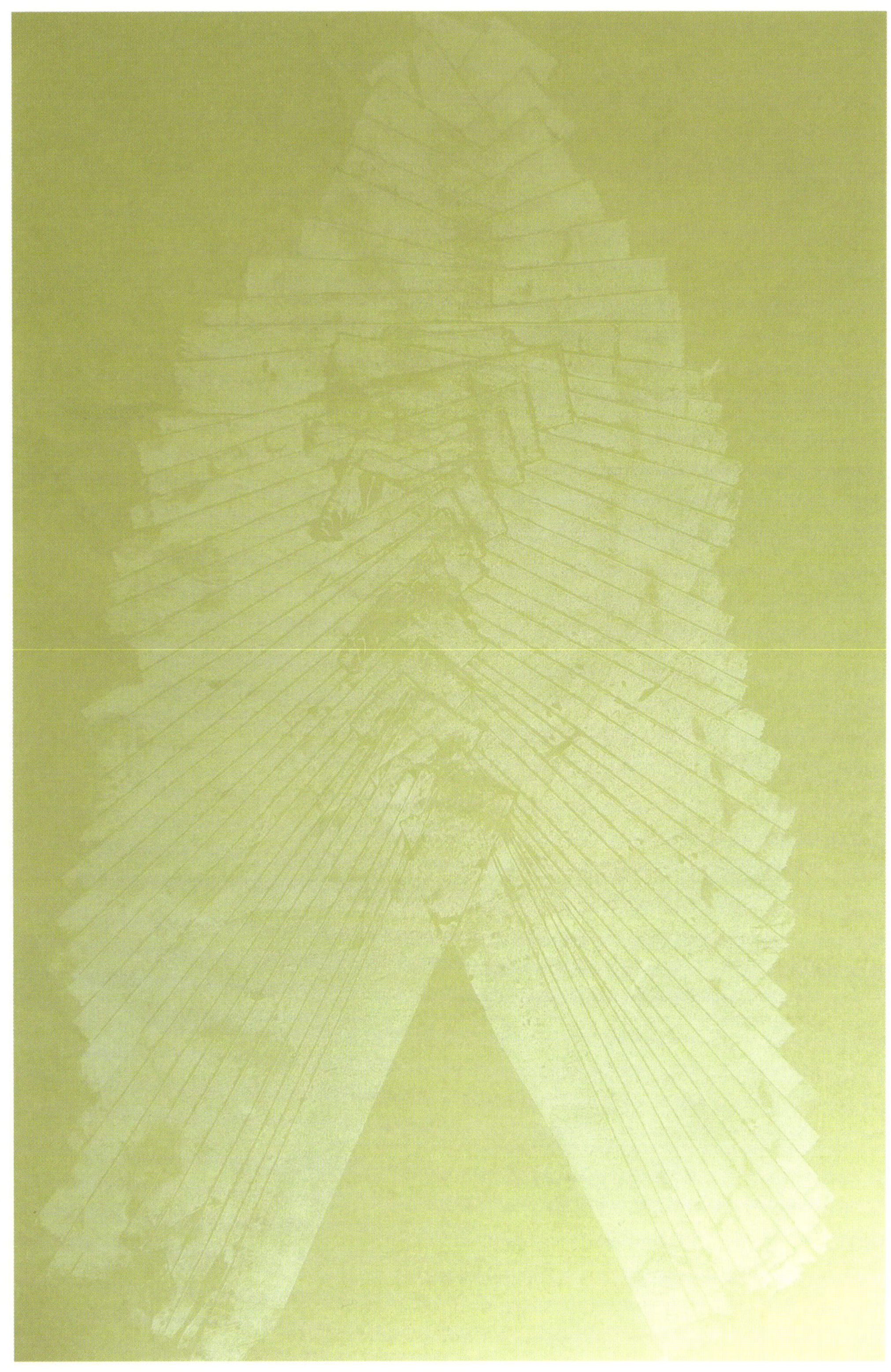

1. *And Plaster Biscuits*, 2015–16
Exercise mats, plaster, unfired clay, and found objects, 180 x 173 cm

2. – 4. *And Plaster Biscuits*, 2015–16 (details)
Exercise mats, plaster, unfired clay, and found objects, 180 x 173 cm

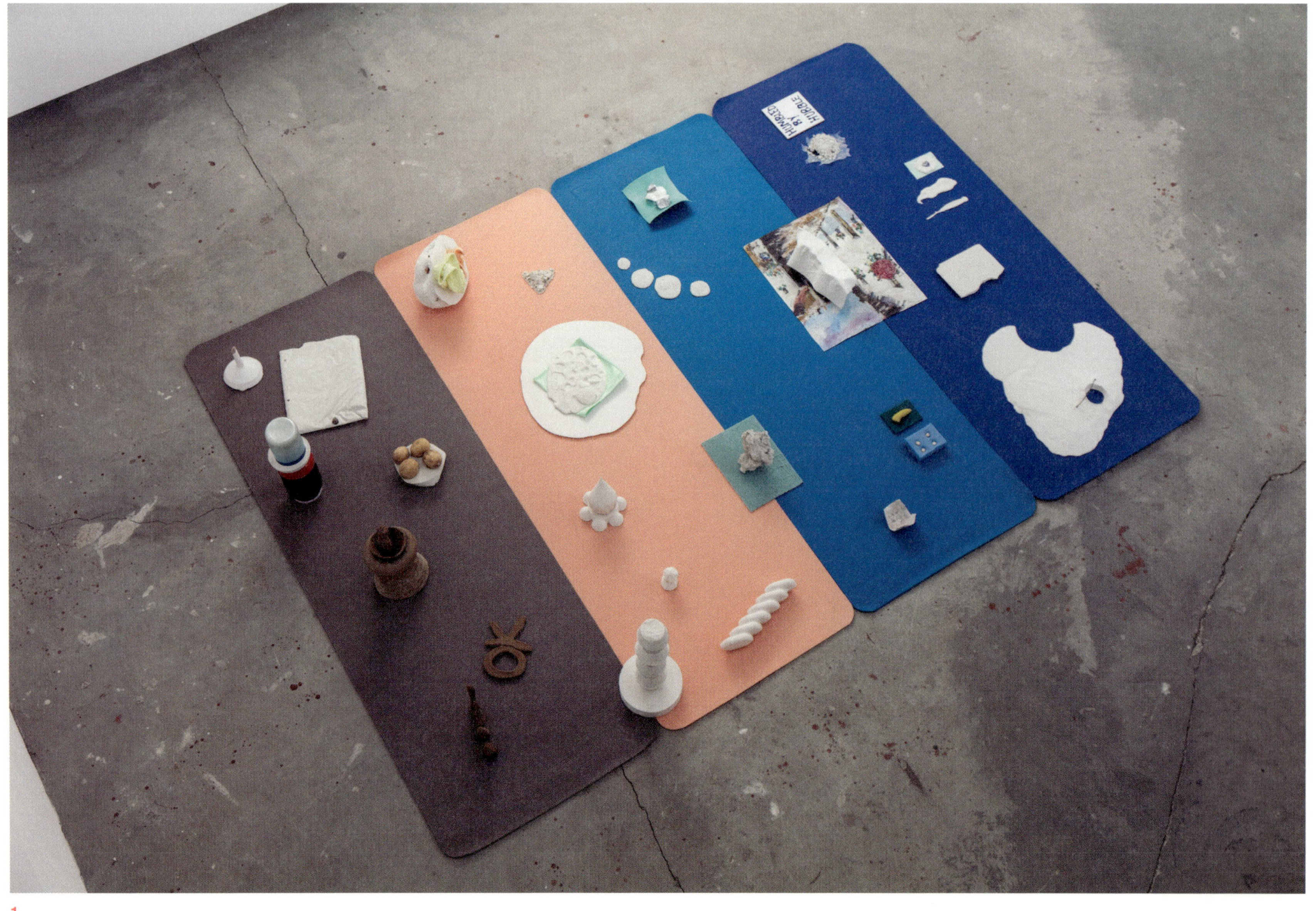

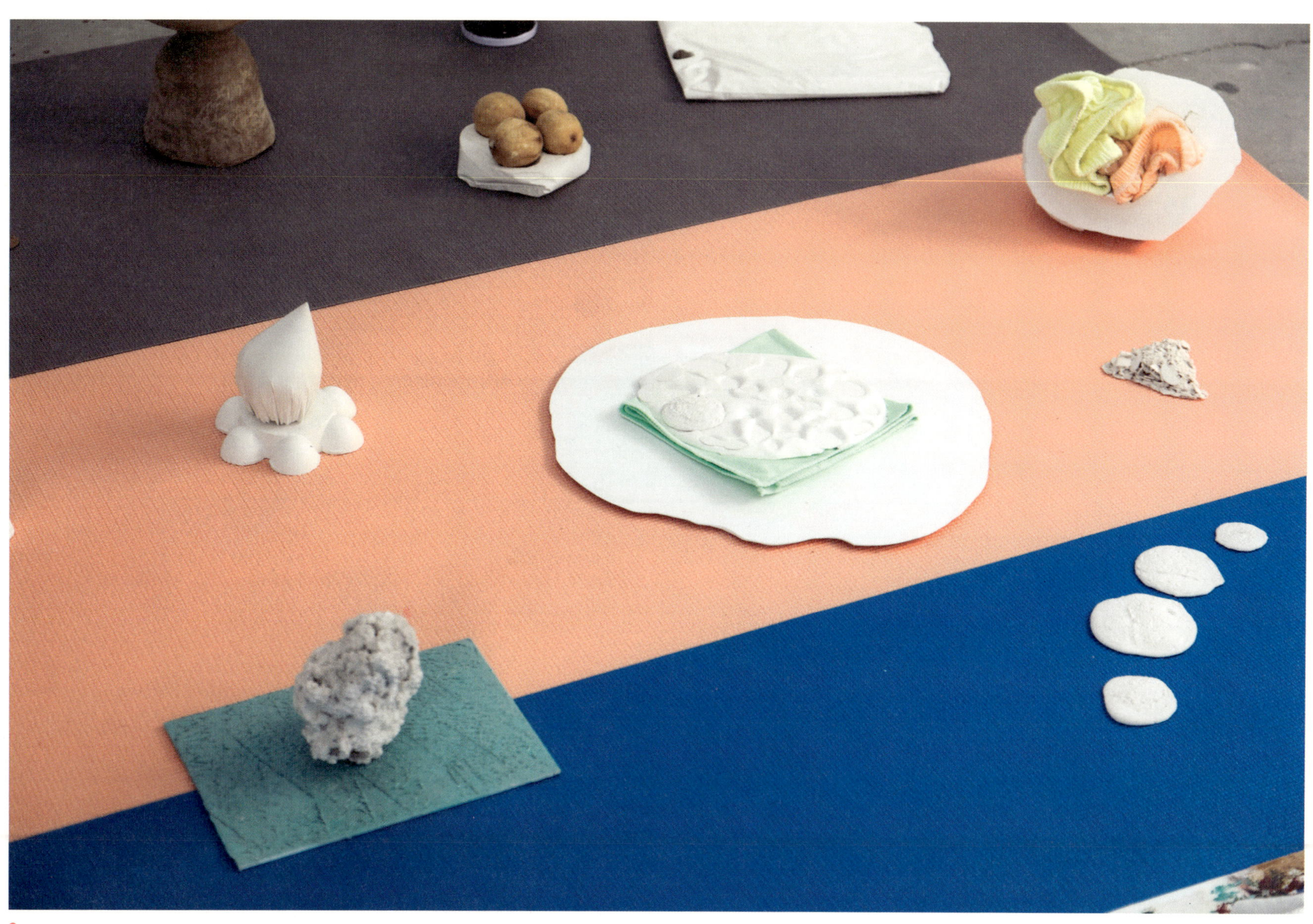

2

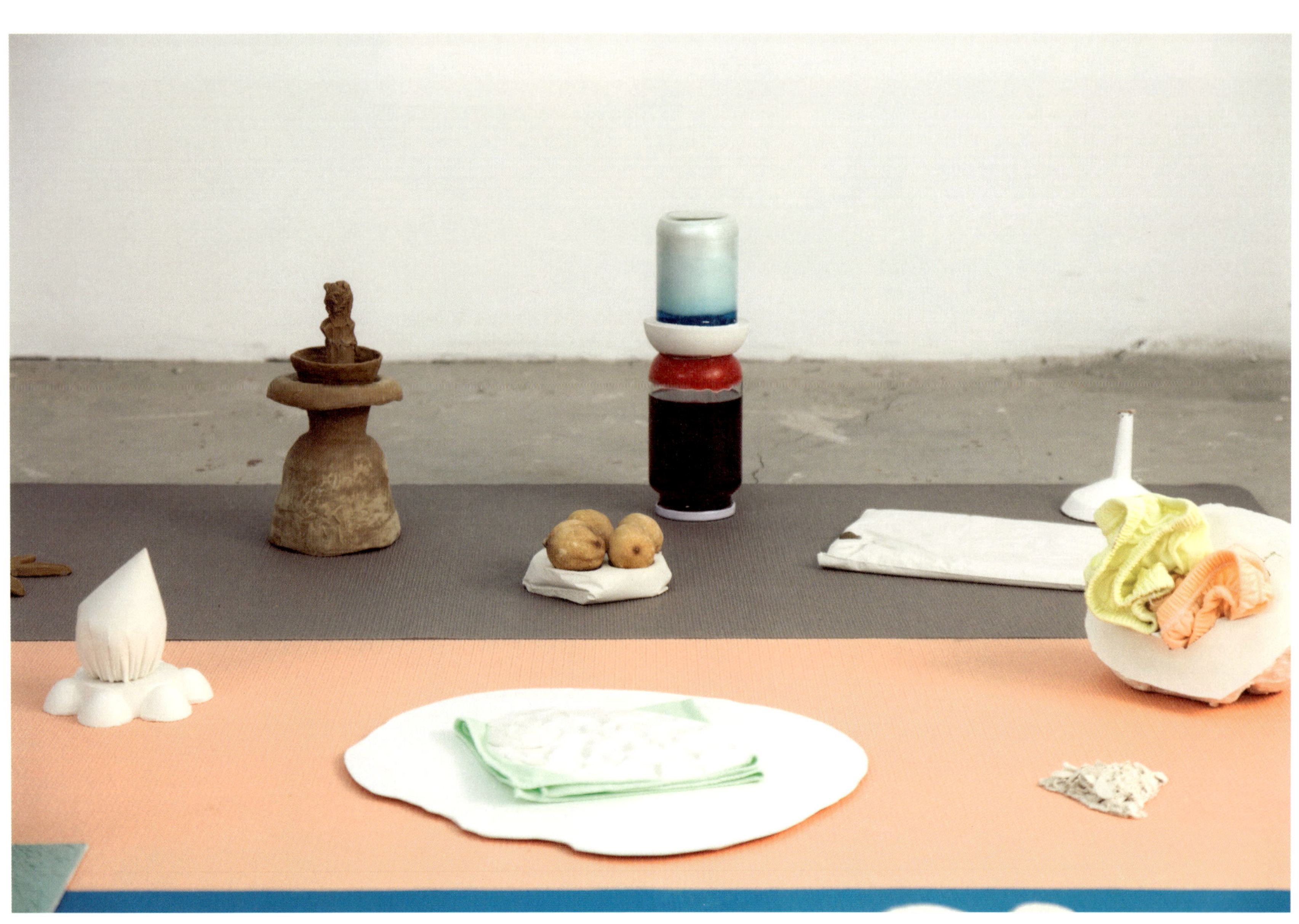

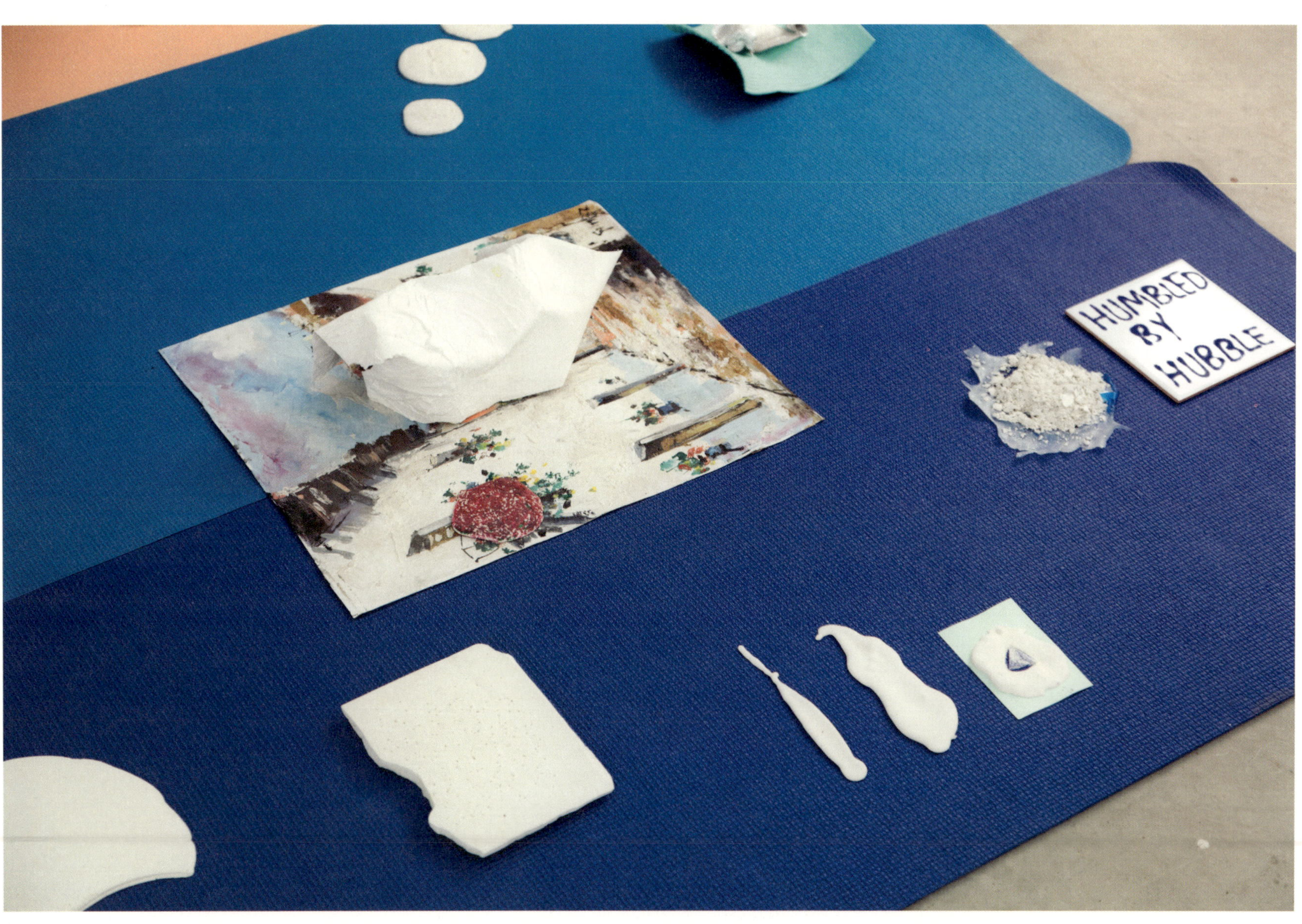
HUMBLED
BY
HUBBLE

LOUKIA ALAVANOU
The Green Room, 2015–16
Stereoscopic 3D video, color,
and sound, 4:07 min
Courtesy the artist

DIMITRIS AMELADIOTIS
Allowing Unpleasant States, 2016
Mixed media, dimensions variable
Courtesy the artist

*How Many Visual Realities Could
Be Recorded in The Brain
of the Creature*, 2016
Mixed media, 60 x 50 x 17 cm
Courtesy the artist

*Numerous Methods into Harms
Disasters*, 2016
Mixed media, 70 x 35 x 28 cm
Courtesy the artist

*How is the 4th Preposition /
Suggestion for a New Sculpture
in This Land?*, 2016
Mixed media, 50 x 42 x 25 cm
Courtesy the artist

*Traditions Matters Lessons vs.
the Abundance of Gestures*, 2016
Mixed media, 60 x 32 x 20 cm
Courtesy the artist

*Small Castles in the Sand As Well
As in My Studio*, 2016
Mixed media, 60 x 54 x 30 cm
Courtesy the artist

MARIA ANASTASSIOU
Gravity, 2015
HD Video, found video, digitized
16 mm film, color, and found sound,
1:38 min
Courtesy the artist

ELENI BAGAKI
*She Was Whistling He Was
Shooting*, 2016
HD video, color, and sound, 2:15 min
Courtesy the artist

*He Fucked Her and Never Talked
To Her Again*, 2016
Audio from WAV file, 3:54 min
Courtesy the artist

*Tears made his dick hard /
He made me drink from the floor /
For his birthday I fucked somebody
else / In my bedroom*, 2016
Customized prints on t-shirts, steel
wire, and steel bases, 90 x 60 x 4 cm
Courtesy the artist

MARGARITA BOFILIOU
Nivea, 2016
Permanent acrylic ink and acrylic
paint on paper, 200 x 300 cm
Courtesy the artist and State
of Concept, Athens

Carnation, 2016
Permanent acrylic ink and sumi
ink on paper, 150 x 200 cm
Courtesy the artist and State
of Concept, Athens

Va te faire voir (chez les Grecs), 2016
Sumi ink and acrylic based hybrid
paint on paper, 200 x 150 cm
Courtesy the artist and State
of Concept, Athens

MARIANNA CHRISTOFIDES
Black Mountain, 2015
HD video, color, and sound, 10:33 min
Courtesy the artist

MANOLIS DASKALAKIS-LEMOS
Silent Hysteria II, 2016
Petroleum and water in iron tanks
Dimensions variable
Courtesy the artist and CAN Christina
Androulidaki Gallery, Athens

Not Yet Titled (Oil Spill Fire), 2016
Oil on canvas and C-print mounted
on DuPont and aluminum frame,
129 x 280 x 4 cm
Courtesy the artist and CAN Christina
Androulidaki Gallery, Athens

PETROS EFSTATHIADIS
Bridge from the series *Gold Rush*, 2016
Inkjet print on paper, 82 x 110 cm
Courtesy the artist and CAN Christina
Androulidaki Gallery, Athens

Interception from the series *Gold
Rush*, 2016
Inkjet print on paper, 110 x 82 cm
Courtesy the artist and CAN Christina
Androulidaki Gallery, Athens

Lucky Numbers from the series *Gold
Rush*, 2016
Inkjet print on paper, 82 x 110 cm
Courtesy the artist and CAN Christina
Androulidaki Gallery, Athens

Thunder from the series *Gold Rush*,
2016
Inkjet print on paper, 110 x 82 cm
Courtesy the artist and CAN Christina
Androulidaki Gallery, Athens

Town Council from the series *Gold
Rush*, 2016
Inkjet print on paper, 82 x 110 cm
Courtesy the artist and CAN Christina
Androulidaki Gallery, Athens

EIRENE EFSTATHIOU
*Other Things Happen in December
Besides Christmas 1*, 2015–16
Oil and screen print on paper
mounted on aluminum, three panels:
33 x 33 cm each
Courtesy the artist and Eleni
Koroneou Gallery

*Other Things Happen in December
Besides Christmas 2*, 2015–16
Oil and screen print on paper
mounted on aluminum, two panels:
33 x 33 cm each
Courtesy the artist and Eleni
Koroneou Gallery

*Other Things Happen in December
Besides Christmas 4*, 2015–16
Oil and screen print on paper
mounted on aluminum, three panels:
33 x 33 cm each
Courtesy the artist and Eleni Koroneou
Gallery

ZOI GAITANIDOU
Betwixt, 2015
Acrylic and thread on canvas,
135 x 188 cm
Courtesy The Breeder, Athens

Ritual, 2016
Acrylic and thread on canvas,
115 x 200 cm
Courtesy The Breeder, Athens

Guardian, 2016
Acrylic and thread on canvas,
152 x 79 cm
Courtesy The Breeder, Athens

Passage, 2016
Acrylic and thread on canvas,
240 x 135 cm
Courtesy The Breeder, Athens

GIORGOS GERONTIDES
Who is the man in red? a t(r)opical collection, 2016
Mixed media, dimensions variable
Courtesy the artist

STELIOS KALLINIKOU
Bougainvillea from the series *Local Studies*, 2015
Pigment print, 40 x 60 cm
Courtesy the artist

Bricks from the series *Local Studies*, 2015
Pigment print, 87 x 130 cm
Courtesy the artist

Palm Trees from the series *Local Studies*, 2015
Pigment print, 40 x 60 cm
Courtesy of the artist

Pink House from the series *Local Studies*, 2015
Pigment print, 40 x 60 cm
Courtesy the artist

Skeleton from the series *Local Studies*, 2015
Pigment print, 130 x 87 cm
Courtesy the artist

Stage from the series *Local Studies*, 2015
Pigment print, 30 x 20 cm
Courtesy the artist

Yellow from the series *Local Studies*, 2015
Pigment print, 30 x 20 cm
Courtesy of the artist

Ghost City from the series *Local Studies*, 2016
Pigment print, 66 x 100 cm
Courtesy the artist

Hometown from the series *Local Studies*, 2016
Pigment print, 66 x 100 cm
Courtesy the artist

Red Lake from the series *Local Studies*, 2016
Pigment print, 26 x 40 cm
Courtesy the artist

YANNIS KARPOUZIS
Parallel Crisis: The Immobilized Time Itself, 2010–16
Twenty C-prints, 100 x 100 cm or 150 x 150 cm each
Courtesy the artist

LITO KATTOU
Solar Love for the Rapid Felines, Volume 1: their planets, 2015
Copper and bronze, dimensions variable
Courtesy the artist

Solar Love for the Rapid Felines, Volume 2: them, 2016
Digital embroidery on Lycra, steel, and hematite magnets, dimensions variable
Courtesy the artist

Solar Love for the Rapid Felines, Volume 2: their weapons, 2016
Copper and aluminum, dimensions variable
Courtesy the artist

KERNEL
Bridge Side B (Ofrah Fergal Kasei), 2016
Digital video projection, 5:00 min
Courtesy the artists

IOANNIS KOLIOPOULOS
Blood by Numbers from the series *Primal Objectivities*, 2015
Lambda C-print, inkjet print, postcard, graphite and coffee stains on book cover, and ink and oilon paper, 124 x 174 cm
Courtesy the artist

Partial Flag from the series *Primal Objectivities*, 2015
Lambda C-print, ink, paper burns, embroidery, textile and canvas on paper, 124 x 144 cm
Courtesy the artist

Post Immigrant from the series *Primal Objectivities*, 2016
Lambda C-print, silver gelatin print, and wood block print on paper, 154 x 164 cm
Courtesy the artist

Televised Embrace Is Erotic Embrace of the Nation from the series *Primal Objectivities*, 2015
Lambda C-print, collage on paper, paper burns, and ink and gouache on paper, 124 x 174 cm
Courtesy the artist

Study in Bread Color from the series *Primal Objectivities*, 2015
Lambda C-print, paper burns and wood block print on paper, 124 x 174 cm
Courtesy the artist

My Hand Is Softer than Hammer, Harder than Cucumber from the series *Primal Objectivities*, 2015
Lambda C-print, acrylic, postcard, and graphite and paper burns on paper, 124 x 169 cm
Courtesy the artist

CHRYSANTHI KOUMIANAKI
Notes for someone who is 1.67m or taller and is bored on a bus, 2016
Metal and marker on wall, dimensions variable
Courtesy the artist

ORESTIS MAVROUDIS
Attempt to Fly, 2013
HD video, color, and sound, 5:00 min
Courtesy the artist

IRINI MIGA
A Place From a Different Timeline, 2016 (fragment)
White oak, drywall, metal, glazed ceramic, resin, brass, aluminum, shoelace, wire, duct tape, ink, household paint, tools, pencil, print on tissue, print on paper, Band-Aid, wire from broken iPhone, cigarette butt, marble dust, and leftovers of carbon dioxide, water vapor, oxygen, and nitrogen

OLGA MIGLIARESSI-PHOCA
All the Guys She's Fucked, Part I, 2014
Ink and digital print on fabric, 220 x 140 cm
Courtesy the artist and Dio Horia Art Platform

All the Guys She's Fucked, Part II, 2014
Ink and digital print on fabric, 220 x 140 cm
Courtesy the artist and Dio Horia Art Platform

Koleti Street, 2015
Ink and digital print on canvas, 140 x 100 cm
Courtesy the artist and Dio Horia Art Platform

Nudists, 2015
Ink and digital print on canvas,
145 x 240 cm
Courtesy the artist and
Dio Horia Art Platform

PETROS MORIS
Notes on Recurrent Forms, 2016
Plaster, steel, and video projection,
150 x 500 x 250 cm approx.
and 10:00 min
Courtesy the artist

**PERSEFONI MYRTSOU
& EVA GIANNAKOPOULOU**
Maltepe Gelinler / Maltepe Brides,
2015–ongoing
Video, 13:44 min
Courtesy the artists

MALVINA PANAGIOTIDI
*Ghost Relief I (The Mansion
of the Kontou Family)*, 2015
Paraffin wax, pigment, wick,
and wood, 157 x 60 x 35 cm
Courtesy the artist

*Ghost Relief II (The House
on Smolensky Street)*, 2015
Paraffin wax, pigment, wick,
and wood, 147 x 45 x 35 cm
Courtesy the artist

Ghost Relief III (The Red House), 2015
Paraffin wax, pigment, wick,
and wood, 131 x 50 x 35 cm
Courtesy the artist

Ghost Relief IV (Villa Kazouli), 2015
Paraffin wax, pigment, wick,
and wood, 176 x 51 x 35 cm
Courtesy the artist

*Ghost Relief V (The House on Vasilissis
Olgas Avenue)*, 2016
Paraffin wax, pigment, wick,
and wood, 153 x 51 x 35 cm
Courtesy the artist

ALIKI PANAGIOTOPOULOU
Fillers & Markers, 2016
Mixed media, dimensions variable
Courtesy the artist

EVA PAPAMARGARITI
Factitious Imprints, 2016
Seven prints on polar fleece, Lycra
sheen, suede, scroll, and voile fabric
and single-channel video, sound,
and color, dimensions variable
and 9:30 min
Courtesy the artist

ZOË PAUL
*The Taste Of A Cosmopolitan
Shepherd with an Excellent Long
Term Memory*, 2014
Semi-fired ceramic beads
and metal, 200 x 120 cm
Courtesy The Breeder, Athens

Air Conditioning is Destiny, 2016
Marble, metal, pumice stones,
and water, 210 x 145 x 45 cm
Courtesy The Breeder, Athens

/0, 2016
Wool and thread on found fridge
grill, 45 x 45 cm
Courtesy The Breeder, Athens

/<, 2016
Wool and thread on found fridge
grill, 45 x 45 cm
Courtesy The Breeder, Athens

SOFIA STEVI
Untitled (Love), 2015
Sumi ink, acrylic, and gouache
on cotton, 150 x 100 cm
Courtesy the artist

Society Of Observers, 2016
Ink and acrylic on cotton,
150 x 100 cm
Courtesy the artist

*Flamingo Salad (When
We Were Close)*, 2016
Ink and acrylic on cotton,
150 x 100 cm
Courtesy the artist

The Island, 2016
Ink, acrylic on cotton, and
natural sponge, 150 x 100 cm
Courtesy the artist

The Present, 2016
Ink, acrylic on cotton, plaster,
and enamel, 150 x 100 cm
Courtesy the artist

Cabinet, 2016
Ink, acrylic on wooden furniture,
and objects, dimensions variable
Courtesy the artist

Soft Language, Slow Circles, 2016
Found furniture, plaster, acrylic,
felt, natural sponge, and porcelain,
dimensions variable
Courtesy the artist

ANASTASIS STRATAKIS
1:1 (Untitled #5), 2016
Charcoal and graphite on paper,
273 x 385 cm
Courtesy the artist

VALINIA SVORONOU
Gravestone Wolfs, Darkpools, 2016
Concrete, fiber-optic fabric, metallic
stands, screen, and HD video,
160 x 250 x 150 cm and 11:04 min
Courtesy the artist

PAKY VLASSOPOULOU
33,478, 2016
Book spines, wood, marble offcuts,
Plexiglas, glass, and water,
84 x 74 x 554 cm
Courtesy the artist

MYRTO XANTHOPOULOU
Deep Blue (from below), 2016
Black carbon paper, terracotta, bamboo
sticks, plastic, lamps, and installation
on shelf, banner: 200 x 100 x 10 cm
approx.; shelf: 37 x 50 x 30 cm
Courtesy Elika Gallery, Athens

NATALIE YIAXI
And Plaster Biscuits, 2015–16
Exercise mats, plaster, unfired clay,
and found objects, 180 x 173 cm
Courtesy the artist

We would like to extend a special
thanks to the group of advisors whose
invaluable insight was a great help
during the research for this exhibition:

Andreas Angelidakis
Dimitris Antonitsis
Nadja Argyropoulou
Panos Giannikopoulos
Katerina Gregos
Elpida Karaba
Katerina Koskina
Polina Kosmadaki
Christoforos Marinos
Tina Pandi
Helena Papadopoulos
Haris Savvopoulos
Stamatis Schizakis
Maria Stathi
Yorgos Tzirtzilakis
Daphne Vitali
Marina Vranopoulou
Denys Zacharopoulos
Despina Zefkili
Andre Zivanari

PUBLISHED BY
DESTE Foundation
for Contemporary Art
22, Henri Mussard,
1208 Geneva / Switzerland

On the occasion of the
exhibition "The Equilibrists"
June 17 – October 9, 2016
at the Benaki Museum,
138 Pireos St., Athens

CURATORS
Gary Carrion-Murayari
and Helga Christoffersen,
with Massimiliano Gioni

COPY EDITOR
Natalie Bell

GRAPHIC DESIGN
k2 Design, Athens

Printed in Greece
by Alta Grafico S.A.
Printing and Graphic Arts
Copyright © 2016
DESTE Foundation
for Contemporary Art

ISBN: 978–618–5039–21–9

PHOTOGRAPHY CREDITS
Pages 30, 31, 32 (images 4, 5), 33: Courtesy the artist and State of Concept, Athens; Photo © Fotini Lykidi / Page 30 (images 3, 6): Courtesy the artist and State of Concept, Athens; Photo © Pinelopi Gerasimou / Pages 38-41: Courtesy the artist and CAN Christina Androulidaki Gallery, Athens / Pages 42-45: Courtesy the artist and CAN Christina Androulidaki Gallery, Athens / Pages 46-49: Courtesy the artist and Eleni Koroneou Gallery, Athens; Photo © Nikos Alexopoulos / Pages: 50-53: Courtesy The Breeder, Athens / Pages 70, 71 (image 2): Courtesy the artists and Union Pacific, London / Page 72: Courtesy the artists and SPACE, London / Page 73: Courtesy the artists and V22 Collection, London / Pages 90-93: Courtesy the artist and Dio Horia Art Platform / Page 97: Courtesy the artist; Photo© Giorgos Sfakianakis / Pages 112-115: Courtesy The Breeder, Athens; Photo© Giovanni Savi / Page 121: Courtesy the artist and AD Gallery, Athens / Page 122: Courtesy the artist and SMCA – State Museum of Contemporary Art Collection, Thessaloniki / Pages 128-130: Courtesy the artist; Photo© Mariza Nikolaou / Pages 132-135: Courtesy Elika Gallery, Athens